Corporate Governance

ACKNOWLEDGEMENTS

My book is drawn from my experience in the corporate world, findings of my research and understanding of corporate governance from other published works. I would like to acknowledge all researchers and scholars whose work has contributed to the vast body of knowledge on corporate governance. Thanks to them a comparatively newer discipline has grown by leaps and bounds in the last 50 years. Material has been reproduced or adopted from my previous writings, Diversity and the Effective board, Elsevier, Tata Sons and the mystery of Mistry, Vikalpa: The Journal for Decision Makers and Intertwining CSR with strategy—the way ahead, corporate governance with kind permission.

This book would not have happened without the constant guidance and encouragement of my mentor Prof. R K Mishra, Senior Professor, ONGC Subir Raha Chair at the Institute of Public Enterprise. Throughout my professional journey, he constantly pushes me to expand my boundaries and better myself. Many thanks to Prof J.P. Sharma, Global Research Foundation for Corporate Governance for paving the way for new research opportunities. It would be amiss to not mention my research students who intellectually stimulate me. And last but not the least, I am extremely grateful for the love and unconditional support of my family, particularly during these two years of the pandemic.

November, 2022   Shital Jhunjhunwala

DISCLAIMER

This book is not intended, and should not be relied upon, as legal advice.

CONTENTS

LIST OF FIGURES

LIST OF TABLES

CHAPTER 1

Corporate Governance: An Introduction

To Be or Not to Be—Is Not the Question, the Question Is: The What, Why and How of Corporate Governance

SH Company:

Sushil and Harish decide to start a business together. They approach a lawyer who suggests they form a company so that their liabilities are limited. They agree to invest Rs. 1,00,000 each. SH Private Limited Company is formed with Sushil and Harish as shareholders each owning shares worth Rs. 1,00,000. As promoters of the company, Sushil and Harish also become directors in the company. After a year, the business is doing well and to expand further they require more money. Their friends Premlata and Harshita are impressed with the success of the business and agree to buy shares of Rs. 50,000 each. Over the next couple of years, the business keeps growing. Few more friends and family members invest in the company and become shareholders.

Sushil and Harish are finding it difficult to manage the company as the business is getting complex and would like to bring someone on board who has experience of managing a large company. They appoint Ramkumar another friend as a director and agree to pay him a monthly salary. With the expertise of Ramkumar, the company grows by leaps and bounds. The board decides that it is time to go

© The Author(s), under exclusive license to Springer Nature Singapore Pte Ltd. 2023
S. Jhunjhunwala, *Corporate Governance*,
https://doi.org/10.1007/978-981-99-2707-4_1

international and they need someone who can guide them. After several months of search, they finally invite Prasad a CEO of a fortune 500 company to join the board as a non-executive director.

Prasad recommends that to raise money, the company should convert to a public limited company and then have an initial public offering. He also advises that they should appoint a company secretary who will ensure that all legal compliances are met. Ramkumar is made the chief executive officer and given a huge salary hike.

Questions

1. What do you understand by the terms shareholders, directors and promoters? Identify them.
2. What is the benefit of forming a company?
3. What is the cost–benefit analysis of appointing Ramkumar as a director?
4. Differentiate between the governance structure in the beginning and now.

What Is Corporate Governance?

Corporate governance refers to the governance of a corporate. Hence, it is important to examine these two words 'corporate' and 'governance'.

Corporate: Corporate is a very large company, having a sizable number of shareholders. It is formed by association of those having a common objective and endowed by law with the rights and liabilities of an individual. It thus has a legal entity separate from the persons that form it. The owners (shareholders) delegate control of the company to a board of directors.

The distinct characteristics of a corporate are:

- *Separate Legal Personality* of the company different from its owners (i.e. the right to own property, enter into a contract, sue and be sued in its own name, etc.).
- *Ownership* by large number of *shareholders*.

- *Delegated management*, in other words, control of the company placed in the hands of a **board of directors** who oversee the company on behalf of shareholders.
- *Limited liability* of the shareholders (so that if the company becomes insolvent, they only owe the money that they subscribed for in shares).
- *Transferable shares*, usually on a listed exchange.

Since a company is a legal entity it comes into existence only when incorporated under law of a country. See Table 1.1 for some examples.

Governance: Governance is the act of governing, i.e. conducting the affairs and actions or controlling a country, organization or a company. The word governance is derived from the Latin word "gubernare" and from Greek "kubernan" which mean 'to steer'. Governance is how the head of the country or a company steers it and gives it direction to achieve its goal or destination. It is the process by which power is exercised to acquire and use resources for the good of the entity.

Table 1.1 Examples of company law in different countries

Country	Laws under which a company is incorporated
Australia	Australia Corporations Act 2001
China	Company Law of the People's Republic of China
India	Companies Act 2013
Japan	Companies Act (Act No. of 86 of 2005)
Mexico	Federal Mexican Ministry of Foreign Affairs
UK	Companies Act 2006 (c46)
France	The Commercial Code
UAE	UAE Federal Law No. 2 of 2015
Uganda	Companies Act, 2012
Canada	Canada Business Corporations Act (CBCA)
Sri Lanka	The Companies Act (No. 7 of 2007)
Germany	German Company Law (Gesellschaftsrecht)
USA	Model Business Corporation Act

Source Compiled by Author

Corporate Governance: Corporate governance is the manner in which corporates are governed. It "is the system by which companies are directed and controlled" (Sir Adrian Cadbury, 1992). "The corporate governance structure specifies the distribution of rights and responsibilities among different participants in the corporation - the board, managers, employees, shareholders and other stakeholders. It also spells out the rules and procedures for making decisions on corporate affairs. In so doing, corporate governance also provides the structure through which the company objectives are set, and the means of attaining those objectives and monitoring performance is determined" (OECD, 2004, 2015). It is the way shareholders (owners) of the company who invest in it ensure their interests in the long term are achieved. Hence "corporate governance deals with the way suppliers of finance assure themselves of getting a return on their investment" (Shleifer & Vishny, 1997). Good governance is thus in the interest and the responsibility of shareholders.

Because of their size corporates, impact a large number of stakeholders, which is why their governance is a matter of huge concern (see Fig. 1.1).

In the example of SH Company, Sushil and Harish as promoters start the company and become shareholders and directors. Soon Premlata and Harshita invest in the company and become shareholders. By creating a company, the liability of the shareholders is limited to the amount of shares they have bought. By appointing Ramkumar as the director, they benefit from his expertise, but the original founders have to give up control. The benefit must be more than they have to pay him. As the company expands, the governance structure becomes complex and more formalized.

THE BIRTH OF CORPORATE GOVERNANCE

The stages of evolution of corporate governance is shown in Fig. 1.2.

Governance: Governance in terms of government for the country is an ancient concept. Kauṭilya's *Arthashastra* considered as the "science of governance" believed to be written in the second century BCE describes how kings can achieve good governance. The moral duty of a ruler is happiness and welfare of its people. The happiness of his subjects is his happiness. One of the greatest Indian treatises, it describes how to run an effective government, duties of the kings, ministers and officials, the

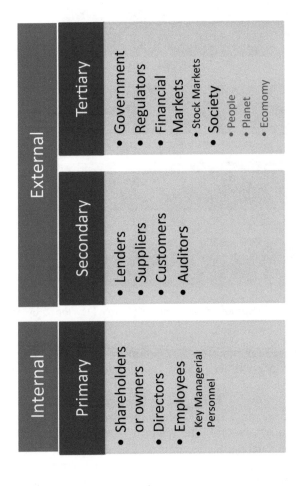

Fig. 1.1 Stakeholders (participants) of corporate governance (*Source* Developed by Author)

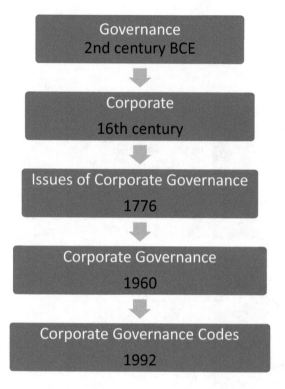

Fig. 1.2 Evolution of corporate governance (*Source* Developed by Author)

methods for screening ministers and among others ethics and trade—
lessons which hold good even today, not just for governments but also
for companies.

Company: Company is a comparatively newer concept originating in
the sixteenth century in England. The joint-stock company, the basis of
the modern company, was first chartered in 1600s by Queen Elizabeth I
to pursue trading interest of the country. The East India Company had
over 1000 shareholders who elected a governing body of 24 directors
each year. Private companies came later where shares were sold to high
net worth investors who provided capital with limited risk. France was the
first in 1807 to create a law for the formation of company with limited

liability to external investors. It was the British Companies Act of 1855 that finally gave rise to companies with limited liability for all shareholders.

Corporate Governance Issues: The world witnessed its first corporate scam in 1700s when the South Sea company went under and the wealthy English who had invested lost fortunes. Adam Smith in 1776 in Wealth of Nations questioned whether directors would take proper care of other peoples' (shareholders) money. This raised the issue of corporate governance for the first time. By the early twentieth century companies became large, had numerous shareholders who were geographically dispersed and became complex. Berle and Means (1932) in their seminal work on corporate governance highlighted the growing 'separation of owners and management'. They also realized the growing economic power that large public companies held and thus the need for governments to regulate them for the good of society. For the next forty years, the dialogue revolved around the role of directors, and measures that shareholders need to adopt to monitors them.

Corporate Governance: The term 'corporate governance' was first used by Richard Eells (1960), and till the 1980s, the discussion on corporate governance was limited primarily to academicians.

Corporate Governance Codes: In 1990, major corporate scams in the UK shook the investment world and the first code of corporate governance was introduced by Sir Adrian Cadbury to check excessive powers of the executives in the form of what is popularly known as the Cadbury Report (1992). Influenced by the Cadbury Report and because of the corporate failures during the 1990s across Europe and others parts of the world, corporate governance frameworks were coded in France, South Africa, Canada, The Netherlands, Hong Kong and India. These codes were recommendatory and voluntary in nature. In 2001, Enron and WorldCom collapsed in the USA leading to stock market investors seeing their money disappear and even common people losing their retirement funds in 401K (for more details, see Chapters 4 and 5). In response, USA enacted the Sarbanes–Oxley Act in 2002 which made it mandatory for American listed companies to comply with very stringent rules of corporate governance. Rest of the world began to follow. For instance, Securities and Exchange Board of India (the regulator of capital markets) put in place Clause 49 of the listing agreement effective 2005. (Table 1.2)

Table 1.2 Beginning of corporate governance

Year	Event
1600s	The East India Company introduces a Court of Directors, separating ownership and control (U.K.)
1776	Adam Smith in the Wealth of Nations warns of weak controls over management
1844	First Joint Stock Company Act (U.K.)
1932	Berle and Means seminal work on separation and control (U.S)
1933	The Securities Act of 1933 is the first act to regulate the securities markets (U.S.)
1968	The EU adopts the first company law directive (EU)
1990/91	Polly Peck, BCCI and Maxwell Business empires collapse (UK)
1992	The Cadbury Committee introduces the first code on corporate governance; and in 1993, companies listed on U.K.'s Stock Exchanges are required to disclose governance on a 'comply or explain' basis (U.K.)
1994	The King Report (S. Africa)
1995	Greenbury (on Executive Remuneration), and Hampel (on Corporate Governance) reports (U.K) The Russian Law on Joint Stock Companies (Russia), The Vienot Report (France)
1996	Publication of the Peters Report (the Netherlands)
1998	The Combined Code (U.K.) CII Code of 1998 (India)
1999	OECD Principles of Corporate Governance Birla Committee Report (India)
2000	Clause 49 of the Listing Agreement (India)
2001	Enron Corporation, then the seventh largest listed company in the U.S., declares bankruptcy (U.S.)
2002	World.Com Collapses
2002	The Sarbanes-Oxley Act (U.S.)
2002	The Winter report on company law reform in Europe German Corporate Governance Code (Germany) ; Russian Code of Corporate Conduct (Russia) Naresh Chandra Committee (India)
	The Journey Continues ....

Source Compiled by Author

THE HOW: MODELS OF CORPORATE GOVERNANCE

How are companies governed? Stakeholders select their representatives, namely board of directors, who in turn choose the management to run the company. While this basic structure is same how stakeholders are defined and the role and form of board varies across regions depending on their cultural and historical background. Different models have been adopted across the world (Table 1.3) institutionalizing the legal, economic, political and social environment of the country (Table 1.4) Significant among these are:

- One-tier Anglo-Saxon model.
- Two-tier Continental (German) model.
- Hybrid (Japanese Business Network) model.
- Communist Chinese model.
- Family-based model.

Anglo-Saxon or One-Tier Model

Anglo-Saxon model or one-tier mode is followed in countries such as USA and UK where stock markets are well developed, and hence, large amounts can be raised from the capital (stock) market. Ownership is dispersed over a large number of shareholders who appoint a board of directors to manage the affairs of the company. A shareholder

Table 1.3 Models adopted in different countries

Model	Country
One-tier	Australia, Belgium, Canada, Chile, Colombia, Greece, Hong Kong, Iceland, Ireland, Israel, Korea, Mexico, Saudi Arabia, Singapore, Spain, Sweden, Turkey, UK, USA
Two-tier	Argentina, Austria, China, Estonia, Germany, Indonesia, Latvia, Poland, Russia, South Africa
Optional (one or two)	Brazil, Czech Republic, Denmark, Finland, France, Hungary, Luxembourg, The Netherlands, Norway, Slovenia, Slovak, Switzerland
Hybrid (a separate body for audit purpose)	Italy, Japan, Portugal

Source Compiled by Author

Table 1.4 Governance models across different institutional settings

CG model	Anglo-Saxon	Continental Europe	Japan	Communist	Family-based
Country	USA, UK, Canada	German, Poland, Indonesia	Japan	China, Russia	South Korea/India
Political environment	Democratic	Moved from authoritarian to democratic	Democratic Single party dominance	Authoritarian	Democratic
Law	Common	Civil	Civil	Socialist	Mostly common, partly civil
Governance approach	Shareholder centric	Stakeholder centric with focus on employees	Business network	Mix of communism and capitalism	Feudalistic (family controlled)
Structure	One-tier	Two-tier	Hybrid		
Shareholding pattern	Dispersed	Banks, few Shareholders	Cross-holding	State-owned	Concentrated
Directors	Focus on independent directors	Executives and non-executive are separated	Inter-locking directors	Govt representatives	Family members

Source Developed by Author

centric model focuses on creating shareholder value. There is a single board which consists of both executive or inside directors (involved in day-to-day affairs) and non-executive or outside directors.

Both managerial and supervisory responsibilities are unified in one board. The chairman leads the board and chief executive officer (CEO) heads the management. Both these positions were usually combined in one person. Post-1990s to reduce agency problems (discussed in Chapter 3) and abuse of powers, there has been a shift towards increasing board independence with countries requiring boards to have a minimum proportion of independent directors (who does not have a material or pecuniary relationship with company) and separation of the post of board chairperson and chief executive officer (CEO). With the growing independence on boards, the CEO is often the only executive on the board (Fig. 1.3) (see Chapter 2 for a better understanding of board constituents).

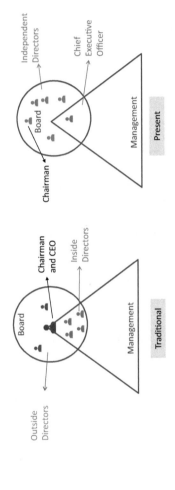

Fig. 1.3 Single-tier model (*Source* Developed by Author)

Continental European (German) or Two-Tier Model

The German model or two-tier model is followed in European countries such as Germany, Poland and Austria where banks are the major financer of the company. There are two boards the supervisory board and the management board. The supervisory board consists of the non-executive directors and the management board consists of executive directors thereby separating the two functions. The supervisory board appoints and removes members of the management board. The management board executes strategies approved by the supervisory board. This to a great extend eliminates agency conflicts (Fig. 1.4).

Strong and large banks have traditionally been the primary long-term financer of companies. Over time, they acquired significant shares in the company and as a major stakeholder have representatives on the supervisory board. The demand for 'industrial democracy' and resultant codetermination law (codetermination is a Germany concept that involves the right of workers to participate in management of the companies they work for) lead to stronger influence of workers on boards. With large block holdings and banks as the major source of financing, there is limited public shareholding. This is a more stakeholder-centric model where the supervisory board has representatives of employees and shareholders that complement the economic legitimacy of a company with a social one.

Several EU countries have necessitated employee representation on board. In Germany, if a company has more than 2000 employees, 50%

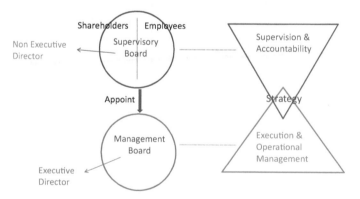

Fig. 1.4 Two-tier model (*Source* Developed by Author)

of board members are elected by employees, else 33%. One-third of the board should consist of employee representation in Austria, Czech Republic, Hungary, Luxembourg, Norway (more than 50 employees), Slovak Republic and Slovenia. Swedish companies with more than 1000 employees have 3 representations on the board, otherwise 2. Companies in Denmark with 35 or more employees can have 2 employee representatives on the board. Employees are allowed to appoint 1 director on the board in Estonia and Norway (with 30–50 employees.)

Hybrid (Japanese Business Network) Model

Japanese businesses generally work through a network of companies called as Keiretsu (family of companies) that are linked through cross holding, common directors and shared business interest. Mitsubishi and Toyota are well-known Japanese Keiretsu with a conglomerate of businesses. Companies hold significant ownership in suppliers and customer companies. They facilitate each other's business and provide support when needed. After World War II, the Japanese government focused on industrial development and got involved in promoting big companies. At that time, they were few banks and each bank formed strong relationships with one group. Thus, all the companies in the Keiretsu have support of a common bank. The concept of outside directors was quite alien (Fig. 1.5).

In recent years, there have been some outside shareholders particularly foreign investors. To attract foreign investments, a comparably more transparent governance system has been developed. Three board structures are permitted in Japan. Most companies have adopted a hybrid model (amalgam of one-tier and two-tier) with two boards. The shareholders appoint the board of directors and directors of the audit and supervisory board. The board of directors appoints representative director(s) from among them who take up the function of CEO or President. The audit and supervisory board must comprise of at least three members and majority should be outsiders. They are to monitor management of the company by the directors. Current regulations also discourage cross holding and require presence of independent directors.

Communist (Chinese) Model

Based on the political set-up, major companies in China are government or state-owned enterprises. The governments' shareholdings are held by

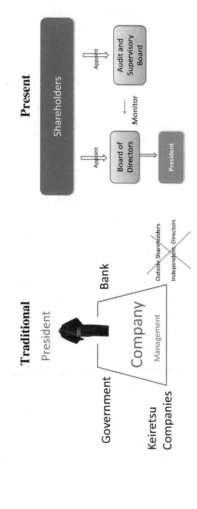

Fig. 1.5 Japanese model (*Source* Developed by Author)

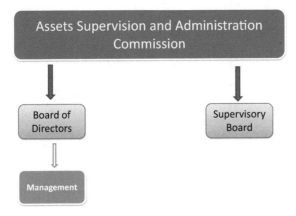

Fig. 1.6   Chinese model (*Source* Developed by Author)

the State-Owned Assets Supervision and Administrative Commission. The Commission is mandated to preserve and enhance the value of these companies. It acts as a shareholder, appoints the board and promotes the interest of the government. It establishes targets/objectives, determines assessment criteria and is involved in devising management policy, operational budgets and executive remuneration of the state-owned enterprises (Fig. 1.6).

The Indian Model

India has adopted the one-tier model combining executive and independent directors in a unitary board. Additionally, they may have nominee directors who may represent interests of financing banks or major institutional holder or government. Each listed and large public company is also required to have a women director. Unlike the Western counterparts which have a large number of shareholders, Indian companies are mainly family-owned or government companies with controlling shareholding. The boards have comparatively more executive directors and non-executive non-independent directors (Fig. 1.7).

Family Based: In family run business, the family members have controlling stake, have many board seats and are able to dominate the board influencing all major decisions (family business will be discussed in detail in Chapter 11). South Korea's corporate model of chaebol is

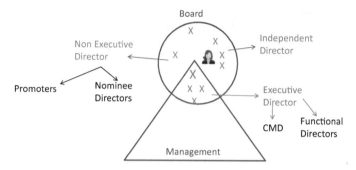

Fig. 1.7 Indian model (*Source* Developed by Author)

a network of companies with one holding company having number of subsidiaries (we will discuss corporate groups in Chapter 12). Chaebols such as Samsung are generally family controlled and operate in diverse industries.

Public Sector Undertakings: Government companies are known as public sector undertakings in India. Their board is selected by the ministry under which they operated. Representatives of the ministry are nominee directors on the board. Independent directors are also chosen by the government. Government's policies and agendas influence board decisions. The post of Chairman and Managing Director (CEO) are held by the same person. Other executive directors representing heads of different business functions are referred to as functional directors.

WHY CORPORATE GOVERNANCE

Good corporate governance improves board decision-making resulting in better corporate performance. Higher compliance minimizes risks, enhances the efficiency of the financial and business operations of the company and avoids costly litigation. Better oversight and accountability help built the reputation of the company in the eyes of customers, suppliers, financiers and business partners ultimately leading to more business. It creates shareholder value and strengthens investor confidence reducing cost of capital. Companies with good governance practices are able to align employee goals with company goals and create a culture that help retain talented and productive employees. Society also looks at such companies more favourably. The purpose of corporate governance is to help organizations realize effective entrepreneurship and sound management that can deliver sustainability and long-term success for an organization.

To enable countries and companies to strengthen their corporate governance framework, the Principles of Corporate Governance have been established.

PRINCIPLES OF CORPORATE GOVERNANCE

The Organisation for Economic Co-operation and Development (OECD) has been recommending Principles of Corporate Governance since 1999 to 'improve the legal, regulatory, and institutional framework for corporate governance, with a view to supporting economic efficiency, sustainable growth and financial stability'.

These principles are internationally accepted benchmarks and have been adopted by renowned institutions such as Financial Stability Board's (FSB) Key Standards for Sound Financial Systems and World Bank Group. OECD Principles of Corporate Governance were revised in the year 2015 in consultation with G20 countries for greater acceptability. The revised principles are more comprehensive and can be adopted by small, big, listed as well as unlisted companies. It provides a gist of six most important aspects of the corporate governance Framework for a country (see Box).

These six principles are not country specific. They take into account the different board structures across the globe as well as the regulatory frameworks present in different regions. The non-binding nature of the principles provides flexibility for adoption to meet changing scenarios.

OECD Principles 2015

Effective Framework: Promoting transparent and efficient markets—a sound legal, regulatory and institutional framework that supports effective supervision and enforcement.

Shareholders: Protecting and facilitating the exercise of rights and equitable treatment of all shareholders and effective redressal.

Market and Intermediaries: Stock markets to enable fair price discovery, fiduciary role of institutional investors and maintaining the integrity of proxy advisors, analysts, brokers and rating agencies.

Stakeholders: Recognizing the rights of stakeholders—cooperation for creating wealth, jobs and the sustainability of financially sound enterprises.

Disclosure and Transparency: Ensuring that timely and accurate disclosure is made on all material matters—financial situation, performance, ownership, and governance.

Board Responsibility: Ensuring strategic guidance of the company, effective monitoring of management and accountability to the company and the shareholders.

Principle 1: The corporate governance framework should promote transparent and fair markets, and the efficient allocation of resources. It should be consistent with the rule of law and support effective supervision and enforcement.

This principle emphasizes on the need of each country to have a corporate governance Framework which complements its history, ethnicities and environments. It propagates flexibility in implementation of the corporate governance Framework so that they are adoptive for large as well as small companies and not curtail upon an organization's economic motives yet promote an environment of accountability, transparency and self-discipline.

'The corporate governance framework should be developed with a view to its impact on overall economic performance, market integrity and the incentives it creates for market participants and the promotion of transparent and well-functioning markets'. The rules and regulations to be implemented should be after consultation with all possible stakeholders including governments, regulatory authorities and corporate representatives. Responsibilities should be clearly divided avoiding overlap and enforcement should be monitored. Effective implementation should be ensured by giving the regulations national status and ensuring the implementing institution is committed towards public interest. The regulatory authorities should be provided with political freedom to perform their duties independently. Necessary resources must be available at their disposal for them to accomplish their objectives, timely and effectively.

Stock market can also play an important role in supervision by introducing strict rules towards adopting the practices. Including the condition to follow the principles as one of the necessary requirements for trading on a particular stock exchange can help improve the corporate governance Standards of the companies being traded on a particular exchange.

> *Principle 2*: The corporate governance framework should protect and facilitate the exercise of shareholders' rights and ensure the equitable treatment of all shareholders, including minority and foreign shareholders. All shareholders should have the opportunity to obtain effective redress for violation of their rights.

Equity shareholders, on account of holding shares of the company, are called owners. However, they cannot directly manage the firms in which they own shares since they vary in their investment objectives as well as their qualification and interests. Instead, they have the right to participate in the affairs of the companies by electing the board of directors and influencing important company decisions such as election of auditors, compensation of directors/executives, distribution of dividends and approving related party transactions.

Investors as shareholders are protected by both ex-ante and ex-post rights. Ex-ante rights are pre-emptive rights such as access to timely information and disclosures and right to participate in company decisions by the way of voting. Timely information about general meetings and their agenda, facility of proxy voting and electronic voting are to be provided for effective shareholder participation in key corporate governance decisions. Ex-post rights give shareholders redressal measures including law suits against the firms as a remedy against the actions of the management which are detrimental to the interest of the shareholders. One such popular tool is class action suit (see Chapter 6 for more detail).

There should be equitable treatment of shareholders and any arrangement that gives any class disproportionate influence must be disclosed. There should not be no discrimination between foreign shareholders and domestic shareholders. Equal opportunity must be provided to all types of shareholders to vote on resolutions.

The principles also advocate smooth functioning of Market for Corporate Control. Transactions of mergers and acquisitions should occur at transparent prices and under fair conditions that protect the rights of all shareholders according to their class. Companies should not employ anti-takeover devices to shield ineffective boards.

> *Principle 3*: The corporate governance framework should provide sound incentives throughout the investment chain and provide for stock markets to function in a way that contributes to good corporate governance.

For corporate governance framework to function effectively, cooperation from various intermediaries is necessary. One of the most important intermediaries is institutional investors consisting of mutual funds, pension funds, insurance companies and hedge funds. They being large investors have the power to influence company decisions by taking a strong stand on the firm's governance issues.

The principles advocate active engagement of institutional investors through voting, direct dialogue and other appropriate means. Their policy towards corporate governance and voting practices should be disclosed. This is particularly important as they have a fiduciary duty towards their client on whose behalf they invest. Institutional investors should be encouraged to sign stewardship codes (will be discussed further in Chapter 6). If there exists a conflict of interest arising from an existing business relations with a company, the institutional investor must disclose how they will manage such conflict.

Various custodian institutions can act as per instructions of the shareholders, if the shareholder is not voting directly. Holders of the depository receipts can also be given the rights of the underlining shareholders. This will help to increase in the participation of the decisions of the companies.

Various other players such as proxy advisors, analysts, brokers and rating agencies should regularly highlight corporate governance flaws which can increase the level of awareness of investors and be instrumental in more effective voting. They should disclose and minimize any conflict of interest. Necessary regulations should be put in place to prevent insider trading (discussed in Chapter 9).

> *Principle 4*: The corporate governance framework should recognize the rights of stakeholder established by law or through mutual agreements and encourage active cooperation between corporations and stakeholders in creating wealth, jobs and the sustainability of financially sound enterprises.

For ensuring long-term survival of a company, it is necessary to take into account the interest of all its stakeholders. The success of a company is the result of teamwork that embodies contributions from a range of different resource providers including investors, employees, creditors, customers, suppliers and other stakeholders (Chapter 7). The rights of stakeholders are either protected by law (e.g. labour laws, insolvency laws) or established by contractual relations that companies must respect. Stakeholders must be provided with regular and timely information to enable their participation (Chapter 8).

The employees of the company must be allowed to participate in the corporate governance of the company. This could be by way of employee representation on board, formation of work councils, profit sharing mechanisms, stock options and any other suitable means.

Unethical behaviour should not violate rights of the stakeholders. Adequate whistle-blower mechanism should be put in place to voice their concerns (Chapter 9). Stakeholders must be provided with adequate avenues for registration and resolutions of their grievances/complaints such as having an ombudsman.

Creditors being important stakeholders' group must be provided with fair treatment with equal rights as other stakeholders. A strong mechanism must be in place to help them recover their money on time. In case of insolvency, priority must be given for meeting the claims of the creditors—both secured and unsecured.

> *Principle 5*: The corporate governance framework should ensure that timely and accurate disclosure is made on all material matters regarding the corporation, including the financial situation, performance, ownership and governance of the company.

Disclosure brings transparency in companies' operations and is a primary right of both the shareholders and stakeholders of the company. Companies are required to adhere to disclosure requirements by bringing out monthly/quarterly and annual reports. Timely disclosures of all material developments help a company improve its market credibility, attract capital and help investor make informed choices. However, companies are not expected to reveal any competitive or price-sensitive information. The information must be equally available to all uses and channels of communication cost efficient.

The disclosures recommended are:

1. The financial and operating results of the company.
2. Company objectives and non-financial information.
3. Major share ownership, including beneficial owners and voting rights.
4. Remuneration of members of the board and key executives.
5. Information about board members, including their qualifications, the selection process, other company directorships and whether they are regarded as independent by the board.
6. Related party transactions.
7. Foreseeable risk factors.
8. Issues regarding employees and other stakeholders.
9. Governance structures and policies, including the content of any corporate governance code or policy and the process by which it is implemented.

The information disclosed should be accurate and according to the accounting and financial reporting standards followed in the country. Financial reports should undergo an independent audit by competent auditors ideally selected by the audit committee (Chapter 4).

Principle 6:   The corporate governance framework should ensure the strategic guidance of the company, the effective monitoring of management by the board and the board's accountability to the company and the shareholders.

The structure of the board of directors may vary from country to country. However, their basic function of governance, strategy and monitoring remain the same. They are responsible for enhancing value of the investments made by the shareholders by ensuring consistent performance by the company along with meeting the expectations of creditors, employees and other stakeholders. The board has a fiduciary duty to act in good faith and be loyal, not pursue personal objectives or serve the interest of a particular group, but work for the larger interest of the company.

In order for boards to effectively fulfil their responsibilities, they must be able to exercise objective and independent judgement. Boards should create committees to support the full board in performing its functions, particularly with respect to audit and remuneration (see Chapter 2 for board responsibility). An important board responsibility is to oversee the risk management system and make certain the integrity of financial reporting systems (Chapter 4). Board must treat all shareholders equally, ensure a transparent board election process, minimize conflict among stakeholders, maintain fairness in related party transactions and ensure compliance with regulations.

References

Berle, A. A., & Means, G. (1932). *The modern corporation and private property.* Macmillan.

Cadbury, A. (1992). *Report of the committee on the financial aspects of corporate governance.*

Eells, R. S. F. (1960). *The meaning of modern business: An introduction to the philosophy of large corporate enterprise* (p. 108). Columbia University Press.

OECD. (2004). *OECD principles of corporate governance.*

OECD. (2015). *G20/OECD principles of corporate governance.* https://www.oecd.org/corporate/principles-corporate-governance/

Shleifer, A., & Vishny, R. W. (1997). A survey of corporate governance. *Journal of Finance, 52*(2), 737–783.

CHAPTER 2

Boards and Directors

They Set the Way, Go the Way, Pave the Way

BOARD OF DIRECTORS

A board of directors is a body of elected or appointed members who jointly oversee the activities of a company. They hold the company in 'trust' for the shareholders. As the word itself suggests, the board is a group of persons entrusted with the overall *direction* of a corporate enterprise. Board's activities are determined by the powers, duties and responsibilities delegated to it or conferred on it by an authority outside itself. These matters are typically detailed in law and the organization's by-laws (adopted from S. Jhunjhunwala and K. R. Mishra, Diversity & Effective Board, 2013) (Fig. 2.1).

Does the board actually run the business? The company is owned by shareholders who elect the board of directors to act as trustees and protect their investment and interest. The board of directors in turn appoints the management team, who have operational responsibility of the organization. The management periodically reports to the board of directors on the functioning of the organization. The board is answerable to the shareholders (adopted from S. Jhunjhunwala and R. K. Mishra, Diversity & Effective Board, 2013) (Fig. 2.1).

What does the Board Do? (adopted from R. K. Mishra and S. Jhunjhunwala, Diversity & Effective Board, 2013).

The responsibility of the board is to 'manage the organization' and the responsibility of managers, i.e. the CEO and his team, is to 'manage the

© The Author(s), under exclusive license to Springer Nature Singapore Pte Ltd. 2023
S. Jhunjhunwala, *Corporate Governance*,
https://doi.org/10.1007/978-981-99-2707-4_2

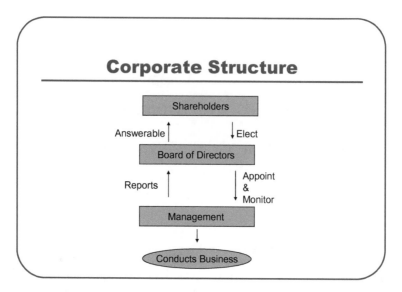

Fig. 2.1 Corporate structure (*Source* R. K. Mishra and S. Jhunjhunwala and Diversity & Effective Board, 2013)

day-to-day activities or work of the organization' based on the guidelines, policies and objectives laid down by the board.

The objective of a company is long-term growth and sustainability. To this end, as representatives of the shareholders, the purpose of the board is to oversee the functioning of the organization and ensure that it continues to operate in the best interests of all stakeholders. The role of the Board of Directors in any company is three-fold. To (Fig. 2.2).

Govern: The board is responsible for governance, i.e. ensuring the organization operates properly and effectively, and achieves its agreed objectives. Governance involves:

- Setting a framework, system, procedures and policies that fulfil the objectives of the organization and needs of all stakeholders.
- Building the ethos and values that underpin the organization enabling and ensuring transparent and accountable decision-making.

Fig. 2.2 Role of board

- Compliance with the laws of the land and in accordance with the regulatory environment.

Direct: The directors are responsible for giving strategic direction to the organization. This entrepreneurial role involves:

- Maintaining a long-term overview of the organization and all its work.
- Making strategic and investment decisions towards achieving organizations objectives.
- Establishing operational policies and providing adequate resources for business activities.

- Appointing the CEO and management team and establishing management goals.

Supervise: Finally, the directors must constantly monitor the progress of the company towards its objectives as defined by shareholders. Supervision encompasses:

- Establishing control and accountability systems that enable risk to be assessed and managed.
- Monitoring use of firms' resources or wealth.
- Assessing progress of implementation of strategy.
- Monitoring the management activities and achievement of the targets set.

These roles in turn require directors to embody three perspectives.

The *inward perspective* allows directors to create the necessary policies and process within the organization and choose the right people to run the business smoothly.

The *outward dimension* required directors to step outside the organization and take care of the concerns of government, customers and society at large. By looking at what's happening around, the board will be able to appreciate the external environment and its impact on company's business.

A *forward-looking* board will be able to build the long-term vision and strategy for the company. Though no one may be able to see the future, it is the role of the board to make certain that the necessary capabilities in terms of people, intellectual property and processes are in place for the company to face new challenges (Fig. 2.3).

This requires a perceptive, level headed and well-balanced board with clairvoyant like ability. Only a well-composed, very vibrant and multi-dimensional board can successfully carry out such a wide range of responsibilities.

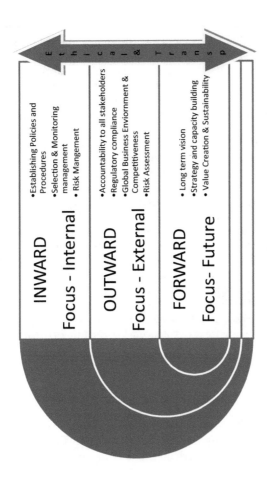

Fig. 2.3 Director's perspectives and role (*Source* R. K. Mishra and S. Jhunjhunwala Diversity and the Effective Board, 2013)

Flying Lufthansa

The Lufthansa Group is a leading global aviation group with more than 550 subsidiaries and affiliated companies. These are organized in the business segments—Passenger Airline Group, Logistics, Technical Equipment, Catering and Other. All business units play a leading role in their respective industries. In 2021, the Lufthansa Group generated annual revenue of EUR 16.8 billion with a little more than 100 thousand employees (www.lufthansagroup.com, 2022).

Deutsche Lufthansa AG has the management and supervisory structures typical for companies in Germany. The Executive Board is responsible for managing the company and defining its strategic direction. In doing so, the aim is to increase company value sustainably. The Supervisory Board appoints, advises and supervises the Executive Board. Deutsche Lufthansa AG is the parent company and the largest single operating company in the Lufthansa Group. The individual business segments are run as separate group companies, with the exception of the Lufthansa Passenger Airlines. They have their own profit and operating responsibility and are monitored by their respective supervisory boards, in which members of Deutsche Lufthansa AG's Executive Board are also represented. The supervisory board consisting of 17 members is led by the chairman. About half the members are employee representatives including the deputy chairman. These include employees such as flight captain, flight attendant, cargo handler and engine mechanic (www.lufthansagroup.com, 2022). The management board consists of the chief executive officer and five other members heading different functional areas such as that of Chief Financial Officer, Fleet and technology and Global Markets & Networks.

Source https://www.lufthansagroup.com accessed in 2018 and 2022.

BOARD COMPOSITION

As discussed in the first chapter, the board may consist of different categories of directors depending on the model adopted. Each has their own role and importance in the governance of a company.

Executive Directors: The Dual Role

Executive directors work for the company as full-time employees. They are involved in the day-to-day operations of the company. They are the senior most officers and form what is known as the 'Top Management'.

They are often referred to as whole-time directors or inside directors. Their leader or head is known as the chief executive officer (Anglo-Saxon model), Managing Director (India) or President (Japan) depending on the governance model. In the one-tier model, other executive directors may be the chief financial officer (CFO) and chief operating officer (COO). In Indian Government companies often functional heads such as Director Finance, Director Marketing are appointed as the executive directors. In the two-tier system, the entire management board consists of executive directors. They could be heads of business divisions or functional heads (see Box—Flying Lufthansa).

In the one-tier model, the executive directors play both the role of management and board member. Technically, they are appointing and supervising themselves. It is the executive directors who are responsible for strategy formulation and its implementation. As we will see in the next chapter, this dual role creates conflict.

Non-Executive Directors

Board members who are not executive directors or senior officers of the company are non-executive directors. They are not part of the management and not involved in the day-to-day operations. In the Anglo-Saxon model, they offer a more advisory role and are often chosen for their expertise and experience. In the two-tier model, members of the supervisory board are non-executive directors. It may be noted that employees may be members of the supervisory board as employee representatives, but they are not part of the top management and hence not executive directors (see Box—Flying Lufthansa).

Bajaj Auto

Bajaj Auto is ranked as the world's fourth largest three and two-wheeler manufacturer. Founded in 1926 in India by Jamnalal Bajaj, founder of the group. His son, Kamalnayan Bajaj, then 27, took over the reigns of the business in 1942 and not only consolidated the group, but also diversified into various manufacturing activities. His son, the present Chairman of the group, Rahul Bajaj, took charge of the business in 1965. Under his leadership, the turnover of the Bajaj Auto the flagship company has gone up from INR.72 million to INR. 120 billion, its product portfolio has

expanded and the brand has found a global market (https://www.bajaja
uto.com/about-us/the-company).

The board structure in 2017 (Bajaj Auto Ltd Annual Report March
2017):

	Name of Director	Category	Relationship with other directors
1	Rahul Bajaj	Chairman, Executive	Father of Rajiv Bajaj and Sanjiv Bajaj, father in law of Manish Kejriwal, Cousin of Madhur, Shekhar and Niraj Bajaj
2	Madhur Bajaj	Vice Chairman, Executive	Brother of Shekhar Bajaj and Niraj Bajaj, Cousin of Rahul Bajaj
3	Rajiv Bajaj	Managing Director, Executive	Son of Rahul Bajaj, brother of Sanjiv Bajaj, brother in law of Manish Kejriwal
4	Shekhar Bajaj	Non- Executive	Brother of Madhur Bajaj and Niraj Bajaj, Cousin of Rahul Bajaj
5	Niraj Bajaj	Non-Executive	Brother of Madhur Bajaj and Shekhar Bajaj, Cousin of Rahul Bajaj
6	Sanjiv Bajaj	Non-Executive	Son of Rahul Bajaj, brother of Rajiv Bajaj, brother in law of Manish Kejriwal
7	Manish Kejriwal	Non-Executive	Son in law of Rahul Bajaj, brother in law of Rajiv Bajaj and Sanjiv Bajaj
8	Pradeep Shrivastava	Executive Director	–
9	D. S. Mehta	Non- Executive	–
10	Kantikumar R. Podar[a]	Non-Executive	
11	D. J. Balaji Rao	Non-Executive	–
12	J. N. Godrej	Non-Executive	–
13	Naresh Chandra	Non-Executive	–
14	Nanoo Pamnani	Non-Executive	–
15	P. Murari	Non-Executive	–
16	Dr. Gita Piramal	Non-Executive	–

[a]Kanti Kumar R. Podar Resigned as a director of the company w.e.f. 15 march
2017

Inside Directors

Board members who are closely associated with the company are considered as inside directors. They may be executive directors or non-executive directors who were previously executive directors but have retired from the company. Directors who have significant shareholding in the company are also referred to as inside directors. In family run firms, the owners may be non-executive but have a strong understanding of the company and wield significant influence on management. The Chairman, Vice Chairman and Managing Director on board of Bajaj Auto Ltd (see Box) all belong to the Bajaj Family. Seven of the sixteen board members are family members and would be considered insiders. Almost half the board members are inside directors. It should be noted that inside directors may be executive or non-executive directors. Inside directors yield enormous unchecked power which allows them to mismanage company affairs and siphon corporate funds (see Box—Pension Raider Maxwell).

Nominee Directors

Nominee directors are representative of a principal shareholder such as the government in a government company, or a holding company of a subsidiary, or a partner in a joint venture or a major institutional investor. They may also be representatives of a large stakeholder, a bank that have financed a large loan or a major customer. They are directors of the company and have a fiduciary duty towards the company. Still their primary responsibility is towards the parent organization they represent, and this can cause a conflict of interest.

Outside Directors

Board members who are neither employees nor stake holders in the company are outside directors and hence necessarily non-executive directors. They generally do not receive any remuneration except sitting fees for attending board meetings. As they are not closely involved with the company, they bring a different perspective and board deliberations benefit from their experience and specialized expertise. They are able to critically evaluate proposals put to the board by inside directors. Another benefit of outside directors is that they help the company network with outside world for acquiring resources and creating business opportunities. Corporate scams during the 1990s showed how insider directors could abuse their powers and misappropriate corporate finds for their self-indulgence. This leads to a call for more outside directors by policy makers to monitor and reduce dominance of insiders on the board. It may be recalled that German, Japanese and Chinese models traditionally did not have outside directors.

Pension Raider Maxwell

"Maxwell was missing from his yacht ..... the publisher of the Daily Mirror, Sunday Mirror, The People, Daily Record, New York Daily News and a raft of titles elsewhere across the world plus several book publishers, including Macmillan - had fallen overboard and drowned" (Greenslade, 2011). Born into poverty in Czechoslovakia, Robert Maxwell build a vast media and publishing empire. A Member of British Parliament he lived a flamboyant lifestyle—helicopter, luxury yacht and all. In 1991, the company's survival became questionable as it reeled under a £3bn debt (Laurance et al., 1991). His body was discovered floating in the Atlantic Ocean and at the time was believed to be a suicide. After his demise, investigations revealed that the media mogul had plundered £440 million from the pension fund of his Mirror Group newspaper business affecting 30,000 people (Faulkner, 2010).

When banks began to close in for repayments, Maxwell began transferring funds from the pension fund into his privately owned companies. Incidentally, two of Robert Maxwell's sons, Ian and Kevin, were also directors in Bishopsgate Investment Management Ltd, the corporate trustee of the pension money as well as directors in their father's company ("A Notorious Fraud – the Robert Maxwell Farrago", n.d.). The Investment Management Regulatory Organisation (IMRO), the watchdog for the fund management industry, was criticised in a long-awaited report into the collapse of Maxwell's empire. The report, which cost £10m and took almost 10 years, attacks IMRO for its "cosmetic" supervision of Bishopsgate Investment Management Ltd. and London & Bishopsgate International Investment, two of Maxwell's pension management companies. Some suggest that for some time IMRO had repeatedly been warning the Securities and Investments Board, to tighten controls on how pension funds were managed, but their warnings were ignored (Ringshaw, 2001).

The Department of Trade and Industry (DTI) report into Maxwell's fraud observed ("A Notorious Fraud—The Robert Maxwell Farrago", n.d.):

- Labour peer Lord Donaghue, a Maxwell director, ought to have been able to find out what was going on. But he never asked the obvious questions.
- Coopers & Lybrand Deloitte accountants "*failed to report abuses*" to pension fund trustees.

The UK Court of Appeal, considering the obligations of the Directors of Corporates in ***Bishopsgate Investment Management Ltd {in liq} v Maxwell (no.2)*** [1994] 1 All ER CA 261; [1993] BCLC 814 stated at p. 265:

> If a director chooses to participate in the management of the company and exercises powers on its behalf, he owes a duty to act bona fide in the interests of the company. He must exercise the power solely for the purpose for which it is conferred. To exercise the power for another purpose is a breach of fiduciary duty....... Mr Ian Maxwell was in breach of his fiduciary duty because he gave away the company's assets for no consideration to a private family company of which he was a director. This was prima facie a use of his powers as a director for an improper purpose and in my judgement the burden was upon him to demonstrate the propriety of the transaction.

Points to Ponder:

1. How did Maxwell funded his flamboyant lifestyle? Did Maxwell and his sons behave appropriately as directors?
2. What is the risk associated with inside directors?
3. What about the role of other members of the board, do you thing having a large number of outside directors would have prevented the fraud?
4. Do you thing think regulators and auditors did their job properly?
5. What were the consequences of corporate governance failure at Maxwell Corporation?

Independent Directors

Independent directors are outside directors who exercise 'independent judgement'. They should not have any direct or indirect pecuniary interest in the company. "They should be independent of management and free from any business or other relationship which could materially interfere with the exercise of their independent judgement" (Financial Aspects of Corporate Governance, 1992). For instance, if an outside director provides consultancy to the company, he is not independent. If he has business ties with the CEO, he would not be independent. A director is considered independent when free from any business, family or other relationship—with the company, its controlling shareholder or the management—which might jeopardise his or her judgement (European Commission, 6 October 2004).

The concept of independent directors was introduced by Securities and Exchange Commission (SEC), USA, as early as 1940, and since 1978, all companies listed on New York Stock Exchange are required to have independent directors as a solution to agency problem caused by inside directors. To monitor management and minimize executive mismanagement, such independent directors should not feel obligated to CEO and be willing to speak their mind against management if needed.

The statutory definition by different regulators (see Table 2.1) don't really say who an independent director is, but who cannot be considered as independent. The question is their ability to take independent judgement. If the director is a very close friend of an inside director or is some way obliged by him would that influence his decisions. If a company appoints retired bureaucrats, retired CEOs or current CEOs of other companies or academicians, they may meet the legal requirements but does that mean they will exercise 'independent judgement'. What if the bureaucrat was offered the seat in return for a favour or the CEO of the other company was for many years a subordinate of the company's CEO. Suppose some of the executive directors and independent directors were school buddies. Their families go for vacations together. Can they be considered independent?

BOARD INDEPENDENCE

To reduce mismanagement by inside directors and the resultant corporate collapses, countries have begun to require boards to be more independent. The Cadbury Report suggested that companies have at least 2 independent directors. Many countries expect 30% or more directors to

Table 2.1 Legal qualification for independent director

Listing Agreements NSYE, USA	No director qualifies as "independent" unless the board of directors affirmatively determines that the director has no material relationship with the listed company (either directly or as a partner, shareholder or officer of an organization that has a relationship with the company). Companies must disclose these determinations In addition i. A director who receives, or whose immediate family member receives, more than $100,000 per year in direct compensation from the listed company, other than director and committee fees and pension or other forms of deferred compensation for prior service (provided such compensation is not contingent in any way on continued service), is presumed not to be independent until five years after he or she ceases to receive more than $100,000 per year in such compensation ii. A director who is affiliated with or employed by, or whose immediate family member is affiliated with or employed in a professional capacity by, a present or former internal or external auditor of the company is not "independent" until five years after the end of either the affiliation or the auditing relationship iii. A director who is employed, or whose immediate family member is employed, as an executive officer of another company where any of the listed company's present executives serves on that company's compensation committee is not "independent" until five years after the end of such service or the employment relationship iv. A director who is an executive officer or an employee, or whose immediate family member is an executive officer, of another company (A) that accounts for at least 2% or $1 million, whichever is greater, of the listed company's consolidated gross revenues, or (B) for which the listed company accounts for at least 2% or $1 million, whichever is greater, of such other company's consolidated gross revenues, in each case is not "independent" until five years after falling below such threshold

(continued)

Table 2.1 (continued)

The UK Corporate Governance Code	The board should determine whether the director is independent in character and judgement and whether there are relationships or circumstances which are likely to affect, or could appear to affect, the director's judgement. The board should state its reasons if it determines that a director is independent notwithstanding the existence of relationships or circumstances which may appear relevant to its determination, including if the director:

- has been an employee of the company or group within the last five years;
- has, or has had within the last three years, a material business relationship with the company either directly, or as a partner, shareholder, director or senior employee of a body that has such a relationship with the company;
- has received or receives additional remuneration from the company apart from a director's fee, participates in the company's share option or a performance-related pay scheme, or is a member of the company's pension scheme;
- has close family ties with any of the company's advisers, directors or senior employees;
- holds cross-directorships or has significant links with other directors through involvement in other companies or bodies;
- represents a significant shareholder; or
- has served on the board for more than nine years from the date of their first election

| Listing Obligation and Disclosure Requirement, SEBI India | An independent director means a non-executive director other than a nominee director: (i) who, in the opinion of the board, is a person of integrity and possesses relevant expertise and experience; (ii) who is or was not a promoter of the company or its holding, subsidiary or associate company; (iii) who is not related to promoters or directors in the company, its holding, subsidiary or associate company; (iv) who apart from director's remuneration has or had no material or pecuniary relationship with the company, its holding, subsidiary or associate company, or their promoters, or directors, during the two immediately preceding financial years or during the current financial year; (v) none of whose relatives has or had pecuniary relationship or transaction with the company, its holding, subsidiary or associate company, or their promoters, or directors, amounting to two per cent or more of its gross turnover or total income or fifty lakh rupees or such higher amount as may be prescribed, whichever is lower, during the two immediately preceding financial years or during the current financial year; (vi) who, neither himself nor any of his relatives, (a) holds or has held the position of a key managerial personnel or is or has been employee of the company or its holding, subsidiary or associate company in any of the three financial years immediately preceding the financial year in which he is proposed to be appointed; (b) is or has been an employee or proprietor or a partner, in any of the three financial years immediately preceding the financial year in which he is proposed to be appointed, of (1) a firm of auditors or company secretaries in practice or cost auditors of the company or its holding, subsidiary or associate company; or (2) any legal or a consulting firm that has or had any transaction with the company, its holding, subsidiary or associate company amounting to ten per cent or more of the gross turnover of such firm; (c) holds together with his relatives two per cent or more of the total voting power of the company; or (d) is a chief executive or director, by whatever name called, of any non-profit organization that receives 25% or more of its receipts from the Company, any of its promoters, directors or its holding, subsidiary or associate company or that holds 2% or more of the total voting power of the Company; or (e) is a material supplier, service provider or customer or a lessor or lessee of the company; (vii) who is not less than 21 years of age |

Source Listing Obligation and Disclosure Requirement, SEBI, India, The UK Corporate Governance Code, Listing Agreements NSYE, USA

be independent (Table 2.2). Enhanced independence it is argued will strengthen corporate governance of the company, enhance performance and finally protect shareholders as well as other stakeholders. The European Commission in 2004 recommended member states to strengthen the presence and role of independent directors on listed companies. "Protecting shareholders, employees and the public against potential conflicts of interest, by an independent check on management decisions, is particularly important to restore confidence in financial markets after recent scandals" (European Commission, 6 October 2004). An independent board it is believed can act as a countervailing force to CEO power, making them more accountable.

Board of directors has been blamed for corporate misdeeds. Independent directors are expected to monitor the actions of executive directors and increase executive accountability. Independent boards were to be the means for improving corporate governance. Independent boards, however, have had limited success in preventing corporate scams. The concept of independent directors has some inherent shortcomings.

"Independent Director" an Oxymoron

Independent directors, who were originally outside directors, were brought in for their professional or business acumen. Their role was to give advice. There function was more of a consultant. They were someone you got to know on the golf course or at cricket club and invited to join the board. When selecting an independent director, familiarity is vital even today. Though the nomination committee undergoes at least on paper some sort of formal process, they normally windup selecting a new member who is vouched for by someone they know. If the function of independent directors is only advisory why not hire them as consultants. And if some directors give more or better advice than others, would they deserve higher remuneration. The question that then arises is, if directors are paid based on the advice they provide, can they be considered independent (Clarke, 2007).

The most important reason companies have independent directors is to meet regulatory requirements. The role of independent directors has become about ensuring compliance. This was why in the 1990s and 2000s when corporate governance codes came around, boards saw a surge in lawyers and finance professionals (certified / chartered accountants). They wanted people with legal background who could ensure the company was compliant legally. Financial experts were necessary to carry out the functions of audit committee. It is important and in many countries even a mandatory requirement that audit committee consists of independent directors who possess adequate financial expertise.

Table 2.2 Board independence

Independent directors	Country	Maximum term for ID (in years)	Substantial shareholding for determining ID	Separation of chair of the board and CEO
One-tier Boards				
More than 50%	Australia		5%	Recommended
	Korea		10%	
	Sweden		10%	Required
50%	Iceland	7	10%	
	UK	9		Recommended
33% or 50%	India	10	2%	If multiple businesses
	Israel	9	5%	Required
	Singapore	9	10%	Recommended
30% / 33%	Brazil		50%	Required/Recommended
	Greece	12		
	Hong Kong	9	10%	Recommended
	Turkey	6	5%	
25%	Columbia		50%	Required
	Mexico		20%	Required
1/2/3	Belgium	12	10%	Recommended
	Canada			
	Chile		10%	Required
	Spain	12	3%	Recommended
Two-tier (Supervisory Board)				
More than 50%	Argentina	5	15%	The Chairman heads the supervisory board and CEO is part of management board
50%	Austria			
	Estonia	10		
	Latvia	10		
33%	China	6	5%	
30%	Indonesia	10	20%	
2	Poland		5%	

(continued)

Table 2.2   (continued)

Independent directors	Country	Maximum term for ID (in years)	Substantial shareholding for determining ID	Separation of chair of the board and CEO
Option (one or two) Board				
More than 50%	Finland		10%	Recommended
	Netherlands		10%	Required
	Norway		10%	Required
	Slovenia	12		Required
	Switzerland			Recommended
50%	Denmark	12	50%	
	Hungary		30%	
33% or 50%	France	12	10%	

Source OECD Corporate Governance Fact Book 2017 available at www.oecd.org

Once selected independent directors stay on for many decades, often till death. There are independent directors who have been on boards for more than half a century. Long association builds a friendly and cohesive relationship with not only management but other independent directors. Restricting tenure of independent directors is one way of putting a check on this. But is number of years the right measure? An independent director may get cosy with management in six months or it may not happen even in decades.

With the failure of policy makers to clearly establish who can be considered as 'independent director', they have shifted the responsibility to the board. As the UK code puts it, 'The board should identify in the annual report each non-executive director it considers to be independent'. The NYSE and Nasdaq stock exchanges also rely on the board to determine independence. The nomination and remuneration committees of Indian companies are required to formulate the criteria for determining 'qualifications, positive attributes and independence of a director'. Further, the onus of independence is on directors themselves, as they are to give a declaration that they meet the criteria of independence.

As this is not their full-time work, independent directors are able to devote limited time and energy to the role. Often, they are on boards of many companies at the same time. At one time, Sanjay Asher a highly reputed Indian lawyer was on the board of more than 50 companies—as independent and non-independent director (Layak, 2017). Limiting their directorship to some extend ensures they commit reasonable time to the company. Directors on Indian boards can be on a maximum of ten listed companies of which maximum seven could be as independent director (LODR, 2015). Resources allocated to them are generally minimal. They are completely dependent on management for information, and their decisions are as good as the information provided to them.

Independent directors' remuneration, even if only sitting fees, is a delicate balancing act. If the fee is too low, why should anyone agree to be on the board, and if it is very large, there is an incentive to want to continue on the board and not displease executive directors by asking too many questions. If they constantly challenge them, they may not be reappointed. To address this issue, Indian Companies Act 2013, has fixed the term of the independent director at 5 years with a maximum of two terms.

A primary responsibility on independent directors is the responsibility of protecting minority shareholders. However, as we will discuss in detail in the chapter on family business, as majority shareholders dominate the board, independent directors' views can easily be side-lined. As seen in the case of Tata companies in 2016, independent directors who assert their 'independence judgement' and go against majority shareholder may be forced to resign or may even be removed.

"The qualities that make a director truly independent do not come from a statutory definition, but rather come from intelligence, experience, and a strong sense of ethical responsibility. The ability to challenge the conventional wisdom, to tell truth to power, is rare, and even rarer, is the director who can do so but not destroy the collegiality of the boardroom" (Karmel, 2013). The problem is finding such directors. After all, as the famous Indian poet Tagore puts it—Independence is "Where the mind is without fear".

BOARD LEADERSHIP

The board is headed by a chairperson. The chairperson is one of the directors that the board chooses as their leader. The most obvious role played by the chairperson is to govern the workings of the board. As the Cadbury Report states, the chairman's role in securing good corporate governance is crucial. He is responsible for running the board smoothly and efficiently. A good chairperson is one who can bring out the best from the board members and maximize its effectiveness. The chairperson decides the agenda of the meeting and steers the direction of discussions. As the leader, he should encourage all directors (executive and non-executive) to contribute to the board. He should create an environment where everyone can express views in healthy deliberations and disputes if any are resolved amicably.

CEO-Chairman Duality

In the two-tier model, the Chairman is the head of the supervisory board and the CEO heads the management position. Hence, the roles are clearly segregated. Historically, in the one-tier board, the chairperson and CEO position was held by the same person. As the Cadbury Report states given the importance of the chairman's role, it should be separate from that of the chief executive. If the two roles are combined in one person, it represents a considerable concentration of power. The Stewardship Theory (theories will be discussed in Chapter 3) suggests that the combined position gives an ethical and responsible leader ability to make swift and effective decisions. This can be extremely useful in period of high uncertainty and turmoil.

According to the managerial hegemony and agency theory, this can lead to abuse and misuse of power (see Box—Pension Raider Maxwell) CEOs often exercise such dominance by means of managerial entrenchment, that is, by making themselves valuable to shareholders and costly to replace. They invest the company's resources in those ventures where they have expertise and skill, though this may not be the best investment alternative for the firm. By doing so, they increase their value to and dependence of shareholders. As a result of such entrenchment, CEOs can raise their remuneration in negotiations with the board of directors, as well as obtain more latitude in running the firm (Shleifer & Vishny, 1989). A root cause of many corporate scams has been this unfettered power in the hands of one person.

Hence, governance regulations in many countries either require or recommend separation of Chair and CEO (Table 2.2) so that no one individual has absolute and unconditional powers. The chairperson 'leads the board' and the CEO 'runs the business'.

Independent Chair

To enhance independence of board and prevent excessive power in the hands of executives, there has been a growing demand that the board chair and CEO not only be separate but the chairperson be independent. This will give confidence to the independent directors and help build an effective independent board. The independence of the chairman is paramount to the successful implementation of good corporate governance practices at board level. The chairman is obliged to use his power appropriately and not to influence the outcome of the meetings towards a specific agenda. To ensure the chairman acts in an independent manner, internationally recognized governance codes state that the chairman should not have previously been the CEO of the company. If the chairperson is not independent, the board should appoint a lead independent director and have a strong pool of independent directors to maintain a strong independent element on the board. In India and Singapore, one-third of the board is required to be independent, but if the chairperson is executive to ensure board independence half the directors must be independent.

BOARD COMMITTEES

As the board has enormous responsibilities to reduce the burden and increase efficiency, some of the functions are delegated to Committees. It is a small working group identified by the board to carry out a specific task. Each committee will consist of a few directors as members and a chairperson and will oversee a particular function. To enable better and more focused attention, the board delegates particular matters to the committees. Committees review the matter in great detail before making specific recommendations to the board. The board can thus take better informed decisions. Some committees may be mandatory under different regulations. Audit committee is essential almost in all country codes. Nomination and remuneration committees are also generally recommended (Table 2.3).

Table 2.3 Board committees in India

Audit Committee Nomination and Remuneration Committee Stakeholders Relationship Committee	Companies Act 2013 and Listing Obligation and Disclosure Requirements (LODR), 2015
Corporate Social Responsibility Committee	Companies Act 2013
Risk Management Committee (required by top 1000 companies by market capitalization)	LODR, 2015

Source Developed by Author

SELECTING A DIRECTOR: THE NOMINATION COMMITTEE

The purpose of the nomination committee is to discourage appointment of family and friends as directors and instead select the most capable and best fit for the board. Most importantly, they are to ensure that the independent directors they choose will in fact be able to act independently. They lay down skills and characteristics that are needed in board candidates and define the parameters of independence. It is important to remember that directors are appointed by shareholders. Nomination committee's function is to search, identify and recommend suitable candidates. The nomination committee is also entrusted with the responsibility of evaluating the performance of the board and individual members. It makes recommendation to the board not only on the appointment, but based on evaluation reappointment of directors. The committee is responsible for succession planning particular for the chairman and the chief executive officer. The committee may also be made responsible for selection of senior management. The committee may be required to review the structure and composition of the board and compliance of the directors with the Code of Conduct.

Since a primary role of the committee is determining criteria for independence and choosing independence directors, it is essential that the nomination committee be predominately independent. Thus, countries such as USA, Canada and Germany require that nomination committee to be 100% independent and chaired by an independent director. Australia, China, India, Indonesia, Russia, Singapore and several other countries require or recommend that 50% or more members of the committee be independent and the committee be chaired by an independent director while most countries including Finland, France, Hungary, Italy, Japan, New Zealand, Norway, Sweden, Switzerland and UK desire 50% to be independent but do not insist that the chair be independent (OECD Corporate Governance Fact Book, 2017 available at www.oecd.org).

Sikka's Sikka

Vishal Sikka, the former SAP Chief Technology Officer who joined Infosys as its first non-founder chief executive officer in June 2014, is in the eye of a storm. Inducted as a full-time director of the board and CEO and MD, his annual compensation was set at $6 million with stock options worth $5 million. His salary for 2017 was Rs. 45. 11 crores, inclusive of a 50% hike in remuneration (Govindraj, 2017). The remuneration of Sikka was 283.07 times higher than the median remuneration of employees (MRE) prompting the founder members to voice concerns ("Infosys CEO Vishal Sikka's annual salary drops due to lower bonus payout", 2017). Infosys had held that ratio between the highest salary paid by the company to any executive and the company's median salary should be 50 to 60 (Sharma, 2017). Several other executives also received significant hike in their pay packages. Sikka while justifying the same said "It has been my personal endeavour since joining Infosys to enable all employees to share in the successes of the company ...... we restructured the compensation of senior leaders to be more performance-based, with a significant portion of their compensation now coming through stock incentives, creating a more direct alignment with the interest shareholders" (Sengupta, 2017).

Points to Ponder:

1. Was Sikka's hike in Salary justified?
2. Should there be parity between senior executives pay and other employees?
3. What are the merits and demerits of stock options?

DIRECTORS' REMUNERATION

Executive compensation has always been a contentious issue. Entrenched CEOs often draw very exorbitant pay packages and perquisite such as use of private jets. There has been a growing discontent of the disparity of pay between top management and the rest of the employees. Bringing people of high calibre onto the board requires that directors be adequately compensated, but at the same time their remuneration should not be in excess and should justify their contribution to the company. "Microsoft CEO Satya Nadella made just over $20 million in cash and stock in 2017...... half of Nadella's pay package is based on how well he performs in three key areas: 'Product & Strategy', 'Customers & Stakeholders' and 'Culture & Organizational leadership'. Scoring well in all areas netted him a $7,032,406 bonus on his base salary of $1,450,000" (Weinberger, 2017). Gurnani the CEO of the multinational information technology solutions provider Tech Mahindra, and the highest paid in India, earned a salary of Rs. 150.7 crores including perks and bonuses for 2016–2017 (GovindRaj, 2017). Pay must be based on performance. Part of executive compensation is increasingly including stock option so as to align their interest with that of shareholders and forging long-term interest in the company (see Box—Sikka's Sikka). However, managerial ownership acts as an incentive to increase share prices using unethical and sometimes illegal means.

The pay for performance provisions of the Dodd-Frank Act requires companies in USA to disclose the relationship between executive compensation paid and the financial performance of the company. According to the Say on Pay included in the Dodd- Frank Act, it is a mandatory to ask shareholders to approve the compensation package of the company's named executive officers (the CEO, CFO and top three most other highly compensated executive officers). Though a non-binding shareholding resolution, it has increased the influence of shareholders and proxy advisory firms. Nethertheless, these provisions can lead to short-term performance focus at the cost of long-term firm value.

The remuneration of independent directors is equality tricky. It must compensate for their time and effort but should not be so large that they would like to continue on the board for the financial incentive and are therefore hesitant to challenge the executive proposals putting their independence in question. As higher remuneration has a tendency to dilute the effectiveness of independent directors, India has capped board seating fees Rs. 1 Lakh per board or committee meeting (Rule 4 of the Companies (Appointment and Remuneration of Managerial Personnel) Rules, 2014).They can, however, receive profit-related commission subject to resolution of the shareholders duly passed at a general meeting. Total commission paid to all independent directors should not be more than 1% of profits (Companies Act, 2013). With the exception of few directors who earn big payouts, for most the average takeaway is much lower than their counterparts in USA. Increase in duties, higher expectation of accountability and greater risk of liabilities have led to a short supply of pool of independent directors. As companies grow bigger and businesses complex, to attract people of calibre they must be adequately compensated. It has to be relative to their duties and value they bring to board.

Remuneration Committee

To ensure appropriate remuneration is paid to directors and to minimize conflict of interest, a remuneration committee is formed. Naturally, if executive directors decide their own remuneration, they can pay themselves heft compensations. Hence, the committee must be significantly independent. Canada, Italy, Ireland, Korea, Norway, Portugal, Russia, Switzerland, UK and USA among others have 100% independent remuneration committees and the chair must be independent. Australia, China, Finland, France, Greece, Hong Kong, Indonesia, India, Israel, Mexico and Singapore have committees with 50% of more independent directors and is chaired by an independent director. German is among the few countries where remuneration committee is not required.

The remuneration committee is to assist the board in developing and administering a fair and transparent procedure for setting policy for the remuneration of directors. They may also oversee remuneration structure of senior management. The committee is responsible for balancing the remuneration between fixed and variable enough to recruit, motivate and retain the best while compiling with regulations and shareholders' interest. Remuneration packages of directors and senior management must be on the basis of their merit, qualifications, competence and contribution to the company (Table 2.4 illustrates the role of these committees as specified by Indian Regulations).

Table 2.4   Nomination and Remuneration Committees in India

Applicability	In India, the nomination and remuneration committees are combined
	(a) All Listed Companies—LODR is applicable
	(b) Public companies who are not listed and fulfil any one of the conditions (Sec 178 of Companies Act is applicable)
	   i. Paid up capital of Rs.10 Crores or more
	   ii. Turnover of Rs.100 Crores or more
	   iii. Outstanding loans or borrowings or debentures or deposits exceeding Rs.50 Crores or more

Composition	• The nomination and remuneration committees shall consist of three or more non-executive directors • At least half (50%) of the directors must be independent • The chairperson of the company may be a member of the committee but cannot chair this committee *The **chairman** of the Nomination and Remuneration Committees must be **independent in listed** companies*
Functions as nomination committee	• Lay down criteria for selection of directors and senior personnel • Identify persons who are qualified to become directors and to be appointed in senior management • Recommend to the board their appointment or removal • Carry out evaluation of every director's performance • Formulate the criteria for determining qualifications, positive attributes and independence of a director *Listed companies are required to have a board diversity policy to encourage women. Extension of the term of independent directors will be based on their performance evaluation*
Functions as remuneration committee	The nomination and remuneration committees shall recommend to the board a policy, relating to the remuneration for the directors, key managerial personnel and other employees. The policy shall ensure that: (*a*) The level and composition of remuneration is reasonable and sufficient to attract, retain and motivate quality directors required to run the company successfully; (*b*) The relationship of remuneration to performance is clear and meets appropriate performance benchmarks; and (*c*) Remuneration to directors, key managerial personnel and senior management involves a balance between fixed and incentive pay reflecting short- and long-term performance objectives of the company The remuneration policy shall be disclosed in the board's report

Source Listing Obligation and Disclosure Requirement, SEBI, India and Companies Act 2013, India

References

Australian Guardians. (n.d.). *A notorious fraud—the Robert Maxwell Farrago*. http://australian-guardians.org/?page_id=808. Accessed 12 December 2017.

Bajaj Auto Ltd. *Annual Report 2016–17*, p. 30. https://www.bajajauto.com/about-us/the-company. Accessed 7 December 2017.

Companies Act 2013, India.

Corporate governance: Commission urges Member States to ensure a strong role for independent directors, European Commission, Press Release 6th October 2004. http://europa.eu/rapid/press-release_IP-04-1182_en.htm?locale=en. Accessed 9 December 2017.

Dodd-Frank Wall Street Reform and Consumer Protection Act, USA.

Clarke, D. C. (2007). *Three concepts of ID*. https://scholarship.law.gwu.edu/cgi/viewcontent.cgi?article=1045&context=faculty_publications. Accessed 11 May 2021.

Faulkner, N. (2010). *The five biggest pension scandals*. https://www.lovemoney.com/news/4133/the-five-biggest-pension-scandals. Accessed 12 December 2017.

Financial Aspects of Corporate Governance. (1992). https://www.frc.org.uk/getattachment/9c19ea6f-bcc7-434c-b481-f2e29c1c271a/The-Financial-Aspects-of-Corporate-Governance-(the-Cadbury-Code).pdf. Accessed 18 February 2021.

Govindraj, R. (2017). *Top 10 highest paid CEO's of India*. https://www.startupstories.in/STORIES/INSPIRATIONAL-STORIES/TOP-10-HIGHEST-PAID-CEOS-OF-INDIA

Greenslade, R. (2011). *Pension plunderer Robert Maxwell remembered 20 years after his death*. https://www.theguardian.com/media/greenslade/2011/nov/03/pressandpublishing-daily-mirror. Accessed 12 December 2017.

Jhunjhunwala, S., & Mishra, K. R. (2013). *Diversity & effective board*. Elsevier.

Karmel, R. S. (2013). *Is the independent director model broken?* Harvard Law School Forum on Corporate Governance and Financial Regulation. https://corpgov.law.harvard.edu/2013/11/14/is-the-independent-director-model-broken/. Accessed 9 December 2017.

Laurance, B., et al. (1991). *Maxwell's body found in sea*. https://www.theguardian.com/fromthearchive/story/0,,1078193,00.html. Accessed 12 December 2017.

Layak, S. (2017). *Why independent directors neither burn out nor fade away*. ET Bureau. https://economictimes.indiatimes.com/news/company/corporate-trends/why-independent-directors-neither-burn-out-nor-fade-away/articleshow/56541369.cms?utm_source=contentofinterest&utm_medium=text&utm_campaign=cppst. Accessed 11 May 2021.

Livemint (2017, May 24). *Infosys CEO Vishal Sikka's annual salary drops due to lower bonus payout.* http://www.livemint.com/Companies/Oior8QMrpnwj 54j4WLbpdM/Infosys-CEO-Vishal-Sikkas-annual-salary-drops-due-to-lower. html

OECD Corporate Governance Fact Book. (2017). https://www.oecd.org/daf/ca/OECD-Corporate-Governance-Factbook-2017.pdf. Accessed 18 February 2021.

Ringshaw, G. (2001). *Mirror pension warnings ignored.* http://www.telegraph.co.uk/finance/4487800/Mirror-pension-warnings-ignored.html

SEBI, Listing and Obligation Disclosure Requirements (LODR), 2015.

Sengupta, R. (2017). *Why Infosys CEO Vishal Sikka's salary fell drastically.* https://timesofindia.indiatimes.com/business/india-business/why-infosys-ceo-vishal-sikkas-salary-fell-drastically/articleshow/58839068.cms

Sharma, R. (2017). *Vishal Sikka's salary: The controversy behind Infosys CEO's Rs. 73.4-crore pay package.* https://gadgets.ndtv.com/others/features/vishal-sikkas-salary-the-controversy-behind-infosys-ceos-pay-package-1658096

Shleifer, A., & Vishny, R. W. (1989). Management entrenchment the case of manager-specific investments. *Journal of Financial Economics, 25,* 123–139.

Weinberger, M. (2017, October 17). *Microsoft CEO Satya Nadella nailed his annual report card—Netting him a cool $20 million.* https://www.businessinsider.in/Microsoft-CEO-Satya-Nadella-nailed-his-annual-report-card-netting-him-a-cool-20-million/articleshow/61109826.cms. Accessed 12 December 2017.

CHAPTER 3

Theoretical Perspectives of Corporate Governance

The Foundation

THEORIES AND DEVELOPMENT OF CORPORATE GOVERNANCE

As corporate governance evolved, various theories helped the development of corporate governance. These theories (see Fig. 3.1) are based on a combination of financial, economics and behavioural sciences. These theories explain the relationship between different stakeholders and shape the governance systems.

PROPERTY RIGHT THEORY: OWNERSHIP AND CONTROL

Property implies assets and can be tangible such as land and building or intangible such as trademarks and copyrights. Property rights theory is concerned with owners' rights to use, enjoy the benefits and dispose of property. When ownership is well defined, control on assets and its returns are with the owner. However, in large corporations, different forms of shareholdings can result in alternative control structures (Fig. 3.2).

Concentrated or Dispersed Ownership

Ownership of the company may be dispersed, spread across a large number of shareholders, with no one person owning a bulk of the shares such as in UK or Australia or may be concentrated in the hands of few as

© The Author(s), under exclusive license to Springer Nature Singapore Pte Ltd. 2023
S. Jhunjhunwala, *Corporate Governance*,
https://doi.org/10.1007/978-981-99-2707-4_3

Broad Theories   Sub Theories

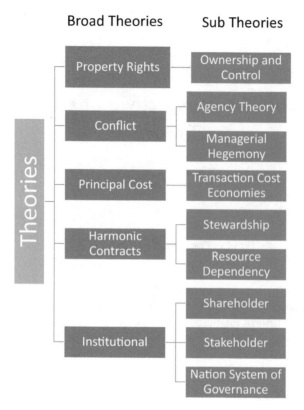

Fig. 3.1 Theories of corporate governance (*Source* Developed by Author)

seen in Indian or Japanese companies. Concentrated ownership can give rise to block shareholders. Block shareholders own a very large number of shares and can influence the way company will be managed. A shareholder individually or a group of shareholders (e.g. promoter and his family) can become majority shareholder by owning more than 50%. As controlling shareholders, they can dictate corporate decisions and may act in a manner oppressive to the minority shareholders or small shareholders.

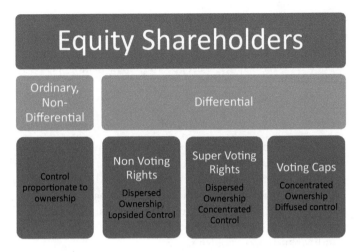

Fig. 3.2 Shareholders and control (*Source* Developed by Author)

Differential Voting Rights

Each shareholder, large or small, should be treated equally and have equal rights (OECD, 2015). Hence, the principle of 'one share one vote' is adopted. This means the more shares an investor owns the more is his voting power and the more he can influence the company affairs. Occasionally shares with differential voting rights may be issued. This restricted or grants additional voting rights to a class of shares. *Non-voting rights* shares may be issued that do not entitle owners voting rights or preferred dividend. This prevents dilution of control by promoters or founders and can prevent takeovers. In India, private companies may issue such shares. Though several countries such as Australia and Italy allow it, it is not popular.

Multiple Voting Rights gives the shareholders more voting rights than other shareholders. In France and Italy, shareholders who are loyal and hold the shares for more than two years have double voting power (OECD, 2017). In USA, prior to listing dual classes of shares may be issued with one class having "super voting" powers. When internet company Google went public, a lot of investors were upset that it issued a second class of shares to ensure that the firm's founders and top executives maintained control. Each of the Class B shares reserved for Google insiders would carry 10 votes, while ordinary Class A shares sold to the public would get just one vote (McClure, n.d.). *Voting Caps* on the other hand limits the number of votes a shareholder may cast. So even though a shareholder may have large shareholding, their voting powers will be restricted. This reduces block holder dominance.

Control

The basis of a company is separation of ownership and control (Adam Smith, 1776). The shareholders as principal delegate control to the board of directors (managers) their agents (Jensen & Meckling, 1976). The extent of control that shareholders are able to have on the company would primarily depend on the ownership pattern and voting rights. The different forms of control prevalent are Managerial Control, Working Control and Majority Control (Fig. 3.3).

Managerial Control

In companies with widely disperse shareholders who are often geographically scattered, shareholders exercise limited direct control. Additionally, information asymmetry in favour of the directors (executive) grants them excessive authority (Berle & Means, 1932). Directors begin to believe they are an elite class to whom the company belongs. This sense of superiority creates a desire to accumulate wealth and display power. CEOs start building empires by diversifying and expanding rapidly to create huge

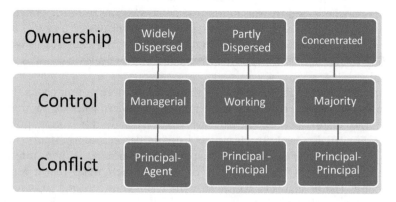

Fig. 3.3 Ownership, control and conflict (*Source* Developed by author)

asset bases and big size companies. This exponentially raises the executives' power, prestige and perks often at the cost of huge debts, efficiency and profits ultimately resulting in loss of value for shareholders—the genesis of many corporate scams.

Working Control
In case of dispersed shareholding, it is possible for a block shareholder with a not very large holding, as less as 20% or even 5% to exercise enough control to shape corporate decisions. Often promoters or founders as original value creators are able to continue to hold the reigns even after their ownership has been diluted. This is because the rest of the shareholders are not exercising their monitoring rights either because of lack of competency or limited excess to information or the paradox of voting; that is, they consider cost and effort of voting are more than the benefit of voting as it will not impact the decision taken by the company. The investors may find it more beneficial to shift portfolio rather than to vote. The founding Raju brothers of infamous Satyam scam which shook the Indian stock market in 2008 were able to manipulate the board and control the company even though by then they were holding less than 9% of the total shares. Though institutional shareholders together held more than 50% since 2003, they do not ever seriously review the promoters' actions till the Maytas deal was approved by the board causing significant reduction in shareholders' value. Differential shares give promoters or initial investors excess power putting constraints on the rights of other shareholders. Issuing shares with non-voting rights to outside shareholders or super voting rights to inside shareholders may create lopsided control in favour of a block shareholder. Block shareholders with working control may be more interested in creating wealth for themselves rather than all shareholders creating a principal-principal conflict.

Majority Control
When a shareholder or group of shareholders own more than 50% shares, they have controlling interest. Group of shareholders could be members of a family or a group of companies owned or controlled by an individual or family. Governments directly or through government bodies may also own majority shares. China and India have a large number of state-owned listed companies. Issue of shares with super voting power may create a situation of majority control. An extreme example is Echostar Communication's CEO Charlie Ergen's holding 5% of the company's stock, yet

controlling 90% of the vote with his powerful class-A shares (McClure, n.d.). Similar to block holding, majority shareholders may take decisions that are not in the interest of the minority shareholders. Government companies are known to take actions that promote government policies which may benefit the society but may not create direct value for the shareholders. For instance, government-owned (public sector) banks in India are required to finance small farmers which more than often become non-performing assets. Thus, a situation of majority-minority conflict arises.

Hence, a governance mechanism needs to be put in place to ensure that the rightful owners (all shareholders) benefit equitably from the company.

Conflict Theory of Corporate Governance

> A house may be large or small; as long as the neighbouring houses are likewise small, it satisfies all social requirement for a residence. But let there arise next to the little house a palace, and the little house shrinks to a hut.
>
> Karl Marx in *Wage Labour and Capital* (1847)

Conflict theory proposed by Karl Marx states that tensions and conflicts arise when resources, status and power are unevenly distributed between groups in society. Those with economic, political or social power try to hold on to it by any means possible, chiefly by suppressing the poor and powerless. A basic premise of conflict theory is that individuals and groups work to maximize their own benefits. Conflict arises because the interests of the various groups are at odds. When the oppressed class revolts, demanding changes, reforms to political and social institutions are required to smoothen the conflict.

This theory holds equally good in companies. Each stakeholder has its own interest. Employee wants more salary and customer wants lower price. These diverging interests create conflict. The function of the governance is to minimize these conflicts. For the time being, we will focus on only two main stakeholders—shareholders and the directors.

Each form of ownership and control creates its own set of conflicts. These can be classified into three broad categories: principal-agent, principal-principal and agent-agent conflict (Jhunjhunwala, 2018).

Principal-Agent Conflict: The Agency Theory

The principal agency problem is well documented in literature as the agency theory. The agency theory marks the advent of corporate governance and presents the underlying problem of separation of ownership and control built into the very structure of the company. Adam Smith was the first to question the fact that directors of the company cannot be expected to take care of others' wealth with the 'same vigilance as the watch their own' (Wealth of Nations, 1776).

The principal agency problem was elaborated by Jensen and Meckling (1976). Shareholders, who are the owners of the company and invest their money, become the principal and appoint the directors as their agents to manage the affair of the company. The governance in a company is established as a relationship between shareholders and directors through a principal-agent contract (Fig. 3.4).

Agency Problem

The agency dilemma is that the agents may not always act in the best interest of the principal (Jensen & Meckling, 1976). Managers (in the agency theory implies inside directors) look after the firm and are privy to all the business information, while owners depend upon the managers to get the information. This information asymmetry allows directors to

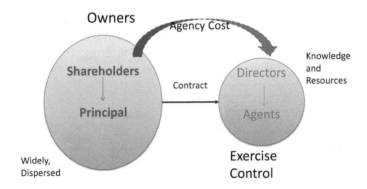

Fig. 3.4 Agency theory (*Source* Developed by Author)

exercise control. In large public companies as shareholders become large and dispersed, powers shift to the directors who often abuse it (Berle & Means, 1932).

Managers are likely to promote self-interest. Managerial decisions depart from those required to maximize shareholders return. Agents may reward themselves more than the value they create for investors. For instance, directors may pay themselves excess remuneration or enter into related party transactions which are not the most beneficial for the company but profitable to them (Shall discuss more in Chapter 9). Directors work for the organization for a limited period and hence have a short-term horizon. There remuneration may be linked to performance (profits). They tend to maximizing profits in the short run at the determent to the long-term interest of the shareholders. Thus, the agency theory is plagued with "conflict of interest" between principal and agents. Agents turned rouge may even siphon corporate assets. The self-interest of both parties can only be satisfied, if the firm exists. Agency conflict is to be managed for survival of firm.

Agency Cost

Agency cost (Jensen & Meckling, 1976) is the cost associated with reducing the conflict of interest between agents and principal. To minimize agency problem, the following costs (Fig. 3.5) are incurred.

- **The monitoring expenditures by the principal**: The wealth maximizing principal makes effort to control the behaviour of rent-seeking agents. It may restrict decision powers of the directors such as the amount they borrow or introduce compensation policy of performance-based incentives. Monitoring cost is incurred on annual or quarterly reporting and shareholder meetings as measures of watching over the agent.

Fig. 3.5 Agency costs (*Source* Developed by Author)

- *The bonding expenditures by the agent*: The cost borne by agents to guarantee that they will act in the interest of the principal or compensate them if they don't. For example, they may accept a non-compete or minimum service agreements.
- *The residual loss*: Even after monitoring and bonding costs, there will be some divergence between the agent's decisions and those decisions which would maximize the welfare of the principal known as the residual or agency loss.

Corporate governance structures and processes are meant to reduce the conflict of interest between these two parties and enable effecting monitoring of directors by shareholders. One such mechanism has been to issue shares to managers to develop in them a sense of ownership, thereby creating alignment of interest with shareholders. Managerial ownership, however, as seen in Enron and other cases, creates the risk of manipulating financials to increase share prices.

Principal-Principal Conflict

Principal-principal conflict occurs between two classes of shareholders. Dual class shares where one class has less voting rights; then, the other can cause a principal-principal conflict. The expectations of return among shareholders may differ. A short-term investor may prefer quick rise in profits as against long-term appreciation in value. Outside investors may look for dividends or buybacks where as an insider may choose to invest cash surplus in a new project. Free rider problem results in some shareholders taking the efforts and cost to monitor the company activities, while others enjoy the spoils. Block holders and small holders may have divergent interests. Examples of abuse of power by a majority holder at the cost of interest of the minority holder is very prevalent where the majority shareholders use the company resources to promote their own interests at the cost of the minority owners. For instance, the majority owners may decide to retain the earnings of the firm and invest in a risky project instead of distributing them as dividends. This may not be what other shareholders want. In family-controlled firms, majority shareholders may take decisions that are in the interest of their family rather than of the company to the detriment of minority shareholders.

Agent-Agent Conflict

Companies with managerial control may see diminishing returns as a result of conflict among agents. Even though the individual directors may be very competent, the board as a whole may lack certain competencies. Due to bias in selection of directors, boards tend to be homogenous in nature which implies that directors may have similar knowledge base, skills and traits. For instance, if all the board members are engineers, they may have high level of intelligence, logical and analytical skills and technical expertise but may lack creativity or negotiation skills. On the other hand, diverging views among directors could lead to delay or even absence of corporate decisions severely affecting firm's performance. Conflict among directors due to personal rivalry or bias would reduce board effectiveness. Individual directors such as long-time serving CEO or a chairman cum CEO can dominate both agenda and discussions in the boardroom. This would mean that investors' returns are primarily based on competence of just one agent, with the contribution of other mangers being insignificant. Notwithstanding that they would still receive their incentive. As witnessed by history the concentration of power in Kenneth Lay was devastating for all the stakeholders of Enron. This kind of behaviour suggests Managerial Hegemony.

Managerial Hegemony Theory

Hegemony is the political, economic, or cultural predominance of one group over others. Marx's suggested that the ruling class exercises hegemony by manipulating the belief and expectations of society. Directors view themselves as an elite class. They appoint new directors who meet the requirements of this elite class. This occurs when there is managerial control. Executive directors with their sense of superiority, access to inside information and financial control exercise dominance over others. If managerial hegemony is exercised by few, boards become ineffective merely rubber stamping the decisions already taken. Appointment of significant proportion of independent directors could be one way of countering their power. The separation of Chairman and CEO is another measure adopted to address this.

PRINCIPAL COST THEORY

The principal cost theory presented by Goshen and Squire (2017) states governance is about minimizing *the 'sum of* principal costs, *produced when investors exercise control, and* agent costs, *produced when managers exercise control. Both principal costs and agent costs can arise from honest mistakes (which generate* competence costs*) and from disloyal conduct (which generate* conflict costs*). Because the expected costs of competence and conflict are firm-specific, the optimal division of control is firm-specific as well'.*

Principal Costs

Principal costs are the costs incurred when shareholders exercise control. Shareholders will appoint managers as agents when they believe that they are more capable than themselves to increase to the firm value for shareholders, else they will act as directors themselves. Principal costs are higher when control (working or majority) is retained by investors themselves as directors. The competency cost of the principal is his limited experience, knowledge and talent in comparison with the manager he may hire with greater expertise and competence (Goshen & Squire, 2017). The value of the firm would then be subject to the competence of those shareholders who are managing the company hands on. When shareholders decide to delegate, the appropriateness of managers would be dependent on the ability of the principal to make the right choice. The frequent firing and replacing of CEOs is testament that shareholders don't always get it right. The majority shareholder Ratan Tata as trustee of the Tata Trust controlled 66% of Tata Sons. After an extensive search, he chose Cyrus Mistry to be the CEO of the Tata empire. However, soon he was dissatisfied with Mistry's management style and fired him. The principal's competence will determine the efficiency with which he is able to monitor the agents, which in turn will impact the benefits derived from delegation.

Agent Costs

Agent costs are incurred when managers exercise control. The degree to which managerial control will result in value enhancement of investors' return depends on the robustness of the strategy decided by the managers and their ability to successfully execute it. The higher the competence of the mangers greater will be the firm's value. Overconfidence of successful managers may cause them to undertake extremely risky projects or make number of unforced errors causing harm to investors' value. Another cost associated with agents is the transaction cost.

Transaction Cost Economics

The transaction cost economics advocated by Williamson (1975) addresses concerns of cost incurred by shareholders in searching for the best directors, negotiating the contract, monitoring their actions and enforcing implementation of the contract (Fig. 3.6). So the choice of governance structure will affect the transaction cost of having directors. It will at the same time influence their behaviour.

For instance, huge incentives would encourage directors to perform better enhancing shareholder wealth, but means more outflow to directors in form of remuneration. Enforcing of the contract through regular audits or director's evaluation has a cost. The costs must not outweigh the benefits due to improved implementation of contract.

Each control structure and the resulting conflict creates a different set of costs for the company (Table 3.1). Corporate governance structures and processes are meant to reduce the conflict of interest caused by different ownership and control structures. Similar to the benefits of reduced cost brought about by economies of scale, the right internal and external governance mechanism can reduce control costs. As human

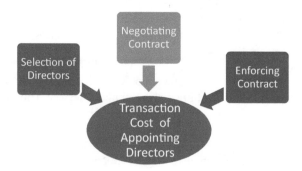

Fig. 3.6 Transaction cost theory (*Source* Developed by Author)

Table 3.1 Control costs

Principal Costs	Competency Cost—Strategy, Manager selection, monitoring inefficiency
Agency Costs	Competency Cost
	Transaction Cost
	Overconfidence Cost
Principal Agent Costs	Monitoring Cost
	Bonding Cost
Agent-Agent Costs	Board Competency
	Inter-personal relations
	Over dominance
Principal-Principal Costs	Divergent expectation of returns
	Free Rider problem
	Differential voting rights
	Majority/Family interest

Source Jhunjhunwala (2018)

behaviour is complex and each individual reacts differently to a stimuli or situation, getting it correct is not easy.

THEORIES OF HARMONIC CONTRACT

The agency theory argues that directors don't always work in their interest and monitoring them has a cost. If so, why appoint directors in the first place, because shareholders expect directors will create more value for the firm. The relationship between directors and shareholders can be one of harmony that is beneficial to shareholders' interest.

Stewardship Theory

The agency theory has been criticized on the grounds that it assumes people always work in their self-interest. The stewardship theory developed by Donaldson and Davis in 1991 suggests that directors are selfless people who act as stewards of the shareholders' interest. Stewardship is the job of taking care of a property or organization. Directors can be trusted and as stewards of the company will fulfil their fiduciary duty to act in the interest of the shareholders. Directors act pro-organization and believe in greater benefits (utility) from collaborative behaviour with

Fig. 3.7   Stewardship theory (*Source* Developed by Author)

shareholders rather than from individualistic behaviour. They are self-actualizing leaders desiring growth and achievement. Directors conduct themselves responsibly and with integrity and can be given greater autonomy and empowered with authority. This theory thus supports combining Chairman / CEO position. An empowered board focuses on strategy and performance resulting in value creation for the company (Fig. 3.7).

Resource Dependency Theory

The resource dependency theory (Pfeffer & Salancik, 1978) specifies that firms need external resources to achieve the objectives of the company and directors facilitate these necessary resources. Shareholders are dependent on directors for obtaining resources such as access to finance, technology, business knowledge, customers and business networks. Directors act as the linkage between company business and external environment and help reduce uncertainty (Fig. 3.8). Therefore, good governance is achieved when board members are appointed for their expertise to help firms successfully cope with environmental uncertainty.

Institutional Theories of Corporate Governance

Institutions are the principles recognized in law, culture, customs, tradition, common practices and conventions of a social structure. Institutional theory highlights the impact of institutional environment on the culture and behaviour of a company including its governance structure (Fig. 3.9). This external pressure to institutionalize creates the need for companies to seek legitimacy.

At the same time, companies like any other organization are themselves a social entity whose organizational practices arise from imitative and firm traditions. It creates an internal pressure to institutionalize. Actions evolve over time and become legitimated within an organization.

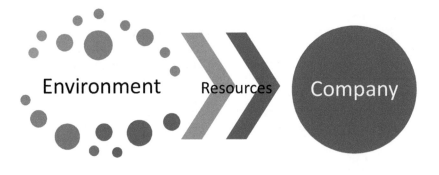

Fig. 3.8 Resource dependency theory (*Source* Developed by Author)

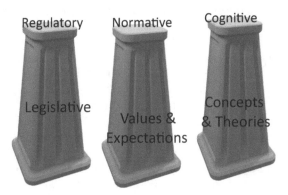

Fig. 3.9 Institutionalization of corporate governance (*Source* Adopted from Scott's three Pillars of Institution)

Shareholder Primacy: Internal Pressure

Traditionally, companies have been shareholder centric. The shareholder theory was formally introduced by Milton Friedman in 1970. Companies are owned by shareholders. As owners, their interest is paramount. The primary function of a business is to maximize the return on investments to the owners of the business; in case of companies, it is the shareholders. Shareholders advance capital to a company's managers, who are supposed to spend corporate funds only in ways that have been authorized by the shareholders and create value for them. The directors have a duty to maximize shareholders' interest subject to law and social value. Legislation, industry and firm traditions, processes and practices define and legitimate the relationship between shareholders and directors in a company. The theory therefore encompasses all the other theories discussed so far.

Stakeholder Theory: External Pressure

Legitimacy theory is defined by Suchman (1995) as "a generalized perception that the actions of an entity are considered appropriate and desirable with some socially construed systems of values, norms, beliefs and definitions in which it operates". Since the firm receives permission to operate as well as its resources from the society, it holds accountability towards society. Legitimacy theory challenges the traditional profit maximization objective of organizations and emphasized upon considering the rights of all stakeholders and not merely the investors. The word stakeholder, coined in 1963, refers to "those groups without whose support the organization would cease to exist".

The stakeholder theory was advocated by Edward Freeman in 1988. Stakeholders are all those that have a 'stake' in the company. As such, they are affected by the decisions and actives of the company and include shareholders, directors, managers, employees, customers, suppliers, business partners, government, local community, environment and society at large (see Fig. 1.1 Stakeholders of Corporate Governance). Social contracts are as important as business contracts. Stakeholder expectations influence firms' behaviour. Primary stakeholders (shareholders and directors) decide corporate actions but participation by secondary stakeholders (customers, suppliers) can help improve corporate governance and strategy to enhance performance.

While shareholder value is the primary goal of a company, it cannot be achieved without taking care of all the stakeholders. A company cannot survive without its employees, customers and suppliers. If a company as part of its production process pollutes the water making it poisonous, the people in the area will get sick, may even die. The company will soon have no employees to work in its plant. Directors' decisions should focus on stakeholders' welfare and long-term sustainability of the company.

This theory is the foundation for Corporate Social Responsibility and Sustainable Development (we shall cover them in later chapters).

National Systems Governance (NSG) Theory: Isomorphic Pressure

From institutional theory perspective, companies should become isomorphic over time. The need for legitimacy within a similar political and regulatory institutional setting creates a universal applicability of governance mechanisms within a country. Institutional environment exerts pressures to meet certain standards of corporate governance. Hence, companies with a country develop the same governance system. However, companies in a different country will establish a different form of governance. The differences in legal origin, government capabilities and social structures result in a different set of governance practices. The theory is based on the premise of heterogeneous governance systems in diverse institutional settings. This explains the difference in corporate governance of a Japanese company as against an American company. Multinational companies that operate in several countries with dissimilar institutional environment thus find it very difficult to build their governance frameworks (we will cover MNC's in Chapter 12).

Vivendi: Getting Messier

Jean-Marie Messier became the chairman and chief executive of Vivendi Universal (Now Vivendi), a French company at the age of 39 in 1996 ("Timeline: the rise and fall of Jean-Marie Messier", 2002). In a short time, he transformed a water utility into a global media giant. He created a dazzling multimedia business through several acquisitions including Universal Studio while piling up increasingly unmanageable debts. The French "rock star CEO" set up lavish offices in New York which he flew to in the corporate jet ("A French exception", 2002). The company paid $17.5 million for his plush 5,300-square-foot duplex Manhattan abode (Netburn & McGeveran, 2001). His reign was brought to an abrupt end in 2002 when he brought the company to the brink of bankruptcy. He had kept the other directors in dark by discounting his failures and portraying a picture of corporate synergies and soaring revenue. He was accused of share price manipulation and misleading stock market by authorizing false financial statements and misappropriation of media group's funds (Davies, 2010).

Points to Ponder:

1. Which theory best explains Messier's behaviour?
2. Whether different theories can be used to address the problems faced by Vivendi?
3. What were the flaws in the governance model of Vivendi? How can it be improved?

Each of these theories provide a different relationship between the participants, and their behaviour defines the function of governance and role of directors. For instance, the agency theory suggests that governance function is to focus on minimizing conflict while the stakeholder theory proposes it is to maximize all stakeholders' welfare (see Fig. 3.10).

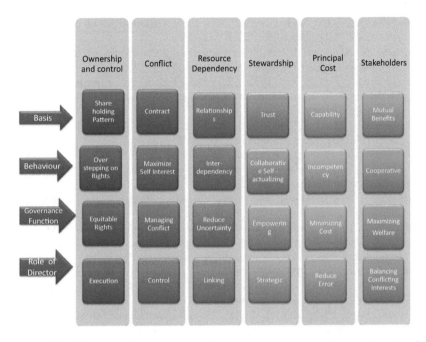

Fig. 3.10 Theoretical perspectives of corporate governance (*Source* Developed by Author)

REFERENCES

Adam Smith. (1776). *An inquiry into the nature and causes of the wealth of nations.* W Strahan.

Berle, A. A., & Means, G. (1932). *The modern corporation and private property.* The Macmillan Company.

Collin, S.-O., & Stafsudd, E. M. A. *Corporate governance through the creation of a managerial class.* http://www.svencollin.se/class.pdf

Davies, L. (2010). *Former Vivendi boss Messier admits making 'mistakes' as he faces fraud trial.* https://www.theguardian.com/business/2010/jun/02/messier-fraud-trial-begins. Accessed 5 December 2017.

Donaldson, L., & Davis, J. H. (1991). Stewardship theory or agency theory: CEO governance and shareholder returns. *Australian Journal of Management, 16,* 49–65.

Evan, W. M., & Freeman, R. E. (1988). *A stakeholder theory of the modern corporation: Kantian capitalism.*

Friedman, M. (1970, September 13). The social responsibility of business is to increase its profits. *New York Times Magazine.*

Goshen, Z., & Squire, R. (2017). Principal costs: A new theory for corporate law and governance. *Columbia Law Review, 117*(767).

Grossman, S., & Hart, O. (1980). Takeover bids, the free-rider problem, and the theory of the corporation. *Bell Journal of Economics, 11*(I), 42–64, Spring. The Rand Corporation.

The Economist (2002, July 4). A French exception. http://www.economist.com/node/1213423. Accessed 5 December 2017.

The Guardian. (2002, July 1). Timeline: The rise and fall of Jean-Marie Messier. https://www.theguardian.com/media/2002/jul/01/citynews.viv endi1. Accessed 5 December 2017.

McClure, B. (n.d.). *The two sides of dual-class shares.* https://www.investopedia.com/articles/fundamental/04/092204.asp

Michael C. J., & Meckling, W. H. (1976). Theory of the firm: Managerial behavior, agency costs and ownership structure. *Journal of Financial Economics 3*, 305–360. Q North-Holland Publishing Company.

Jhunjhunwala, S. (2018). Control conflict and activism. *IUP Journal of Corporate Governance, XVII*(4).

Karl Marx. (1847). *Wage labour and capital.*

Netburn, D., & McGeveran, T. (2001). *Vivendi universal guy buys outbronfmans, then $17.5 M. duplex.* http://observer.com/2001/04/vivendi-universal-guy-buys-out-bronfmans-then-175-m-duplex/. Accessed 5 December 2017.

OECD. (2015). G20/OECD Principles of Corporate Governance, (OECD). https://www.oecd.org/corporate/principles-corporate-governance/

OECD. (2017). Corporate Governance Factbook.

Pfeffer, J., & Salancik, G. R. (1978). *The external control of organizations: A resource dependence perspective.* Stanford University Press.

Suchman, M. (1995). Managing legitimacy: Strategic and institutional approaches. *Academy of Management Review, 20*(3), 571–610.

Williamson. (1975). *Markets and hierarchies: Analysis and antitrust implications: A study in the economics of internal organization* (286 p.). Free Press, University of Pennsylvania.

CHAPTER 4

Internal Control, Financial Oversight and Risk Management

The Winning Board: Assurance and Reliability with Big Profits

FINANCIAL OVERSIGHT

Financial oversight is integral and indispensable to good governance. Robust financial oversight is essential for a company to remain financial healthy. It includes (i) establishing a proper internal control system, (ii) ensuring reliability of financial records and statements, (iii) having an effective audit process and (iv) creating an appropriate risk management system. Though the shareholders have delegated control to the board, they should regularly keep a watch on the company and its financials. For this purpose, they appoint auditors who examine the financial reports of the company and appraise them on its fair representativeness.

The shareholders should review the audit report along with various other reports and disclosures that are made by the company as required by law of the land. The regulators too should be vigilance for any irregularities (see Fig. 4.1).

The board is entrusted with the responsibility of good corporate governance. It must actively oversee the financial systems and structures of the company to ensure present and future financial stability. This function is primarily carried out through the audit committee. As the CEO and CFO supervise the day-to-day activities they are directly responsible for the firm's financial integrity.

S. Jhunjhunwala, *Corporate Governance*, https://doi.org/10.1007/978-981-99-2707-4_4

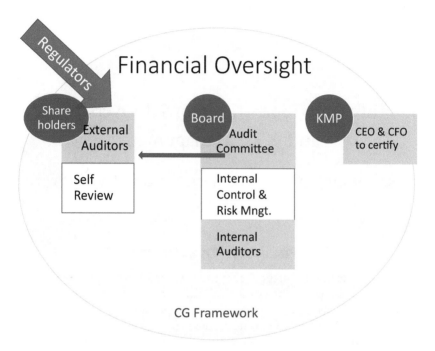

Fig. 4.1   CG framework for financial oversight (*Source* Developed by Author)

The Queen's Bank Falls

Barings Bank, Britain's oldest merchant bank and Queen Elizabeth's personal bank, was brought to its knees by a rogue trader Nick Leeson. Leeson came from humble beginnings, the son of a plasterer from Watford with an average academic record. He joined the bank's back office but soon built a successful track record as a trader.

He was transferred as branch manager to Singapore office to benefit from arbitrage opportunities between derivatives contracts on the Singapore Mercantile Exchange and Japan's Osaka Exchange. Such arbitrage, referred to inside Barings as "switching", was seen as "essentially risk-free and very profitable" (Titcomb, 2015). He oversaw both trades and back office operations. The 28-year-old Nick Leeson promptly started unauthorized speculation in Nikkei 225 stock index. In 1993, Lesson made £10m—10% of the bank's profits for that year. He earned a bonus of

£130,000 on his salary of £50,000. As Lesson himself put it "We were all driven to make profits, profits, and more profits ... I was the rising star" (Business: The Economy How Leeson broke the bank, 1999). He had the confidence of the management and was transferred funds without questions. He opened the infamous "Error Account 88888" where he began to book loses. This account was never reported.

In January 1995, a powerful earthquake shook Japan, dropping the Nikkei 1000 points. The total damage suffered by Barings was £827 million, or $1.4 billion (Rodrigues, 2015). Dutch bank, ING, purchased Barings for a mere £1 and assumed all of its liabilities (Rodrigues, 2015). 232 years of history of one of the finest banks was erased (Titcomb, 2015). Investors lost it all. The Bank of England (regulating authority), in their report, pointed out how lack of internal controls and management supervision led to the fall of the bank. Management had no clue of what Leeson was doing and were happy to turn a blind eye as long as the money came in. These were the early days of derivative trading and 'old boys' on the board had no understanding of the various strategies and products and the risks associated that finally saw the Barings collapse.

Points to Ponder:

1. If Leeson did not oversee both trading and settlement would the crisis been avoided?
2. What led to the collapse of the bank?
3. Could auditors have done something that may have prevented the bank's fall?
4. Can the board be held accountable?

INTERNAL CONTROL [1]

The board is entrusted with the responsibility of establishing sound internal controls. This implies creating the right systems and processes, putting in place the necessary checks and balances to prevent things from going wrong. Internal controls are systemic measures instituted in an organization to ensure business runs in an efficient and effective manner; the integrity of financial and accounting information is maintained; prevention and detection of fraud is fortified; firm's resources and assets are safeguarded; and that company policies and procedures are transmitted and followed throughout the organization. The most common internal control mechanism is segregation of duties. Tasks are delegated among several people to ensure no single individual is in a position to authorize, record and be in custody of a financial transaction and the resulting asset. For instance, the person who authorizes expenses does not make the payments. The Barings Bank broke this cardinal rule (see Box—The Queen's bank falls).

Internal Control: Guidance for Directors on the Combined Code published in UK in 1999 set out the best practices for internal control holding board accountable to "maintain a sound system of internal control to safeguard shareholders' investment and the company's assets". The board is responsible for the establishment and maintenance of internal controls—creating a structure of authority and responsibility; control checks, evaluation processes and surprise verification; and free flow of a two-way communication system (Fig. 4.2). A sound internal control system is the foundation of a good corporate governance structure. It sets the expected standards of conduct, an environment of integrity and ethical values of the company. The board must satisfy itself that an effective internal control system has been put in place such that they are aware of what is happening across the length and breadth of the company and everyone does 'what is right'. This will ensure that the information they receive, which is the base for their decision making, is reliable. The Board of Baring Bank never took the trouble to understand the derivative market or what Leeson was up to.

IT Governance

High-speed information processing has become indispensable to organizations' activities. Given the reliance of information technology (IT) in every aspect of business, it has a direct impact on the overall reliability of financial statements. IT controls act as a critical mechanism for ensuring the integrity of information systems and the reporting of organization. IT governance, employee access, network configuration, disaster recovery plans, physical and logical controls, application controls and various input and output controls will increase accuracy and reliability and help prevent errors and detect fraud. Appropriate IT controls and audit must be put in place and frequently reviewed and if needed, updated (see Box—the 4C Diamond Con).

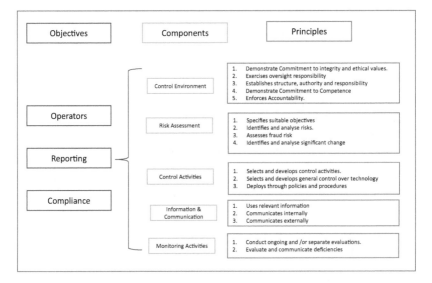

Fig. 4.2 Integrated internal control framework (*Source* Adapted from Internal Control-Integrated framework [2013], https://www.coso.org/pages/ic.aspx accessed on August 13, 2021)

The 4C Diamond Con

The con orchestrated by Diamond Merchant Modi on Punjab National bank's (PNB) Brady House branch in Mumbai that unfolded in February 2018 was no less than a Hollywood movie. Diamonds are valued based on their carat, clarity, cut and colour. In this case the Carats; at least Rs 11,400 crores, were cleverly skimmed through fraudulent transactions.

Nirav Modi and Mehul Choksi of Gitanjali Jewelry at the centre of the PNB fraud had such Clarity of the con that they successfully perpetuated fraud on the bank for almost a decade. A branch official issued Letters of Undertaking (LoU)* on behalf of companies belonging to Nirav Modi Group for availing buyers' credit from overseas branches of Indian Banks. That foreign branch would credit the PNB account with forex which would be used to pay, supposedly, oversee supplier of rough diamonds. They were in fact front companies of Modi. When a LOU became due, a fresh one was issued to clear earlier guarantees.

The Cut in the system—the loophole they exploited. The fake LoU requesting credit transfer to overseas banks was issued through the global messaging system, Society for Worldwide Interbank Financial Telecommunication (SWIFT). The transactions were not routed through CBS[#] which would have given real-time data on transacted business. Unfortunately, the two systems had not been integrated at PNB (Sahgal, 2018). The internal auditors of PNB did not think it fit to tally the entries made on SWIFT daily with those on CBS, which helped in the fraud going undiscovered.

The true Colours of Modi and Choski became clear soon after the con came to light as they immediately fled the country. The colours of the PNB bank and Reserve Bank of India, the banking regulator of India also appear to be Shades of Grey as concerns regarding huge loans to Choski had been raised by an independent director but ignored (Prasad, 2018). In the aftermath of Nirav Modi and the 31 other debtors fleeing India, the government passed the Fugitive Economic Offenders Bill (FEOB), which targets defaulters above Rs 100 crores. All assets—and not just proceeds of crime—can be confiscated from an offender declared a fugitive and he can't pursue any civil disputes (Varma, 2018).

Points to Ponder:

1. Why was the fraud possible?
2. What measures should the bank take to prevent such events in the future?
3. How important is internal control and IT governance in an organization?

*Letter of Undertaking is a bank guarantee issued for overseas import payments of a client. It agrees to repay the principal and interest on the client's loan unconditionally.

#CBS refers to Core Banking System through which all branches are electronically interlinked so that a customer regardless of their home branch—are able to operate their account and transact from any branch anywhere in the world or even online. All transactions are updated real-time.

Financial Controls

Effective financial controls, including the maintenance of proper accounting records, are an important element of internal control enabling reliability of internal and external reporting. Companies listed on a US stock exchange are subject to Section 404 of the Sarbanes-Oxley Act of 2002 which, in response to accounting and financial scandals, requires that companies publish a statement on the effectiveness of internal controls over financial reporting and disclose any material weaknesses they may have identified. Directors are personally responsible for the evaluation of internal controls and the publication of their findings together with their company's SEC filings. Similarly, Sec 134 of Companies Act 2013 requires directors of Indian listed companies to submit a statement that internal financial controls to be followed by the company have been laid down by them and that such internal financial controls are adequate and were operating effectively. Auditors must also report whether the company has adequate internal financial controls with reference to financial statements in place and the operating effectiveness of such controls (Sec 143 Companies Act 2013).

RELIABILITY OF FINANCIAL STATEMENTS

Investors and creditors and to some extend other stakeholders depend on the financial information provided by the company to make their decisions. They must be able to trust the financial statement of the company to give them reliable and relevant information. The board is responsible to ensure that the statements give a true and fair view of the state of affairs of the company—its total assets and liabilities and the financial results—the profits or loss made.

Loose accounting standards allowed managers to implement reporting practices that suited their self-interest such as to bloat revenue and profit figures (see Box—The Rougue E). Accounting standards have since been tightened with most countries adopting International Financial Reporting Standards (IFRS) with some customization for local requirements. Adoption of a particular accounting practice should be justified by the company. Where in the preparation of financial statements, a treatment different from that prescribed in an accounting standard has been followed, the fact shall be disclosed in the financial statements, together with the management's explanation as to why it believes such alternative treatment is more representative of the true and fair view of the underlying business transaction (LODR, 2015). In addition, extensive disclosures, particularly of off-balance sheet transactions, are mandated to prevent window dressing.

The Rogue E

Gary, a young and ambitious graduate from a not so elite business school, got placed in his dream company—Enron, the 7th largest company in the world valued at as $70 billion (*Committee on Governmental Affairs United States Senate*, 2002). On the first day at orientation, he learned that 80% of the energy giant's value was in intangibles. The Enron's board as the corporate brochure showed was composed of many prominent and financially sophisticated people of America including Wendy L. Gramm, a former government regulator and the wife of Senator Phil Gramm, Republican of Texas; John Wakeham, a member of the British House of Lords and a former British cabinet member; Norman P. Blake Jr., the chief executive of Comdisco, a computer services company; Dr. Robert K. Jaedicke, Dean Emeritus of the Stanford Business School, and a former accounting professor (see table). Its founder and chairperson Kennet Lay in his welcome speech emphasized how the company stood for honesty and fairness, did business with integrity, and played by the rules and executives stood by their word. Besides his salary if he performed well, he would earn huge bonus. He was ecstatic at the opportunity, who wouldn't be.

Members	Since	Executive Committee	Finance Committee	Audit and Compliance Committee	Compensation Committee	Nomination Committee
Kennet Lay, Chairman	1986	Member				
Jeff Skilling CEO	February to August 2001	Member				
John H. Duncan (Former UK secretary of state for energy)	1985	Chairman			Member	
Herbert S. Winokur JR	1985	Member	Chairman			
Dr. Robert K. Jaedicke (Professor of accounting emeritus)	1985			Chairman	Member	
Dr. Charles A. LeMaistre	1985	Member			Chairman	
Norman P. Blake, Jr. (Chairman, President and CEO, Comdisco)	1994		Member		Member	
Robert Belfer (Chairman, Belco Oil & Gas Corp.)	Mid 1980s	Member	Member			
Wendy L. Gramm (Former chairwoman, US commodity futures trading commission)	1993			Member		Member
John Wakeham	1994			Member		Chairman

Members	Since	Executive Committee	Finance Committee	Audit and Compliance Committee	Compensation Committee	Nomination Committee
Ronnie Chan (Chairman, Hang Lung group, HK)	1996		Member	Member		
Paulo Ferraz Pereira (Former President and CEO, State Bank of Rio de Janeiro, Brazil)	1999		Member	Member		
Frank Savage (Chairman, Alliance Capital Management International)	1999		Member		Member	
Dr. John Mendelsohn (President, University of Texas. Anderson Cancer Center)	1999			Member		Member
Jerome Meyer, Chairman, Tektronix	1997 Till 2001		Member			Member

Note Data for the above table have been obtained from websites of *The Guardian* (2002), *Committee on Governmental Affairs United States Senate* (2002) and My Plain View (2002)

Enron a global mega company with over $100 billion in revenues and 20,000 employees worldwide over the years had transformed from a traditional power company to one creating high-tech financial products such as trading in online energy contracts (*Committee on Governmental Affairs United States Senate* (2002). Gary was assigned to the bankruptcy insurance division. This insurance protected the buyer if their customer went bankrupt and defaulted.

His team did not welcome him. He was a 'nobody'. Then, one day they saw him speaking to a top brass (actually a family friend, but they did not know that). Mystically he was invited to join them for lunch at this high-end Japanese restaurant that they drove to in a pricey sports car. He learned that based on the deals they close with clients they earn huge bonuses. His team members had bought fancy houses on sizeable monthly loan instalments and flaunted flashy lifestyles funded out of these bonuses.

The Harvard Business School graduate Jeff Skilling, the new CEO had introduced mark to market accounting which meant that assets or liability were valued at current market values. He initiated trading in energy futures that in effect, were valued "as the company accountants thought fit" and booked as revenue. Based on these supposedly earned revenue, hefty bonuses were paid out. The auditors Arthur Andersen and Securities Exchange Commission (SEC) surprisingly gave their approval, considering that both energy trading and mark to market accounting were new ideas. The audit team had their offices inside Enron's premises and drew fees of $1 million every week. Skilling created an aggressive corporate culture where bottom 10% performers were fired. There was a cut throat competition for survival and huge payouts.

Gary soon made his first big deal. But when the final contract was drawn up, his estimates had been upped by his seniors. They brushed aside his concerns explaining that the new figures will give him better rating and a bigger bonus. He felt he had to go along. And that day, after work, Gary went and bought a brand new car (of course to be paid from the bonus he was going to get, he couldn't afford it on his salary). He would take his team tomorrow for a ride. They would be impressed. He had become one of them.

One day Gary's friend who worked as an analyst at Merrill Lynch called him about why Enron was not able to present its balance sheet. He told Gary another analyst John Olson had been fired when he raised questions about why Enron always had a "BUY" recommendation. The rumour in his office was that in return Enron gave Merrill Lynch two analyst jobs that paid $50 million each (Spen & White, 2002).

Gary found this odd. His company was telling all the employees that all was well and encouraging them to even buy shares of the company. He knew Enron spent a lot on building and maintaining its market image; his small division also had their own PR representative. Was all not well. He remembered a few days back when he happened to be riding in the lift with the Chairman he had overhead Lay offering the corporate Jet to President Bush and suggesting he sell his shares of Enron.

However, the next week results were declared and huge profits announced. Everyone was initially happy. Share prices would rise and bonuses paid. But there was a catch. The company had lost over $1 billion (Barton, 2014) on the Dabhol project in India which ran into trouble from the beginning with human right activists, bribery allegations and political controversies. The price at which it decided to sell power was unacceptable to local Indian government and the plant had to be shut down. Meanwhile, Enron executives had already paid themselves bonuses based on the future expected gains from the power plant.

Enron was praised for its expansions and ambitious projects and named "America's Most Innovative Company" by *Fortune* for six consecutive years between 1996 and 2001 (Enron Scandal: The Fall of a Wall Street Darling, 2018). Over the next few months, several such project failures can to light, but due to media campaigns the share price of Enron kept rises reaching a peak of $90. During this time, top executives sold nearly $1 billion in personal stock, led by Ken Lay and Jeff Skilling who sold around $300 million and $200 million of their own shares, respectively (Barton, 2014). At the same time employees were encouraged to pour their entire live savings into buying shares of Enron.

Using his connections to Bush, Lay manipulated energy regulation. Facing over $500 million in losses, Enron decided to shut down power plants in California causing rolling blackouts throughout the state driving the price of energy upward in order to make a profit (Borger, 2005). Public outrage of the energy crisis in California eventually caused the governor to declare a state of emergency, thus regaining control.

Then, one day all employees were called for a meeting where Gary learnt that Skilling had resigned. The stock prices of Enron began to spiral downwards. Gary with the help of his analyst friend began to do some digging. They learned the Enron had taken $ 30 billion in debt to cover losses and show profits. The debt was hidden in shadow companies created by CFO Andew Fastow. Fastow created many off-balance sheet SPVs and raised huge debts through them. The company had hidden its debt by moving its non-performing assets to the SPVs. The board of directors of these SPVs was related to the management of Enron which was a clear conflict of interest (Concept of Special Purpose Vehicle (SPV) and Enron Accounting Fraud Case Study, 2017). In fact, one of the biggest of them belonged to Fastow. These assets were hedged with banks and guaranteed using Enron Stock. 96 of the world's major banks invested as much as $25 million each in the project (Barton, 2014).

Gary wondered why the auditors and lawyers had signed off. He realized they were being paid off $50 million annually to keep quite. But was the board not aware of all this. Why were they approving so risky projects? Why were they quiet? He heard that Meyer was ticked off for asking questions that were too critical of management (Salter, 2008). His research should that Blake sat on the board of Owens Corning Corp., which had signed a $1 billion energy management deal with an associate company of Enron in 1999. Duncan was directly linked to a charity supported by Enron, the Rise Schools of Texas, which includes the Brenda and John Duncan Rise School in Houston. Kenneth Lay is on the schools' governing board. Gramm became a director in Enron, five weeks after leaving the Commodity Futures Trading Commission, where as chairwoman, she passed a regulatory exemption for the trading of energy products, which profited Enron. She is a director of the Regulatory Studies Program of the Mercatus Center at George Mason University, which has received at least $50,000 from Enron since 1996. Over the years, through its officers and employees, Enron made nearly $100,000 in campaign contributions to her husband, a senator. Enron has long been a 'big-hearted' donor, giving around $600,000 to the Houston Institution led by Charles A. Lemaistre. As energy secretary of Britain, Wakeham gave permission to Enron to construct a massive gas-fired power plant at Teeside in the UK. He joined the company's board four years later, in 1994. In addition to directors' fees and reimbursement of expenses amounting to about $79,000 a year, since September 1996 he is paid $6,000 a month as consultancy fees from an Enron's European subsidiary. Winokur is affiliated with National Tank Co., which has made about $2.5 million in sales to Enron since 1997 (Babineck, 2002). The board had suspended Enron's code of ethics to approve the creation of the partnerships between Enron and its chief financial officer (Abelson, 2002).

By now, the whole world realized things were not right. Credit rating agencies downgraded Enron. Stock prices were crashing. One morning as Gary walked into the office, all documents were being put through the shredder. Employees were queuing up to destroy documents. Even the auditors were destroying documents. A SEC investigation was a definite eventuality.

Finally, on 2 December 2001, Enron declared bankruptcy. Shares were not even worth a dollar. Gary lost his 'dream' job. So did his 20,000 colleagues. They lost their houses, cars and all their savings. Their lives were turned upside down. Investors too lost billions. Arthur Andersen, the country's oldest accounting firm, voluntarily gave up their license. Over 22,000 Arthur Andersen employees lost their jobs over night. Enron became 9/11 of the financial world.

Point to Ponder:

1. Can the managers (Directors) of a company such as Enron be trusted to act in the interest of the owners (Shareholders)?
2. Do you think the auditors acted independently? How can auditors' accountability be increased?
3. What steps can be taken to ensure financial statements are "true and fair"?
4. Did political nexus have a role in rise and fall of Enron?
5. What were the causes for Enron's collapse?

Note: Though the case is based on true facts of Enron the story of Gary and his friend is fictitious and drawn from the movie The Crooked E.

Strong internal controls, maintenance of proper and adequate accounting records, and appropriate accounting policies and standards are to be followed so that the financial statements prepared present a correct picture of the company's financial position. CEO and CFO as per regulations in USA and India must certify to the correctness and fairness of the financial statements and that they are not misleading nor any material facts omitted. SOX Act (Sec 304) further requires forfeiture of bonuses and profit from sale of securities of senior executives responsible for financial statements if they have to be restated due to their misconduct.

AUDIT AND AUDITORS

As an assurance that the financial statements are reliable, shareholders appoint auditors to conduct an audit to verify that the financial statements are true and fair. These **external** or **statutory** auditors are independent accounting professionals who examine the financial records and issue an opinion regarding the financial statements of the company. They are to be distinguished from internal auditors who are hired to evaluate and improve the effectiveness of internal control processes, risk management systems and governance of the organization (Fig. 4.3).

Given the separation of ownership from management, the directors are required to report on their stewardship by means of the annual report and financial statements sent to the shareholders. The Cadbury Report emphasized the importance of auditors' role in providing an objective check on the financial reports. The auditors must carry out their work with professional objectivity and due care. They should maintain a professional and independent relationship with the management. Various scams have shown how executive directors manipulated accounts to fill their pockets violating their fiduciary role causing significant loss to investors. The failure of auditors in preventing or even detecting the accounting frauds and in some cases even perpetuating the fraud has raised concerns of auditors' objectivity and audit effectiveness (Fig. 4.4). Several measures can be taken to enhance audit effectiveness.

Audit standards and procedures: To begin with audit standards and procedures need to be well established. This will provide the basis for applying professional skills and act with objectivity. A separate body may be put in place to prepare audit standards and processes.

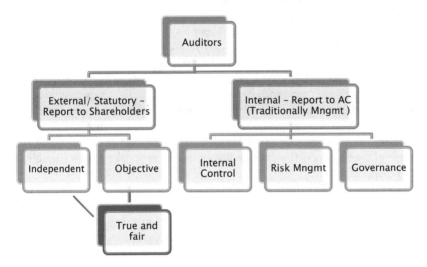

Fig. 4.3 Role of auditors (*Source* Developed by Author)

Fig. 4.4 Audit
effectiveness and scams
(*Source* Developed by
Author)

Audit
Effectiveness

Scams

Independent Oversight: The SOX act of 2002 established the Public
Company Accounting and Oversight board as a regulator to provide independent oversight of public accounting firms in USA. Audit firms of
public companies have to register with it and are subject to regular inspec-
tion. The board can investigate and initiate disciplinary action against
audit firms if needed. An independent regulator aims to protect investors
by overseeing the audits of public companies. The National Financial
Reporting Authority has been set up India to provide oversight over auditors and adopt appropriate audit standards. With increase in regulatory
oversight and penal action against auditors, audit firms have become more
diligent.

Independence of Auditors: Auditors work closely with management
who prepare the financial statements. Maintaining independence of auditors becomes most important. The relationship between the audit firm
and the company has to be at arms-length. Directors or employees,
their relatives, partners and anyone with close ties or business association with the company should not be appointed as auditors. Similarly,
appointment of former partners or employees of the audit firm at senior
positions in the company should be discouraged. Joint audit has also been
suggested to reduce the probability of auditors working hand in glove
with management.

Rotation of Auditors: Another measure to preserve independence is
to restrict the period of association between those who prepare and those
who audit. It was seen that the same auditors continued in a company for
years and years. This resulted in a close relationship developing between
management and auditors increasing the chances of fraud. The Cadbury
Report had recommended rotation of partners of the audit firm. USA

has adopted a five-year rotation of lead audit partner. However, there has been a growing preference for rotation of the audit firm itself, arguing that a fresh pair of eyes would make for more effective audits. Though, initially, the audit quality may get impacted on account of lack of in-depth knowledge of the company and understanding of its complexities. The EU audit legislation since 2016 requires mandatory rotation of the audit firm every ten years, and member states have been advised to adopt shorter terms. India too requires listed companies to rotate audit firms after ten years and individual auditors after five years. On expiry of the term, they cannot be reappointed for five years.

Restriction on Non-Audit services: Audit firms to increase business provide other services to the audit client. Hence, if they lose the audit engagement, they are likely to lose other businesses also and this can cause severe revenue loss. This dependency impacts auditor's independence. Cadbury Report recommended disclosure of remuneration of non-audit work. The SOX act went further and put restrictions on non-audit services. In India and USA, services such as accounting and book keeping services; internal audit; design and implementation of any financial information system; actuarial services; investment banking or advisory services; and management functions are prohibited.

Selection Process: The manner of selection of auditors is also very crucial. Though auditors are appointed by the shareholders by way of voting, they are chosen by the board through the audit committees. EU and UK require auditors to be selected through a tendering procedure. After every 10 years, new auditors are to be appointed only through a tendering process.

Audit Remuneration: The fees paid to auditors should be adequate but not excess. Abnormal large payments can be conceived as bribe or hush money. The lure of huge fees created a situation where Arthur Andersen turn a blind eye to the happenings at Enron.

Audit Committee: An audit committee is to be formed by the board. The audit committee is responsible for the selection, compensation and oversight of the auditors. The auditors will directly report to the audit committee, thereby reducing the authority of the management on auditors.

AUDIT COMMITTEE

Audit committee is one of the main pillars of the corporate governance mechanism in any company. The Securities Exchange Commission of USA required listed companies to have an audit committee of non-executive directors way back in 1977. The Cadbury Report made it the focal point of good governance. Today, if a company is listed on any stock exchange in the world, it probably needs to have an audit committee. Not only listed companies but even other large companies in India are required to have an audit committee (Fig. 4.5). The King Report on Governance for South Africa 2009 (King III) emphasizes the vital role of the committee in ensuring the integrity of financial controls and integrated reporting (both financial and sustainability reporting), and identifying and managing financial risk. The audit committee is responsible for oversight of financial reporting and disclosure, reliability of the company's internal control processes and a strong risk management system.

Composition

The audit committee is generally formed of non-executive directors and as recommended in the Cadbury Report should be predominantly independent. Hence majority or all members are expected to be independent and preferable chairperson should also be independent (see Table 4.1). This ensures that independent directors review financial statements without the presence or influence of executive directors.

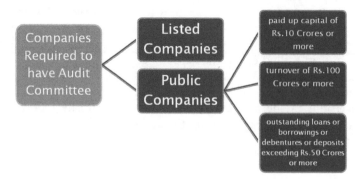

Fig. 4.5 Audit Committee in India (*Source* Developed By Author)

Table 4.1 Independence of Audit Committee

100% Independent and Chair Independent (Mandatory)	Canada, Hungary, Indonesia, Italy, Mexico, Slovenia, South Africa, Turkey, USA
100% Independent and Chair Independent (Recommended)	Brazil, Ireland, Russia, Switzerland, UK
66% Independent and Chair Independent	India, Korea
66% Independent	Argentina, France
50% or more Independent and Chair Independent (Mandatory)	Chile, Denmark, Hong Kong, Israel, Netherlands, Singapore, Spain
50% or more and Chair Independent (Recommended)	Australia, China, Finland, Greece,
50% or more independent	Iceland, Japan, Luxembourg, Norway, Portugal

Source Compiled by Author

In addition, the committee should have the capacity to understand and review financial statements. Thus, in India, all member should be financially literate (read and understand financial statements), and at least, one should have financial expertise (see Fig. 4.6). In USA also, all members should be financially literate, and it is preferred that there be at least one member who is a designated financial expert. In UK besides one member having recent and relevant financial expertise, the committee as a whole must have relevant competence of the sector the company operates in.

Role of Audit Committee

The role of the audit committee is expressly defined in most regulations. The board should specify in details the scope of the audit committee and may lay down additional responsibilities. The committee is charged with oversight of the company's accounting processes and financial reporting, internal control and risk management and auditor's selection, remuneration, independence and effectiveness.

Integrity of financial accounting and reporting: The primary role of audit committees is to oversee the integrity of the financial reporting systems and make sure the financial statements are understandable and reliable. As it is the management that prepares the statements, the committee must engage with them, particularly the CFO or equivalent while reviewing the quarterly and annual financial statements. In

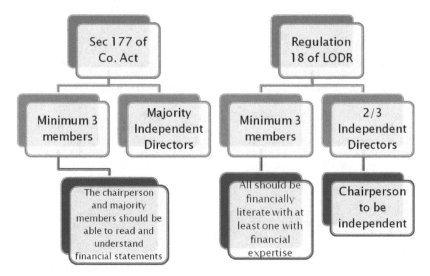

Fig. 4.6 Composition of audit committee: Example of India (*Source* Developed by Author)

addition, they are to assess the quality of the accounting principles and examine reasons for changes in accounting policies and appropriateness of accounting estimates. The committee should examine significant accounting or reporting issue or any new rules and their likely impact on financial statements. They should discuss these matters with the independent auditors as well as their observations in audit report.

Oversight of the external auditor: An important role of the audit committee is to oversee the functioning of the external or statutory auditor and confirm their independence. These responsibilities extend to the auditor's selection, appointment, remuneration, reappointment or termination. It is important that the auditors report directly to the audit committee. This way the auditor's appointment is not in the control of management and they can report without fear of repercussions.

The manner of selection of auditors is critical to ensure independence and competency of the auditors. Transparency of the process builds confidence in the investors. The audit committee should assess the independence of the auditor considering the relationship between the firm networks and group companies. It should evaluate the performance of the independent auditor and make an informed recommendation to the board regarding reappointment.

Another important element for maintaining auditor's independence is that only the audit committee has the power to negotiate the statutory audit fees and audit scope. In determining the fees, the committee should assess the audit scope, audit team's knowledge and experience, industry standards and non-audit service. Any non-audit service provided should be preapproved by audit committee.

The audit committee is to review the objectivity and effectiveness of the auditors and monitor their compliance with professional standards and the amount of non-audit fees paid to the firm. Difficulties faced during audit and management responses to audit queries should be reviewed. To improve oversight of the audit process, they should have frequent interactions with the independent auditor both in formal audit committee meetings as well as separate and less formal meetings to encourage candid and open communication and information flow between the auditor and audit committee. This discussion allows the audit committee to define an adequate audit scope, monitor the progress and make sure auditors are not influenced by pressures from management. Contentious issues from either side can be brought up and addressed.

Effectiveness of internal control and internal audit: Audit committee should evaluate whether their company has created and maintained an internal control system adequate to its business conditions and size, with the ability to detect and prevent fraud. Internal and external auditors are to report to the audit committee regarding the effectiveness and efficiency of internal control.

The audit committee must review the internal audit team's competencies, scope of work, audit plan and frequency of internal audit to assure the quality and adequacy of the internal audit function. It is advisable that internal auditors report directly to the committee. The committee should meet with internal auditors on a regular basis to discuss any matter of concern that may arise.

Regulatory compliance: The audit committee may also assist the board in monitoring compliance with laws and regulations. The audit committee should meet periodically with compliance officers to better understand the company's compliance process. They should periodically review any query or complain received by a regulator, examine company secretarial reports if applicable and take corrective action if needed.

Risk management: Audit committee's main focus is on risks that affect the financial statements. The board oversees strategic and operational risks, although the audit committee may be involved in developing the policies and practices used by the company to identify, prioritize and respond to the risks. Often boards have a separate risk management committee.

To perform all these responsibilities (Table 4.2) adequately, the audit committee must be vigilant, ask intelligent questions and obtain and analyse relevant information to make informed decisions.

RISK MANAGEMENT

A good internal control system helps identify risks. The board is to provide framework which enables risk to be 'assessed and managed'. The Turnbull's report (1999), recommended that the board "provide a balanced assessment of the significant risks and the effectiveness of

Table 4.2   Role of Audit Committee: An example of India

Companies Act (Sec 177)	• Recommendation for appointment remuneration and terms of appointment of auditors • Monitor and review the independence and performance of auditor and effectiveness of audit process • Examination of financial statements and auditors' report • Approval or any subsequent modification of transactions of the company with related parties • Scrutiny of inter-corporate loans and investments • Valuation of undertakings or assets of the company, whenever is necessary • Evaluation of internal financial controls and risk management • Monitoring the end use of funds raised through public offers and related matters • Operate *the vigil mechanism* so that directors and employees can report genuine concerns. The whistle-blower mechanism must provide adequate safeguards against victimization and make provision for direct access to the chairperson of the audit committee if need

(continued)

Table 4.2 (continued)

LODR (Part C Schedule II)	• Provide oversight of the company's financial reporting process and the disclosure of its financial information to ensure that the financial statement is correct, sufficient and credible • Approval of payment to statutory auditors for any other services rendered by the statutory auditors • Reviewing, with the management, the annual financial statements before submission to the board for approval, with particular reference to:

(a) Matters required to be included in the Director's Responsibility Statement

(b) Changes, if any, in accounting policies and practices and reasons for the same

(c) Major accounting entries involving estimates based on the exercise of judgement by management

(d) Significant adjustments made in the financial statements arising out of audit findings

(e) Compliance with listing and other legal requirements relating to financial statements

(f) Disclosure of any related party transactions

(g) Qualifications in the draft audit report

- Reviewing, with the management, the quarterly financial statements before submission to the board for approval
- Reviewing, with the management, the statement of uses / application of funds raised through an issue so that utilization of proceeds is appropriate
- Reviewing, with the management, performance of statutory and internal auditors and adequacy of the internal control systems
- Reviewing the adequacy of internal audit function, including the structure of the internal audit department, staffing and seniority of the official heading the department, reporting structure, coverage and frequency of internal audit
- Discussion with internal auditors any significant findings and follow up there on
- Reviewing the findings of any internal investigations by the internal auditors into matters where there is suspected fraud or irregularity or a failure of internal control systems of a material nature and reporting the matter to the board
- Discussion with statutory auditors before the audit commences about the nature and scope of audit as well as post-audit discussion to ascertain any area of concern
- To look into the reasons for substantial defaults in the payment to the depositors, debenture holders, shareholders (in case of non-payment of declared dividends) and creditors
- Approval of appointment of CFO after assessing the qualifications, experience and background, etc., of the candidate
- Carrying out any other function as is mentioned in the terms of reference of the audit committee

Source Companies Act 2013 and SEBI Listing and Obligation Disclosure Requirements, 2015

the system of internal control in managing those risks" by consider the following factors:

- The nature and extent of the risks facing the company.
- The likelihood that these risks may materialize.
- The types and levels of acceptable risk.
- The company's ability to reduce the likelihood and impact of identified risks.
- The cost-effectiveness of operating individual internal controls relative to the benefit gained by managing the risks.

High-profile corporate failures caused by mismanagement of risks (see Box—Queen's Bank and Crooked E) highlight the consequences of not having an effective risk management in place. The board must design and implement an appropriate risk management system, determine the nature and extent of the principal risks and the companies' risk appetite, agree on how the principal risks should be managed or mitigated to reduce the likelihood of their incidence or their impact and monitor and satisfy itself that the system is functioning effectively (Guidance on Risk Management, Internal Control and Related Financial and Business Reporting, Financial Reporting Council, 2014).

The board may ask the audit committee to carry out the responsibilities of risk management or may set up a separate risk management committee (Table 4.3).

Table 4.3 Risk Management Committee: Example of India

Applicability	As required by LODR top 500 companies by market capitalization shall constitute a Risk Management Committee
Composition	• Committee shall consist of directors and senior executives • Majority should be directors • The chairman shall be a director
Role	The board shall define the roles and responsibilities of the Risk Management Committee and may delegate monitoring and reviewing of the risk management plan to the committee and such other functions as it may seem—to include cyber security

Who Will Choose Your Next Leader?
USA and India are the largest democracies in the world. Are they? Who will choose their next leader—Their people or Facebook? Cambridge Analytica a British political consultancy has allegedly acquired in an unfitting manner data on Facebook's American users to understand their voting preferences that were later used to help elect U.S. President Donald Trump in 2016. In a 2018 congressional hearing, Facebook Inc.'s Mark Zuckerberg was made to testify to explain to the US House how 50 million users' data got into the hands of Cambridge Analytica (Shepardson, 2018). Federal Trade Commission is examining whether Facebook violated an agreement made in 2011 regarding its privacy practices. All this led the company's market value to fall by more than $50 billion (Shepardson, 2018). It has also prompted a few public funds with holdings in Facebook Inc., to back a shareholder proposal to remove Mark Zuckerberg as chairman given these controversies including the possible role of Facebook in promoting violence in countries such as Myanmar. The demand for making the role of chairperson independent has "no practical effect as the social-media chief has a lock on the bulk of Facebook's super voting shares, but it heightens scrutiny of the company's corporate governance" (Seetharaman, 2018).

Note Facebook was renamed Meta in 2021.

Data Protection

An important component of internal control and risk management in a technology-driven world is data protection. Large amounts of data are stored about the company's customers, clients and customers. It is important that this information is not leaked or misused (see—who will choose your next leader). The European Union's (EU's) General Data Protection Regulation (GDPR) took effect in May 2018, harmonizing data protection and privacy requirements across the EU. It is the legal framework that sets guidelines for the collection and processing of personal information from individuals who live in the European Union (EU). The Data Protection Act 2018 of UK controls how your personal information is used by organizations, businesses or the government. Everyone responsible for using personal data has to follow strict rules called 'data protection principles'. They must make sure the information is used fairly, lawfully and transparently. The Information Technology Act (2000) of

India requires consent and provides right to compensation for improper disclosure of personal information.

References

Abelson, R. (2002, January 19). *ENRON'S COLLAPSE: THE DIRECTORS; one enron inquiry suggests board played important role.* Retrieved March 5, 2018, from The New York Times. http://www.nytimes.com/2002/01/19/business/enron-s-collapse-directors-one-enron-inquiry-suggests-board-played-important.html

Babineck, M. (2002, February 16). *Who were Enron's outside directors?* Retrieved March 5, 2018, from My Plain View. https://www.myplainview.com/news/article/Who-were-Enron-s-outside-directors-8924784.php

Barton. (2014). *Enron case.* Retrieved March 5, 2018, from Course Hero. https://www.coursehero.com/file/11937738/barton-enron-case/

Borger, J. (2005, February 5). Tapes reveal Enron's secret role in California's power blackouts. *The Guardian.* Retrieved November 22, 2022 from https://www.theguardian.com/business/2005/feb/05/enron.usnews

Business: The Economy How Leeson Broke the Bank. (1999, June 22). Retrieved March 5, 2018, from BBC News. http://news.bbc.co.uk/2/hi/business/375259.stm

Committee on Governmental Affairs United States Senate, The Role of Board of Directors in ENRON'S Collapse Report. (2002, July 8). Retrieved March 5, 2018 from https://www.gpo.gov/fdsys/pkg/CPRT-107SPRT80393/html/CPRT-107SPRT80393.htm

Companies Act(2013), India.

Concept of Special Purpose Vehicle (SPV) and Enron Accounting Fraud Case Study. (2017, December 10). Retrieved March 5, 2018, from Investxp. https://www.investxp.in/concept-of-special-purpose-vehicle-spv-and-enron-accounting-fraud-case-study/

Enron Scandal: The Fall of a Wall Street Darling. (2018, January 3). Retrieved March 5, 2018, from Investopedia. https://www.investopedia.com/updates/enron-scandal-summary/

Enron's board of directors. (2002, February 1). Retrieved March 5, 2018, from The Guardian. https://www.theguardian.com/business/2002/feb/01/corporatefraud.enron3

(EU's) General Data Protection Regulation (GDPR)(2018). The European Union's.

Nirav Modi case: What is LoU, CBS, SWIFT? Know these terms to understand PNB fraud. (2018, February 18). *Business Today.* Retrieved July 31, 2020, from https://www.businesstoday.in

Prasad, A. (2018, February 16). *Nirav Modi-PNB scam explodes as whistleblower Dinesh Dubey details scope of his interventions made to Allahabad Bank, RBI and UPA government.* Retrieved July 31, 2020, from https://www.republicw orld.com

Rodrigues, J. (2015, February 24). *Barings collapse at 20: How rogue trader Nick Leeson broke the bank.* Retrieved March 5, 2018, from The Guardian. https://www.theguardian.com/business/from-the-archive-blog/2015/feb/24/nick-leeson-barings-bank-1995-20-archive

Sahgal, R. (2018, March 5). An evergreen LoU story: How Shetty & Co pulled the PNB con. *The Economic Times.* Retrieved July 31, 2020, from https://economictimes.indiatimes.com

Salter, M. S. (2008). *Innovation corrupted the origins and legacy of Enron's collapse.*

Sarbanes-Oxley Act (2002), USA.

Seetharaman, D. (2018, October 17). Funds back proposal to remove Zuckerberg as Facebook Chairman. *Wall Street Journal.* Retrieved February 14, 2021 from https://www.wsj.com

Shepardson, D. (2018, March 24). U.S. lawmakers formally ask Facebook CEO to testify on user data. *Reuters.* Retrieved February 14, 2021 from https://www.reuters.com

Span, P., & White, B. (2002, November 15). The Market Scholars' Star Turn. *The Washington Post.* Retrieved November 22, 2022 from https://www.washingtonpost.com/archive/politics/2002/11/15/the-market-scholars-star-turn/c7a137d3-4c33-4bbb-a366-0ba5781ccdcc/

The Information Technology Act (2000), India.

The Data Protection Act (2018), UK.

The EU Audit Reform legislation (2016), European Union.

The King Report on Governance for South Africa 2009 (King III), South Africa.

Titcomb, J. (2015, February 23). *Barings: the collapse that erased 232 years of history.* Retrieved March 5, 2018, from Telegraph. https://www.telegraph.co.uk/finance/newsbysector/banksandfinance/11427501/Barings-the-collapse-that-erased-232-years-of-history.html

Turnbull, Internal Control: Guidance for Directors on the Combined Code. (1999). Institute of Chartered Accountants in England and Wales (ICAEW), UK.

Varma, S. (2018, March 23). PNB Fraud: Nirav Modi case: India has no option but to act. *The Economic Times.* Retrieved July 31, 2020, from https://economictimes.indiatimes.com

CHAPTER 5

Global Corporate Governance Movement

Scams, Codes and Regulations—Issued in Public Interest

THE FIRST SCAMS—UK SHAKEN, WAKESUP

During 1990/91, a wave of three scams unnerved UK—Polly Peck (1990), Maxwell (1991) and Bank of Credit & Commerce International (1991).

Polly Peck International was a small textile company in UK which expanded rapidly in the 1980s becoming one of the top 100 companies before collapsing in 1990 with debts of £1.3bn (https://en.wikipedia. org/wiki/Polly_Peck). Its chief executive Asil Nadir was sentenced for stealing nearly £29m from the company he set up and got listed. He transferred huge funds to his Turkish companies which required only his single signature. He used company money for buying huge properties for himself and funding his lavish lifestyle.

When *Maxwell* started to get into financial difficulties, he started moving funds from the pension fund of the company's employees into his privately owned companies. Maxwell had stolen hundreds of millions of pounds from his own companies' pension fund which he held in trust for his employees. The other directors in the company as well as the auditors did not object. (See Pension Raider Maxwell—Chapter 2).

The collapse of these companies saw investors lose money as stock markets fell. These scams resulted in a loss of confidence of investors and to prevent future scams a Committee was commissioned under the Chairmanship of Sir Adrian Cadbury by the Financial Reporting Council

(FRC) and London Stock Exchange. Their report the **"Financial Aspects of Corporate Governance" popularly known as Cadbury Report of 1992 was the first code on Corporate Governance.**

Meanwhile, a large bank also fell to its knees. *The bank of Credit and Commerce International (BCCI)* was set up in 1972 by Afghan Hasan Abedi, a Pakistani banker. The bank was registered in Luxembourg with head offices in Karachi and London. A decade after opening, BCCI was 7th largest private bank in the world and had over 400 branches in 78 countries (https://en.wikipedia.org/wiki/Bank_of_Credit_and_Com merce_International). It was involved in massive money laundering and other financial crimes. Hasan had close ties with ruler of Abu Dhabi and may be even intelligence agencies.

British regulators realized in 1982 that something was wrong but considered it problem of Luxembourg. The bank used different auditors in each country; hence, no one knew the full picture. Finally, in March 1991, the Bank of England asked Price Waterhouse to carry out an inquiry. On 24 June 1991, Price Waterhouse submitted the Sandstorm report (http://visar.csustan.edu/aaba/BCCISandstormRelease. html) showing that BCCI had engaged in "widespread fraud and manipulation" that made it difficult, if not impossible, to reconstruct BCCI's financial history. The bank of England and other regulators of different countries felt the bank could not be 'cleaned up' and as it had already lost its capital it should be shut down. The court of Luxembourg finally ordered liquidation of BCCI. The report also points out how few individuals exercised full control on all operations of BCCI.

CADBURY REPORT

The "Financial Aspects of Corporate Governance" widely referred to as Cadbury Report was published in 1992. The scandals revealed how board and auditors had failed their responsibilities. Thus, the recommendations of the report covered three major aspects:

- Board Structure and Responsibility of Directors.
- Audit and Auditors.
- Role of Shareholders.

The most important element of the report is the "Code of Best Practices" for board and directors to adopt.

Board Effectiveness

The report emphasized the importance of an efficient board to lead and control. Board is collectively responsible for meeting objectives of the company. It is the responsibility of the chairman to secure good corporate governance. Excess power in the hands of Maxwell and Nadir had been the primary reason such large-scale fraud was possible. Hence, no one person should dominate the company and the post of Chairman and CEO should be held by different people.

The board must have a balance of executive and non-executive directors. Executive directors should have intimate knowledge of business, their term should be limited and their remuneration disclosed.

The other board members of the three companies were conspicuous by their inactiveness. Non-executive directors as outsiders bring a broader perspective. They must play a great role in the board and exercise independent judgement. The "majority of nonexecutives on a board should be independent of the company. This means that apart from their directors' fees and shareholdings, they should be independent of management and free from any business or other relationship which could materially interfere with the exercise of their independent judgement". The fees of independent directors should be adequate to "recognizing value" but not in excess to "affect independence". Every board must have at least 3 non-executive directors of which 2 are independent. The independent directors are to review the board and executive directors' performance.

Board Committees

Every board must have an audit committee, nomination committee and remuneration committee.

Audit Committee: The audit committee should consist of 3 or more non-executive directors with majority being independent. The audit committee's duties should be based on the needs of the company but should normally include:

- Appointment and resignation of auditors and determining their fees.
- Review of the half year and annual financial statements before submission to the board.
- Discussion with the external auditor about the nature and scope of the audit.

- Any problem or reservations arising from the audit, and any matters which the external auditor wishes to discuss, without executive board members present.
- Review of the company's internal control systems prior to endorsement by the board.
- Review of any significant findings of internal investigations.

Nomination Committee: The responsibility of the nomination committee is to recommend to the board new appointments for both executive and non-executive directors. The committee should be composed of a majority of non-executive directors and chaired by a non-executive director.

Remuneration Committee: The report recommended boards have a remuneration committee consisting entirely or mostly of non-executive directors and chaired by a non-executive director. The committee is to recommend to the board the remuneration of the executive directors.

Auditors

The duty of the auditors is to provide the shareholders with an external and objective report on the fairness and correctness of the financial statements presented by the directors. They must ensure an effective internal control system is in place. In each case, the auditors failed the shareholders. Auditors should apply their professional skill and impartially carry out their responsibilities. Audit firms are to disclose remuneration from non-audit services and periodically change partners that are handing a particular audit.

Shareholders

Shareholder can enable good governance by their role in election of director and auditors. They must actively participate in Annual General Meetings and hold board accountable.

Disclosure and Transparency

The report recommended stronger accounting standards and better disclosures so that accounting misrepresentation is discouraged.

UK CORPORATE GOVERNANCE CODE

After the Cadbury Report UK set up many committees to examine different aspects of corporate governance and the code went through several changes to its present form.

Greenbury Report

The Confederation of British Industry (CBI) established the Study Group on directors' remuneration under the chairmanship of Sir Richard Greenbury to address concerns about directors' remuneration. The report usually referred to as the Greenbury Report of 1995 lays down a code of "best practices in determining and accounting for Directors' remuneration". According to the report, "The remuneration committee of non-executive directors to determine on their behalf, and on behalf of the shareholders the remuneration policy of executive remuneration and specific remuneration packages for each of the Executive Directors, including pension rights and any compensation payments". The Chairman of the committee is directly accountable to the shareholders. The members of the committees should have no personal financial interest and no potential conflicts of interest arising from cross-directorships. Full disclosure should be made with regard to remuneration of all directors (Greenbury Report, 1995).

Combined Code

The Hampel Report combined the Cadbury and Greenbury Report that resulted in *the* **Combined Code: Principles of Good Governance and Code of Best Practice** published in 1998. The report has two major components: (i) Principles of Corporate Governance and (ii) a code of good corporate governance. Similar to the earlier codes, it focuses on board structure, director's remuneration, role of shareholders and accountability of auditors. It emphasized the importance of providing quality and timely information to the board so that they can act appropriately (Combined Code, 1998).

Turnbull Report

The Internal Control: Guidance for directors on the Combined Code by Turnbull was published in 1999. It provides guidance on implementing internal controls within companies. The report discusses the importance of internal control, how to establish an internal control system the role of board in reviewing the effectives of the system. The board should disclose the "process for identifying, evaluating and managing the significant risks faced by the company" (Turnbull Report, 1999, 2005).

The Higgs Report

The Higgs Report of 2003 titled a "Review of the role and Effectiveness of non-executive directors" provides best practices for non-executive directors to maximize their effectiveness in the corporate governance framework. The report discusses the importance of independent directors, their definition, tenure, remuneration and role in the board. It suggests identifying a senior independent director to interact with shareholders if they have concerns (Higgs Report, 2003).

The Smith Report

The audit committee's Combined Code Guidance under the chairmanship of Robert Smith of 2003 deals with increasing the effectiveness of audit committee. It discusses the establishing the audit committee, its membership, frequency of meetings, its role and responsibilities. It recommends that the members should have adequate professional qualification, knowledge and experience. At least one member of the audit committee should have recent and relevant financial experience (Smith Report, 2003).

THE SCANDALS OF USA

After the scams in UK and other parts of the world, regulators realized that there is a need to strengthen Corporate Governance regulations. US stock exchanges too increased governance and disclosure requirements. Then, Enron—9/11 of the corporate world happened in 2001. Enron portrayed how easily management can destroy investors' wealth. This was followed by WorldCom in 2002 (See Box). The US investors were completely shaken up by the corporate scandals of Enron (2001) and WorldCom (2002). US government reacted by creating a new law—The Sarbanes-Oxley Act.

WorldCom: The Awakening
WorldCom was a US-based large telecommunications company that its founder and CEO Ebbers had grown through several acquisitions. The Board kept approving loans from the company to the CEO to repay a margin call to prevent his selling his shares in the company bring prices down. The Board eventually forced Ebbers to resigned in April 2002 as he owed $366 million in personal loans he had taken from the company and a probe into its accounting malpractices (CIMA, 2009). The Security Exchange commission investigation found accounting irregularities to the tune of billions of dollars. The company had to file for bankruptcy protection in July 2002. Their auditors, Authur Anderson, said they were not aware of any accounting mis-statements. The company founder and former CEO Bernard Ebbers was sentenced to 25 years in prison, and former CFO Scott Sullivan received a five-year jail sentence.
Point to Ponder: Are the events of WorldCom different from the other scandals. What's the solution?

SARBANES-OXLEY ACT (SOX)

Post Enron and WorldCom, to protect investors from the possibility of fraudulent accounting activities by corporations and improve disclosures, the Sarbanes-Oxley Act named after its writers US Congressmen Paul Sarbanes and Michael Oxley was passed by US regulators in 2002. All publicly traded companies in USA must comply with SOX. The US Securities and Exchange Commission (SEC) administers the act and sets compliance and disclosure requirements.

The act is divided into eleven titles or chapters. Some of the major provisions are:

Public Company Accounting Oversight Board (Title I)

This is the most important provision of the act. A Public Company Accounting Oversight Board (PCAOB) is to provide independent oversight of public accounting firms. All firms are to register with PCAOB.

The board is to establish auditing standards. The board shall conduct regular inspections to assess the degree of compliance by each registered public accounting firm. It also has the power to undertake investigation and disciplinary action against firms if needed. It also will determine accounting standards to be followed.

Auditors Independence (Title II)

To ensure independence of auditors, the Act prohibits certain non-audit services to companies in which they are auditors. All audit and non-audit services are to be approved by the audit committee. All non-audit services shall be disclosed. The partner who is the lead or coordinator of audit services must be rotated every five years. To prevent conflicts of interest registered public accounting firm are not to carry out any audit service if a chief executive officer, controller, chief financial officer, chief accounting officer or any person serving in an equivalent position for the company was employed by that registered independent public accounting firm and participated in audit during the previous year.

Corporate Responsibility (Title III)

This title cast certain important responsibilities on the company. Audit committee is responsible for the appointment, compensation and oversight of the auditors. The audit committee is to be 100% independent that is all the members must be independent directors. CEO and CFO are to certify financial statements are correct; if later found incorrect and accounts have to be restated any bonus received and profit on sale of shares will be recovered. Directors and officers should not mislead or influence the auditors in any way.

Financial Disclosures (Title IV)

The annual and quarterly financial report shall disclose all material off-balance sheet transactions. The act places restriction on loans to directors and executives and any loans given are to be duly disclosed. Any transactions with directors or shareholders who hold more than 10% must be disclosed.

Analyst Conflicts of Interest (Title V)

The act requires segregation of brokers and dealers of investment bankers with security analyst to ensure independence of recommendation. Securities analyst and each registered broker or dealer to disclose to public and in any research report conflicts of interest that exist.

Frauds and Penalties

The act imposes heavy penalties and punishment for fraud. Anyone including auditors who are found guilty of falsifying or destroying documents and records will be fined and can be imprisonment up to 20 years. The act provides for protection for whistle-blowers. To act as a deterrent and enable prosecution, certain corporate fraud can be treated as a criminal offence.

The Satyam Scandal: Truth Behind Lies

Satyam Computer Services Ltd (Satyam) one of the most prominent information technology (IT) firms of India was a family run business headed by Ramalinga Raju as Executive Chairman and his brother B Rama Raju as Managing Director. It was listed on New York Stock exchange alongside Indian stock exchanges. By 2008, Satyam had become a USD \$2.1 billion company demonstrating an annual compound growth rate of 35% having won many big contracts with global organizations such as Microsoft and World Bank. Satyam Computers was awarded the coveted Golden Peacock Global Award for Excellence in Corporate Governance for 2008 by the World Council for Corporate Governance (WCFCG). Investor Relations Global Rankings (IRGR) rated Satyam as the company with Best Corporate Governance Practices for 2006 and 2007 (Businesswire India, 2008).

Satyam probably came to the limelight of the ordinary man when Bill Gates from Microsoft along with the then Chief Minister of former Andhra Pradesh, Mr. Chandra Babu Naidu, met Ramalinga Raju and other senior executives at one of the offices of Satyam in Hyderabad (PTI, 2002).

On 7 January 2009 when Ramalinga Raju confessed to accounting frauds of more than Rs. 7800 crores, the Indian investors and regulators were stunned and outraged. Ironically, Satyam means "truth" in the ancient Indian language "Sanskrit". But it was lies weaved through 'creative accounting' that led to investors losing about \$2.82 billion as the share prices fell from Rs. 541 in January 2008 to Rs. 6.50 on 10 January 2009.

Board Composition

Name	Designation	Qualification	Profile
Ramalinga Raju	Executive chairman, promoter-director	MBA	Promoter of Satyam Computers
Rama Raju	Managing director, promoter-director	MBA	Promoter of Satyam Computers
Ram Mynampati	Executive director, declared interim CEO	MCA	Employee and executive director on board of Satyam
Prof. Krishna G. Palepu	Non-executive director, consultant	Ph.D	Professor at Harvard Business School
Dr. (Mrs) Mangalam Srinivasan	Non-executive director, independent	Ph.D	Management consultant and advisor to Kennedy School of Management
Mr. Vinod K. Dham	Non-executive director, independent	B.E/ M.E(Electrical)	Director of New Path Ventures LLC, NEA—Indo U.S Ventures LLC
Prof. M. Rammohan Rao	Non-executive director, independent	Ph.D	Dean, Indian School of Business
Mr. T. R. Prasad	Non-executive director, independent	M.Sc.(Physics)	Retired bureaucrat (Cabinet Secretary, Government of India)
Prof. V.S. Raju	Non-executive director, independent	Ph.D	Chairman of the Naval Research Board, Defense Research and Development Organization, Government of India

Satyam's "gold-plated" board comprised of nine directors of which five were independent directors (they met the standards set by the NYSE on which Satyam's securities were listed and Clause 49 of SEBI). These included Mangalam Srinivasan (US academician and independent director since 1991), Vinod K. Dham (famously known as father of the Pentium Chip), US Raju (former director of IIT Delhi), M Rammohan Rao (then Dean of Indian School of Business), Krishna Palepu (professor at Harvard

Business School) and T.R. Prasad (former Cabinet Secretary). They were luminaries, men of standing and reputation. Each of the members was on the board on the personal invitation of founder chairman Ramalinga Raju.

On 16 December 2008, a proposal for the acquisition of Maytas Infra Limited and Maytas Properties Limited by Satyam was placed before the board. Maytas companies were controlled by the Raju family ironically 'Satyam' read backward is 'Maytas'. These companies were in the business of real estate and infrastructure development—two industries completely unrelated to Satyam's core information technology business. This related party deal would result *"in a significant amount of cash flowing from Satyam a public listed company to its individual promoters, the Raju family"* (Varottil, 2010), Yet the board approved the proposed acquisition. As required under the listing agreement, the stock exchanges were informed of approved deal. The market reacted badly to the news, and the company quickly withdrew the Maytas proposal.

It is astounding that seven out of the nine directors were present at the board meeting where the unanimous decision to acquire Maytas Infra and Maytas Properties for $1.6 billion was taken. Companies Act and SEBI regulations even then required interested directors not to participate when a deal in which they were associated was to be taken up at a board meeting. To avoid any appearance of bias and comply with legal bindings, the two promoter-directors excused themselves from the meeting.

Close to the heels of the incident, on 18 December 2018 a whistle blower who used a pseudonym of Jose Abraham, and claiming to be a former senior executive of the company involved with Satyam's contract with the World Bank, emailed to an independent board member regarding the company's sorry state of affairs (Sanyal & Tiwari, 2009). On 23 December 2008, the World Bank announced that Satyam has been barred from business with World Bank for eight years for providing bank staff with 'improper benefits' and on charges of data theft (ET Bureau, 2008).

Financial of Satyam for 2008

Items (Rs. in crore)	Actual	Reported	Difference
Cash and Bank Balances	321	5361	5040
Accrued Interest on Bank Fixed Deposits	Nil	376.5	376
Understated Liability	1464	234	1230
Overstated Debtors	2161	2651	490
Total	Nil	Nil	7136
Revenues (July–September 2008)	2112	2700	588
Operating Profits	61	649	588

Sources Corporate Accounting Fraud: A Case Study of Satyam Computers Limited, Madan Lal Bhasin, *Open Journal of Accounting*, 2013, 2, 26–38 (http://dx. doi.org/10.4236/ojacct.2013.22006) Published Online April 2013 (http://www. scirp.org/journal/ojacct) and *The Business Today*, February 8, 2009, p. 50

These chain of events culminated in the Chairman Mr Raju confessing to a financial crime—a colossal fraud in the company's financial statements. On 7 January 2009, in a letter to the board Mr. Raju confessed to a $1.47 billion (or Rs. 7800 crore) fraud, admitted that he had exaggerated profits for years. This created a growing gap in the balance sheet which was filled by reporting debtors (receivables) and cash that did not exist (see table). As Mr. Raju in his letter stated "Every attempt made to eliminate the gap failed.... It was like riding a tiger, not knowing how to get off without being eaten. The aborted Maytas acquisition deal was the last attempt to fill the fictitious assets with real ones".

Very smartly, fictitious invoices were created in Satyam's self-developed ERP models which generated into receivables and then were shown as received by bank accounts outside India. By showing a rosy picture of the company, the promoters were jacking up the share price and simultane-ously selling off their holdings raking in handsome money. The promoters' holdings had gradually decreased from 20.74% in 2003 to 8.74% by 2008 while institutional holding during the same period increased from about 56% to 61% and non-institutional holdings from 23 to 30% which included an increase in share of Indian public from 8.47% to 10.25%. In 2008, Foreign Institutional investors had a 48% share in the company. By December 2008, promoters held only 2.18% holding yet exercised full control. The brothers together with their family members sold most of their shares during April 2000 to 7 January 2009 pocketing more than 3.9 crores shares (SFIO Report).

As per the Enforcement Director's investigations, several gardeners, truck drivers and others, who were working in the mango gardens and orchards belonging to Raju family for meagre salaries of Rs. 4000 to Rs 5000 per month, were made directors in shell companies that possessed more than 4200 acres of land valuing over Rs 4000 crores (Sharma, 2010). The fraud took place to divert company funds into real-estate investment, showcase high earnings per share, raise executive compensation and make huge profits by selling stake at inflated price.

'Why was a company with 5000 crore bank balance even borrowing 200 odd crores? Did the directors need finance degrees to question this? Global auditing firm, PricewaterhouseCoopers (PwC), audited Satyam's books from June 2000 until the discovery of the fraud in 2009. The excess cash should have been a flag to auditors and the directors. The auditors never independently verified the balances with banks. Interestingly between 2003–2008, audit fee from Satyam had increased three times. Price Waterhouse received an annual fee of 4.3 crore for financial year 2007–2008, which is almost twice of what Satyam peers in the IT sector paid their audit firms' (Sharma, 2010).

As a result of the scandal, the Ministry of Corporate Affairs, Government of India, and the Securities Exchange Board of India initiated investigations. Both brothers along with the company's CFO were arrested. The two auditors—partners at Lovelock & Lewis, an Indian affiliate of PwC—were also arrested and suspended by the Institute of Chartered Accounts of India. In an attempt to save the company and its employees, the government nominated six members of its choice to the board. In April 2009, Tech Mahindra purchased the company through a global bidding process for just about a $1.13 per share (Bhasin, 2013). US investors filed a class action suit and were awarded $150 million.

The Satyam scandal had a profound effect on Indian corporates and their stakeholders. It triggered "at least 620 independent directors resigning in 2009 alone, a figure that is... by far without precedent globally" (Afsharipour, 2010). Sweeping changes were made to corporate governance in India. The old Companies Act 1956 was modified in 2000 and replaced by Companies Act 2013 and clause 49 was updated and later replaced with Listing Obligation and Disclosure Regulation (2015). Stringent governance laws were implemented not just for listed companies but also for large public companies.

Points to Ponder

1. Why was a board of such luminaries so ineffective?

2. Why did the auditors fail to verify the correctness of the financial statements?
3. What was the impact of dominance of the promoters?
4. How did different shareholders participate in the company?

THE REACTIVE REGULATOR

Only when a scam happens, frauds unearthed, do governments and regulators wake up and make laws and rules. They never seem to proactively take preventive measures. It's like taking medicine after catching a cold but nor wearing warm clothes beforehand. Rather, it was as if these companies were suffering from cancer yet continued to consume tobacco. And the regulators woke up only when a company was on its deathbed. India has been no different and though corporate governance initiatives began following the Cadbury Report major reforms saw light only after Satyam's setback.

CORPORATE GOVERNANCE INITIATIVES IN INDIA

Background

Till 1991, **Controller of Capital Issues** administered control over capital issues in accordance with the Capital Issues (Control) Act, 1947. Its purpose was to channelize investments in desired directions and helped maintain the health of the capital market. To do so, the Controller of Capital Issues was empowered as the sanctioning authority for any reorganization of the capital structure of public limited companies, raising capital through either initial and follow on public issue, its prices and premium including rights and bonus issues. Debt by way of debentures also needed its approval.

Harshad Mehta, known as the big bull a well-known stock broker, manipulated the stock market in 1992 by drawing out funds from banks fraudulently. He pretended to broker short-term lending and borrowing between banks but used the money of the lending bank to purchase shares. Fake documents and bank receipts were used and bank officials bribed to do this. The shares were sold at profits and money returned. He rigged the market to increase share prices. As a result, the market rose by more than 4500 points. When the scam was exposed, the banks lost a lot of money, the stock market crashed, and small investors lost their savings.

Capital market reforms were undertaken to develop the market. Securities and Exchange Board of India (SEBI) was established to increase transparency and protect investors.

Evolution of Corporate Governance in India

Post-liberalization as the economy developed, companies started to flourish and expand. They began raising capital from the huge Indian investor base. The need for implementing good corporate governance was evident. The scams in UK and other parts of the world in the 1990s made India realize the importance of corporate governance codes (Fig. 5.1). The early initiatives include:

- CII Code (1998)
- Birla Committee (1999)
- Naresh Chandra Committee (2002)
- Murthy Committee (2003)
- Irani Committee (2004).

The Confederation of Indian Industries Code (1988)

India's first major corporate governance reform proposal was launched by the Confederation of Indian Industry (CII) in 1996 with the formation of a task force to develop a corporate governance code for Indian companies. Their report entitled "Desirable Corporate Governance: A Code" of 1998 contained detailed governance provisions related to listed companies. It was voluntary in nature and only a few companies adopted it. It did not result in a broad overhaul of governance norms and practices by Indian companies (CII Code, 1998).

Birla Committee (1999)

Later SEBI appointed the Birla Committee on corporate governance under the chairmanship of Kumar Mangalam Birla. The committee's report divided the recommendations into two categories, namely mandatory and non-mandatory. The mandatory recommendations included

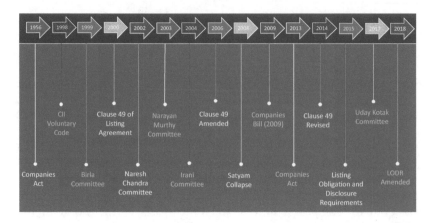

Fig. 5.1 Corporate governance development in India—a timeline (*Source* Developed by Author)

increasing board independence and formation of audit committee. It also made several recommendations regarding disclosure and transparency issues in particular with respect to information provided to shareholders. The committee suggested directors' report to shareholders should contain a Management Discussion and Analysis (MD&A) section describing operations, risks and strategy of the company (Birla Committee, 1999).

Clause 49 (2000)
Based on the recommendations of the Birla committee, SEBI introduced Clause 49 in the listing agreement which give **India** its **first code on corporate governance in 2000**. It provided detailed provisions of corporate governance relating to board composition, independent director and its definition and role of audit committee (Clause 49, 2000).

Naresh Chandra Committee (2002)
After Enron and WorldCom debacle, and the enactment of the Sarbanes-Oxley Act, in 2002 the Department of Company Affairs (DCA) under the Ministry of Finance and Company Affairs appointed a high-level

committee under the chairmanship of Naresh Chandra to examine governance issues specially the role and independence of statutory auditors. It recommended (Naresh Chandra Committee, 2002):

- **Disqualifications for audit assignments:** A firm cannot accept an audit if it or the partners have any direct financial interest in or business relationship or personal relationship with the company, hold more than 2 per cent of the capital, or received any loans and/or guarantees from or on behalf of the audit client. So that no audit firm is unduly dependent on an audit client, the fees received from any one client and its subsidiaries and affiliates, all together, should not exceed 25 per cent of the total revenues of the audit firm. However, to help newer and smaller audit firms, this requirement will not be applicable to audit firms for the first five years from the date of commencement of their activities, and for those whose total revenues are less than Rs.15 lakhs per year.
- **Prohibition of non-audit services:** Firm cannot provide non-audit services such as accounting and book keeping, internal audit design and implementation of financial information systems, actuarial or investment advice, management functions, valuation or recruitment services to audit clients.
- **Audit Partner Rotation:** Partner should be rotated every five years but allowed to return after a break of three years.
- **Independence:** Auditors to provide annual certificate of independence.
- **Audit Committee:** Audit committee to choose auditors and monitor their work.
- **Certification of Account:** CEO and CFO to certify correctness of annual audited accounts.
- **Disclosures:** Qualifications to audit report and contingent liabilities must be clearly spelled out.
- **Replacement of auditors:** Explanation must be provided by management if auditors are proposed to be replaced.

Narayana Murthy Committee Report (2003)
The Narayana Murthy Committee was set up by SEBI, with the objective of further strengthening corporate governance practices in India. The committee proposed certain mandatory recommendations including: (a)

closer monitoring of financial statements, internal control and related party transactions by the audit committee which should be composed of only financially literate members and at least one member to have financial expertise; (b) justification of alternative treatment of a transaction other than those prescribed by accounting standards; (c) all related party transactions to be placed before audit committee and any transaction not at arms-length to be explained; (d) risk assessment and management processes to be evaluated and approved by the board; (e) funds raised by IPO to be reviewed on a quarterly basis by audit committee; (f) a code of conduct to be adopted and complied by board and senior management; (g) nominee directors to be appointed by shareholders and are accountable like any other director; (h) remuneration of non-executive directors to be decided by board, approved by shareholders and disclosed in annual reports; (i) protection of whistle-blowers; (j) audit committee to review appointment, remuneration and removal of internal auditor; and (k) stronger monitoring of subsidiaries. Notable non-mandatory recommendation of the committee was training and evaluation of board members.

Clause 49 (2004)
Based on these recommendations of the Narayan Murthy report, Clause 49 was revised. As per SEBI, the new provisions were to be complied by companies planning to get listed and all listed companies "having a paid up share capital of Rs. 3 crores and above or net worth of Rs. 25 crores or more at any time in the history of the company, by April 1, 2005" (SEBI circular SEBI/CFD/DIL/CG/1/2004/12/10 dated October 29, 2004). According to the revised provisions, companies are to submit quarterly compliance reports.

Irani Committee (2004)
Following changes in governance regulations for listed companies, in December 2004, the Ministry of Corporate Affairs formed the Irani Committee led by J. J. Irani, to revise the Companies Act to improve governance of non-listed companies as well. The objective was to have a common comprehensive framework for all companies that catered to the needs of an emerging economy such as India and was in line with global best practices in corporate governance. In the words of Irani, "our effort has also been aimed at making India globally competitive in attracting investments from abroad, by suggesting systems in the Indian corporate

environment which are transparent, simple and globally acceptable" (Dr J. J. Irani Committee Report on Company Law, 2005). Many of the recommendations of Dr J. J. Irani Committee Report on Company Law, 2005, were incorporated into proposed amendments to the Companies Act. Based on the recommendations of the committee, the Companies Bill 2008 was introduced but it was not passed in parliament.

Clause 49 (2014)
As a result of Satyam sweeping changes were made to corporate governance in India. The old Companies Act 1956 was replaced by Companies Act 2013 and Clause 49 was updated in 2014 with stringent governance laws not just for listed companies but also for large public companies. Clause 49 gives an exhaustive definition of independent directors and enhances their responsibilities. Related party transactions were to be closely monitored and disclosures enhanced (Clause 49, 2014). Later in 2015 SEBI replaced Clause 49 with the Listing Obligations and Disclosure Requirements.

Companies Act 2013

The Companies Act, 2013 came into force on 30 August 2013. It made several changes to corporate governance laws bringing several SEBI guidelines and other voluntary guidelines within the ambit of the act. It focuses on independence of boards, enhances the role an responsibilities of board, lays down the duties and liabilities of directors, defines and sets the term of independent director, and promotes gender diversity by requiring boards to have at least one woman director.

The act recognizing the benefits of technology introduced various e-governance measures such as e-filing, e-voting and attending meetings through video conferencing. Notices can be sent through electronic means and extensive disclosures are required through the company's website.

According to the act, only independent chartered accountant firms can be appointed as auditors. An auditor is to be rotated every five years and an audit firm every ten years. To empower shareholders class action suit has been introduced and to protect investors insider trading prohibited.

LISTING OBLIGATIONS
AND DISCLOSURE REQUIREMENTS (2015)

Securities and Exchange Board of India, Listing Obligations and Disclosure Requirements Regulations (LODR) come into effect from 1 December 2015 and applies to an entity which has listed its securities (shares or others as specified) on any recognized stock exchange. It is not applicable to companies having paid up equity share capital not exceeding Rs. 10 crore and net worth not exceeding Rs. 25 crore, as on the last day of the previous financial year and those companies whose equity share capital is listed exclusively on the SME exchanges. In 2018, based on the recommendations of Uday Kotak Committee, several regulations were further strengthened.

Principles of Corporate Governance

The requirements of LODR are based on the following Principles of Corporate Governance which are similar to the OECD principles broadly in the areas of *The Rights of Shareholders & their Equal Treatment, Role of Stakeholders, Disclosure and Transparency including Timeliness of Information and Responsibility of Board.*

Major Regulations

Regulations 16–27 of Chapter IV, Schedule II and Schedule V of the Regulations specify corporate governance requirements. Some key features are described.

Board of Directors

At least half of the board shall constitute of non-executive director. If the chairman is a non-executive director, at least 1/3 of the board members shall be independent, else half the board shall be formed of independent directors. If the chairman is a promoter or related to the promoter, 50% or more directors should be independent. The board will have at least one independent woman director. If at any time the board falls short of the minimum number of independent director within three month or at the immediate next board meeting, whichever is earlier a new independent director must be appointed. The idea is to ensure higher independence of board and preventing dominance of any individual or group (Reg 17).

The board is to meet at least four times a year, with a maximum time gap of one hundred and twenty days between any two meetings. This way the board meets at regular intervals which is expected to improve board efficiency. So that the board is upraised of major activities and events of the company, information as specified in Part A of schedule II is to be provided (Reg 17).

The board shall lay down a code of conduct for all board members and senior management of the company. The code will contain the duties of independent directors as laid down in the Companies Act 2013, thereby making independent directors more accountable. As independent directors may not be privy to all information, the regulation states " an independent director shall be held liable, only in respect of such acts of omission or commission by a company which had occurred with his knowledge, attributable through board processes, and with his consent or connivance or where he had not acted diligently". The code shall be posted on the website of the company. The annual report of the company shall contain a declaration of compliance signed by the CEO (Reg 17).

Board Committees
Every board will constitute an independent and qualified audit committee, an independent nomination and remuneration and a stake-holder relationship committee to redress security holders' grievances (Reg 18–20).

Risk Management
The board shall be responsible for framing, implementing and monitoring the risk management policy for the company. A proper system will be established to keep the board abreast of the steps taken for risk assessment and mitigation. Top 1000 companies by market capitalization shall also comprise a Risk Management Committee. The Committee shall consist of members of the board of directors and senior executives. The chairman and majority of the members will be directors. This is the only board-level committee where other senior executives may be members as they are more directly involved in the company's risk management process. The board shall specify the roles and responsibilities of the Risk Management Committee and may delegate the task of regular monitoring and reviewing to it (Reg 21).

Whistle-Blower Policy

The company shall establish a Whistle-Blower Policy which will allow all stakeholders including directors to express any concerns about "unethical behaviour, illegal practices, actual or suspected fraud or violation of the company's code of conduct or ethics policy" (Reg 22). The vigil mechanism must provide adequate safeguards against victimization of the whistle-blower. Where required, the complaint may be provided direct access to the Chairman of the audit committee. This is important when the concerns are regarding behaviour of top management. The Whistle-Blower Policy of the company should be disclosed in the board's report and on its website (Reg 22).

Related Party Transactions

Given the risk associated with misuse of managerial discretion in case of related party transactions (RPTs), the board is responsible to formulate a policy to deal with related party transactions (see Chapter 9 for more on RPTs). All RPTs shall require prior approval of the audit committee. The audit committee may choose to grant omnibus approval for certain RPTs which are repetitive in nature and such approval is in the interest of the company. Omnibus approvals shall be valid for a period not exceeding one year and should be reviewed on a quarterly basis (Reg 23).

The board will develop and regularly review the policy for RPTs that are considered material to the company. According to Regulation 23, they shall be considered material "if the transactions / transactions to be entered into individually or taken together with previous transactions during a financial year, exceeds ten percent of the annual turnover as per the last audited financial statements of the company". All material related party transactions are to be approved by the shareholders through a resolution, and the related parties are not to participate in the voting of the said resolution (Reg 23).

Subsidiary Companies

The board should closely monitor 'material' unlisted subsidiaries of the company. (Unlisted companies may not have independent boards and board committes.) A subsidiary shall be considered as material if the investment of the company in the subsidiary exceeds twenty per cent of its consolidated net worth in the previous accounting year or if the subsidiary has generated twenty per cent of the consolidated income of the company during the previous accounting year. An independent director of the holding company will also be appointed as a director of the material non-listed Indian subsidiary company. The minutes of the unlisted subsidiary's board meetings and a statement of all their significant transactions and arrangements are to be placed at the board meeting of the listed holding company (Reg 24).

The audit committee of the holding company shall also review the financial statements, of the unlisted subsidiary company specially all investments made by them. Unless approved by a Court or Tribunal, the company will not sell, dispose or lease more than twenty per cent of the assets of the material subsidiary or reduce its shareholding in such subsidiary to less than 50% without approval of the shareholders by passing a special resolution in its General Meeting (Reg 24).

Independent Director

An exhaustive definition of independent directors is provided by Regulation 16. LODR limits independent directors tenure to two terms of five years each, restricts their remuneration and reappointment is subject to performance evaluation. They must hold one separate meeting a year without any non-independent director present (Reg 25).

Responsibilities

A director shall not act as Chairman of more than five committees nor be a member in more than ten committees across all companies in which he is a director. For this purpose, every director shall keep the company informed about the committee positions he occupies in other companies and any changes thereof (Reg 26).

All board members and senior management personnel are required to confirm compliance with the code of conduct each year (Reg 26).

Quarterly Report

Companies are to submit quarterly corporate governance compliance reports to the stock exchanges duly signed by the chief executive officer or company secretary (Reg 27).

Disclosures

Schedule V specifies the disclosures in annual reports which include details of related party transactions, accounting treatment and a management and discussion analysis.

The Corporate Governance Report will describe the company's philosophy on corporate Governance, board composition and meeting, directors attendance and memberships and their relationships inter-se. It should give a brief description of the terms of reference, composition, meetings and attendance of the audit committee and nomination and remuneration committees. The chairmanship of stakeholders relationship committee is to be disclosed with the number of complaints received and resolved.

Remuneration policy for and shareholding of non-executive directors is to be disclosed in the corporate governance section of the annual report or displayed on the company's website and reference drawn thereto in the annual report. All pecuniary relationship or transactions between the non-executive directors and the company shall also be disclosed. Non-executive directors shall be required to disclose their shareholding in the listed company in which they are proposed to be appointed as directors, prior to their appointment. These details should be disclosed in the notice to the general meeting called for appointment of such director.

In addition to the disclosures required under the Companies Act 2013, remuneration package of each director is to be reported with details such as salary, benefits, bonuses, stock options, pension; performance linked incentives along with the performance criteria; as well as information about service contracts, notice period, severance fees and details of stock options issued.

The CEO will certify compliance by directors and senior management of Code of Conduct. The CG report will give declaration regarding the compliance of CG requirements and be certified by auditor or practising company secretary.

The Movement Continues

The journal that started in the 1990s continues. Over the years, each country has developed some form of governance rules/regulations or codes (see Table 5.1) which is constantly updated or sometimes even overhauled, particularly after a major corporate shock.

Table 5.1 Select codes across the world

Country	Name of code	Year	Link
Europe			
European Union	Corporate Governance Practices in the European Union	2015	https://www.ifc.org/wps/wcm/connect/506d49a2-3763-4fe4-a783-5d58e37b8906/CG_Practices_in_EU_Guide.pdf?MOD=AJPERES&CVID=kNmxTtG
UK	UK Corporate Governance Code	2018	https://lpscdn.linklaters.com/pdfs%2Fpdfns%2F180716_2018_UK_Corporate_Governance_Code_FINAL_published.pdf
Germany	German Corporate Governance Code	2017	https://ecgi.global/sites/default/files/codes/documents/german_corporate_governance_code_2017_english_version_.pdf
Italy	Italian Corporate Governance Code	2020	https://ecgi.global/sites/default/files/codes/documents/2020code_eng.pdf
Netherlands	Dutch Corporate Governance Code	2016	https://ecgi.global/sites/default/files/codes/documents/thenetherlands_cgcode_2016.pdf
Australia			
Australia	Corporate Governance Principles & Recommendations by ASX	2019	https://www.asx.com.au/documents/regulation/cgc-principles-and-recommendations-fourth-edn.pdf
New Zealand	NZX Corporate Governance Code	2017	https://ecgi.global/sites/default/files/codes/documents/180228-corporate-governance-handbook-2018.1.pdf
Asia			
China	The Code of Corporate Governance for Listed Companies	2018	http://www.csrc.gov.cn/pub/csrc_en/laws/rfdm/DepartmentRules/201804/P020180427400739560.pdf

(continued)

Table 5.1   (continued)

Country	Name of code	Year	Link
Hong Kong	Hong Kong Corporate Governance Code	2018	https://en-rules.hkex.com.hk/sites/default/files/net_file_store/HKEX4476_3828_VER10.pdf
Sri Lanka	Sri Lankan Corporate Governance Code	2017	https://www.casrilanka.com/casl/images/stories/content/members/draft-code-of-best-practice-on-corporate-governance-2017.pdf
Japan	Japan Corporate Governance Code	2018	https://www.jpx.co.jp/english/news/1020/b5b4pj000000jvxr-att/20180602_en.pdf
South America			
Brazil	Brazil Corporate Governance Code	2017	https://thelawreviews.co.uk/title/the-corporate-governance-review/brazil
Columbia	Colombian Corporate Governance Best Practices Code	2007	http://www.oecd.org/corporate/ca/corporategovernanceprinciples/39741294.pdf
Africa			
Egypt	Egyptian Code of Corporate Governance	2016	https://ecgi.global/sites/default/files/codes/documents/egypt_cg_code.pdf
Nigeria	Nigerian Code of Corporate Governance	2018	https://nambnigeria.org/Nig_Code_of_Corp._Governance_2018.pdf
South Africa	King Report on Corporate Governance for South Africa. (King IV Report)	2016	https://ecgi.global/sites/default/files/codes/documents/King_Report_On_Corporate_Governance_For_South_Africa_2016.pdf
North America			
USA	USA has not adopted a corporate governance code for US companies Corporate governance matters are provided in state and federal laws, regulations and listing rules such as, Sarbanes-Oxley Act, 2002, the Dodd-Frank Act, 2010, NYSE and NASDAQ listing rules, etc		https://www.lexology.com/library/detail.aspx?g=e295afc9-da23-4824-9025-9772e3438ebe https://www.soxlaw.com/

(continued)

Table 5.1 (continued)

Country	Name of code	Year	Link
CANADA	No jurisdiction in Canada has adopted a corporate governance code in its corporate legislation 1. Toronto Stock Exchange (TSX) Manual on corporate governance 2. Disclosure of Corporate Governance Practices (in accordance with National Instrument 58-101), 2005		https://ecgi.global/sites/default/files/codes/docume nts/tsx_gtgd.pdf https://www.tsx.com/res ource/en/76 https://uk.practicallaw.tho msonreuters.com/2-502-2944?transitionType=Def ault&contextData=(sc.Def ault)&firstPage=true

Source Compiled by Author

REFERENCES

Afsharipour, A. (2010). *A brief overview of corporate governance reforms in India*. Director Notes, The Conference Board.

Bhasin, M. L. (2013). Corporate accounting fraud: A case study of Satyam Computers Limited. *Open Journal of Accounting, 2*, 26–38. http://dx. doi.org/10.4236/ojacct.2013.22006. Published Online April 2013 (http://www.scirp.org/journal/ojacct).

Birla Committee. (1999). *Report of the Kumar Mangalam Birla Committee on Corporate Governance*.

Businesswire India. (2008, September 23). *Satyam receives Golden Peacock Global Award for Excellence in Corporate Governance*. http://www.financialexpress. com/archive/satyam-receives-golden-peacock-global-award-for-excellence-in-corporate-governance/364843/

CIMA. (2009). *Fraud risk management: A guide to good practice*. https://www. cimaglobal.com/Documents/ImportedDocuments/cid_techguide_fraud_risk_management_feb09.pdf

Combined Code, 1998, UK.

Companies Act (2013) India.

Dr J. J. Irani Committee Report on Company Law, 2005.

ET Bureau. (2008, December 24). *World Bank bans Satyam for 8 years*. https://economictimes.indiatimes.com/tech/ites/world-bank-bans-satyam-for-8-years/articleshow/3882667.cms?utm_source=contentofinterest&utm_med ium=text&utm_campaign=cppst

Financial Aspects of Corporate Governance (1992), UK.

Greenbury Report 1995, UK.

Higgs Report of 2003.

http://www.icaew.com/en/technical/corporate-governance/uk-corporate-gov
ernance/uk-codes-and-guidance. Accessed July 10, 2021.

https://en.wikipedia.org/wiki/Polly_Peck. Accessed September 15, 2021.

Letter by Ramalinga Raju to Satyam Board, 2009.

Narayana Murthy Committee, Report of the SEBI Committee on Corporate
Governance Report, 2003, India.

Naresh Chandra Committee Report, 2002, India.

PTI. (2002). Bill Gates visits Satyam Technology Centre. http://timesofindia.
indiatimes.com/articleshow/28274054.cms?utm_source=contentofinterest&
utm_medium=text&utm_campaign=cppst

Report of Investigation, by the Special Investigative Committee of the Board of
Directors of Worldcom Inc. https://www.sec.gov/Archives/edgar/data/723
527/000093176303001862/dex991.htm

Sanyal, S., & Tiwari, D. (2009, April 17). Ex-insider blew the lid off Satyam
scam. *The Economics Times*. https://economictimes.indiatimes.com/tech/
software/ex-insider-blew-the-lid-off-satyam-scam/articleshow/4411924.cms?
utm_source=contentofinterest&utm_medium=text&utm_campaign=cppst

Sarbanes-Oxley Act (2002), USA.

SEBI. Clause 49 of the Listing Agreement (2000, 2004, 2014), India.

Securities and Exchange Board of India. (2015). Listing Obligations and
Disclosure Requirements Regulations (LODR), India.

SFIO Report published in the Pioneer (New Delhi), May 4, 2009, p. 10.

Sharma, J. P. (2010). Corporate governance failure: A case study of Satyam.
Indian Journal of Corporate Governance, 3(2), 136–175. First Published July
1, 2010.

The Business Today. (2009, February 8). p. 50.

The Confederation of Indian Industries Code, Desirable Corporate Governance:
A Code 1998.

The Smith Report, 2003, UK.

Turnbull Report, 1999 and 2005, UK.

Varottil, U. (2010). Evolution and effectiveness of independent directors in
Indian Corporate Governance. *Hastings Business Law Journal*, 334.

CHAPTER 6

Shareholder and Activism

It's is ultimately all about the shareholders

SHAREHOLDERS

Shareholders or stockholders are the owners of the company. They invest in the company by buying shares with expectation of returns. As they are the owners of the companies is in their interest to make sure that the company is being run properly. If the company performs badly or goes bust, it is the shareholders who lose the most.

There are two major types of shareholders—Ordinary or Equity and Preference.

Preference Shares

Preference shareholders have a right to receive a fixed amount of dividend every year usually expressed as a percentage of the face value of the share. If shares are of $10 and dividend rate is 20%, they will receive $2 per share. It is similar to earning interest except they will be paid as long as the company has undistributed profits or reserves. They get preference over equity holders and will be paid before them. On winding up, the holders of preference shares are entitled to any arrears of dividends and their capital ahead of ordinary shareholders. Preference shares usually do not have voting rights. However, they may be entitled to vote if their dividends are in arrears or when the company is winding up or in cases where capital restructuring will affect them. Preference shares are often redeemable either after a fixed time or as determined by the company.

Equity Shares

They are the owners or member of the company. They have the right to vote and elect the Board of Directors. There is no fixed rate of dividend for equity shareholders. The dividend paid on equity capital depends upon boards' recommendation and as approved by the shareholders themselves. They benefit by higher dividend and appreciation in share prices. This in turn depends on how well they monitor the company doings. A shareholders voting right is proportionate to his or her shares. The more shares you have, the more you have a say in the affairs of the company.

Equity Shareholders are the controlling owners and it is in their best interest to ensure the company is governed well. It is their responsibility to closely monitoring corporate actions. For this purpose, several rights have been bestowed on shareholders such as participation in shareholder meetings, conveying meetings and access to information and documents of the company.

Participation in Annual General Meeting (AGM)

Every company is required to have a general meeting annually. This is a meeting for all the shareholders to attend and participate in. It gives them information about the company's performance, and allows shareholders to discuss and deliberate with management and among themselves about the company affairs and be involved in corporate decisions by voting on matters such an appointment of directors and declaration of dividend.

Information of Meeting

Shareholders must be given prior information about the meeting so that they may exercise their voting rights. The information about the venue and time of meeting must be sent to all shareholders well in time. Indian Companies Act permits that the notice of the meeting may be sent electronically. In addition, some countries require that information of the meeting be published in newspaper and/or company website. In Greece, Hong Kong, Portugal and Turkey, it is adequate to just publish on the

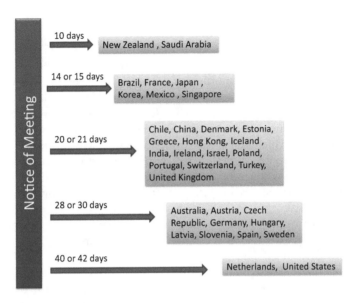

Fig. 6.1 Duration for notice of meeting (*Source* Developed by Author)

firm's website. The minimum time period for a notice ranges from 10 days
to six weeks across countries with most requiring at least 3 weeks (see
Fig. 6.1).

Agenda of Meeting

The notice of the meeting must specify the agenda of the meeting.
Agenda contains the list of activities of the meeting in the order in
which they will be conducted. It provides the businesses to be transacted including proposals that will be voted on. The agenda in a general
meeting are commonly, appointment and remuneration of directors and
auditors, adoption of financial statements and approval of dividend. Any
corporate action which requires shareholder approval is to be discussed
and voted in general meetings. Essentially, no major decision can be made
without shareholder approval. The relevant supporting information to
agenda items must also be provided. For instance, if a director is proposed
to be appointed, then his profile must be available so that shareholders can
take an informed decision.

Voting Rights

Shareholders have a right to vote in the general meeting. Voting can be done through show of hands or poll. In show of hands there is a head count, whereas in poll the number of shares/votes held will be counted. The OECD principals advocate that every shareholder should have equal rights. Thus, generally most countries follow the 'one share one vote' rule. Equity shareholders may sometimes be issued shares with differential voting rights which may either restrict or give them additional voting rights (Discussed in chapter III). Differential shares goes against the principle of good governance of providing equal rights to all shareholders. Even with one share one vote, lack of participation by shareholders allows promoters or executives to unilaterally control corporate actions.

The **Quorum,** the minimum number of members that must be present at the meetings to make the proceedings of that meeting valid is not large (see Table 6.1). Thus, those who attend are able to determine the course of action. Some who do attend, either do not bother to vote or blindly vote in favour of proposals of the management. Most decisions require majority approval of those attending. Few situations may even require special majority. Hence, if shareholders actively attend and vote in the general meetings, they can to a great extent protect their interest and influence management decisions. They can replace the entire board if they are unsatisfied with their performance (see Firing the Board).

Firing the Board
In a dramatic move the shareholders of struggling Lakshmi Vilas bank have voted against the appointment of seven directors to its board including that of ES Sundar as the managing director and chief executive officer as well as promoters K.R. Pradeep and N. Sai Prasad.

Table 6.1 Quorum for AGM in Indian companies

Private Company: 2 members
Public Company:
- 5 members if < 1000 members
- 15 members if between 1000 to 5000 members
- 30 members if > 5000 members

Source Based on Companies Act, 2013

This has triggered a fresh crisis at the beleaguered Lakshmi Vilas bank which has been in the middle of a merger process with PE fund backed by Clix Capital. The bank is looking for capital at this juncture quite desperately as the bank's capital adequacy ratio or CAR according to Basel 3 guidelines contracted to 0.17 as on 30th June as against the regulatory minimum of 10.87.

The promoter group holds only 6.8 stake in the private bank and the bank reported a net loss of 112 crore rupees in the June quarter of FY 21 compared to a loss of 237 crore rupees in the same period last year. Deposits in the June quarter also stood at 21,161 crore rupees, down twenty-seven per cent from a year ago level.

The coup at the annual general meeting on 25th September left the bank completely leaderless and investors and depositors as well as employees are likely to face a few anxious days. Nearly 100 institutional investors voted against these directors, even 19 percent of promoters' votes went against them. Shareholders also voted against BK Manchunath, Gorinka Jagan Mohan Rao and YN Lakshmi Narayan Murthy as non-executive and independent directors. They also rejected the reappointment of statutory auditors. This is the first time that shareholders have boarded out as many as seven board members including its promoters and the CEO who was appointed by the RBI.

The Reserve bank of India stepped in to address the issue at Lakshmi Vilas bank approving a committee of directors composed of three independent directors—Mita Makhan who is the chairperson of the committee of directors, Shakti Sinha (member) and Satish Kumar Kara (member) of the panel, who would run the day-to-day affairs of the lender. A regulatory filing by the bank said the panel will exercise the discretionary powers of managing director and CEO in the ad-interm. The bank also assured the deposit holders, bondholders, account holders and creditors that they are well safeguarded as the liquidity coverage ratio the bank is of about 262 per cent as on September 27th of 2020 as against the minimum hundred percent required by the RBI.

Reference: Money control. (2020, September 28). What's next for Lakshmi Vilas Bank as Shareholders Vote out 7 Directors from The Board? | Big Story [Video], YouTube.

Alternate Voting Mechanisms

Exercising of the voting rights is the primary tool with shareholders to hold the board accountable. If a shareholder is unable to attend a meeting, he may either appoint a proxy to vote on his behalf, or vote through postal ballot or vote electronically.

Proxy: Rather than physically attend the shareholder meeting, shareholders may vote by proxy. *Proxy voting* is a form of *voting* whereby a shareholder delegates his or her *voting* power to a representative to attend the meeting and vote on his behalf.

Postal Voting: The ballot papers are sent by post to shareholders and those who cannot attend can cast their vote through them and post them back. This is time-consuming and costly and they may reach the company too late to be counted.

Electronic Voting: Electronic Voting or E-voting allows shareholders to use electronic means to vote from wherever they are located as per their convenience. In a globalized world, where shareholders may be in any corner of the world, E- voting can increase shareholder participation manifold. E-voting improves transparency, reduces administrative costs of postal ballot and increases efficiency in declaring voting results. The drawback of E-voting is that it has to be exercised before the meeting which means decision is taken prior to deliberations.

Postal ballot or Electronic voting may be used to take a decision on a resolution when it cannot wait and conducting a meeting may not be feasible.

ADDING AN AGENDA

Besides voting in meeting, shareholders have the right to add an item in the agenda of the general meeting. Shareholders with 3–10% shares may propose a resolution within the stipulated time (Table 6.2). In India 10% shareholders can add an item on the agenda if requested 6 weeks before the AGM.

In Korea and Japan, only 0.5 and 1% shareholders respectively can add an item on the agenda provided they have been holding the shares for at least 6 months. This gives shareholders not just the right to monitor corporate management but power to proactively steer the direction of the company affairs.

Table 6.2 Adding an agenda

Deadline for Request		No minimum Requirement	Upto 1%	2–3%	5%	10%
No Deadline		Denmark Finland Iceland New Zealand Norway	Hungry		Argentina Australia Greece Saudi Arabia	Mexico
Days before AGM	10 days			China		Chile
	14–15 days				Poland	Estonia
	20–25 days			Belgium	France Turkey	Luxemburg
	28–32 days		Israel Japan	Russia	Indonesia	
	42 days		Korea	Ireland	Singapore	India
	49–60 days	Sweden		Netherlands	UK	
Days after notice	5–7 days			Portugal Spain	Slovenia	
	10 days			Italy	Germany	

Source Developed by Author

CONVEYING A MEETING

Shareholders have a right to convey an Extra-Ordinary meeting (Meeting other than AGM) by putting a request to the company. Generally investors with 5 to 10% shareholding can request for a general meeting (Fig. 6.2). In Korea owners holding as less as 1.5% of the total shares can call a meeting provided, they are holding them for at least 6 months and on request the meeting must be held promptly.

RIGHT TO INFORMATION

Shareholders have a fundamental right to information. The primary source of information is the Annual Report, a summary of the activities of the company during the financial year which is sent to all shareholders and presented in the AGM. It provides extensive information through the Directors' Report, Management and Discussion Analysis, Corporate Governance Report, Auditors Report, financial statements, Executive compensation, etc. These reports can become very lengthy running into few hundred pages. A vast variety of detailed disclosures are required such

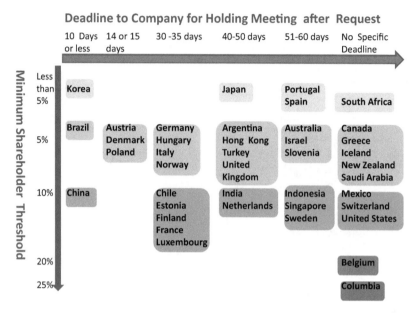

Fig. 6.2 Requesting a meeting (*Source* Developed by Author)

as accounting standards adopted and related party transactions. Sifting through them for the average shareholder can become a herculean task. In addition, a large range of other information may be mandated to be disclosed to investors such as details of shareholders, debenture holders, directors, senior executives and minutes of general meetings. Most of this information may also be required to be displayed on the company website or a common platform.

Shareholder Activism

We have already seen that the control on the company and the use of their rights by shareholders depends on multiple factors such as their proportion of ownership, expectations as an investor, willingness to participate and ability to comprehend company affairs.

The lack of active participation by shareholder allows managers to push forward their own interests. The shareholder whose interests are being trampled upon can seek redressal through activism. Shareholder activism may be defined as the various actions undertaken by investors to influence and monitor corporate management and boards and to bring about changes in the organizational control structure of firms not perceived to be pursuing shareholder-wealth-maximizing goals. When a shareholder views that companies' activities are not in alignment with their interests, they may either exit or voice their dissent in an attempt to change the situation.

Exit Strategy

When investors feel their interests are alienated they may prefer to exit the company by selling their shares and shifting their investment to a more profitable choice. Monitoring requires time and effort and the cost may exceed the expected benefits. Small investors experience the paradox of voting and prefer to exit. When large shareholders exit, it not only shows their dissatisfaction but causes share prices to fall. This risk encourages management to be more accountable to shareholders especially if they are incentivised through shares or stock options.

Threat of Exit

The threat of exit can be a very powerful form of activism. Exit by a block shareholder and the resultant decrease in prices would have an even more potent impact on the shareholder(s) with control and may make them rethink their actions. The risk that large shareholders may exit bringing down prices can be an effective form of disciplining managers. Institutional Investors (mutual funds, pension funds, etc.) as block holders are in a better position to monitor corporate actions due to their sheer size and expertise. The benefits of monitoring are expected to be greater than the cost. Exit of an institutional shareholder can create reputational hazards and other shareholders may follow, causing prices to spiral down. Institutional Shareholders together hold a significant voting share and can be a powerful force in ensuring that companies work in the interest off all shareholders even in family firms with majority control.

Voice

Voice is an expression of dissatisfaction of shareholders with the performance of the company directed at those controlling it. The effectiveness of voice crucially depends on the credibility of the message, the manner in which it is presented and who has raised the voice. The voice may be either a nudge or a shove or sometimes even a punch depending on the level of activism (Fig. 6.3).

Shareholder Engagement: Shareholders can gently *nudge* those in control to change course of action through dialogue, private conversations and letters. Shareholder engagement helps to bridge the gap between owners and managers. Institutional investors are increasingly engaging in direct discussions with the management or the board of directors of their portfolio companies, mostly behind closed door. Private negotiation can resolve divergence of opinions and encourage companies to act in the best interest of all shareholders. This give and take could be a long-drawn process and success would depend on the activist's communication and negotiation skills and the size of his investment in the company. The benefit of this form of activism is that the absence of public display of dissatisfaction prevents prices from moving downwards.

Public Disapproval: When this nudge does not generate the desired results, investors give a hefty *shove to* management with more aggressive forms of activism to protect their interests. Publicizing the issue using media can be a powerful tool to change the status quo. Founder member and long-term erstwhile chairman Narayana Murthy with a sizeable block of voting power had been engaging with the Infosys board questioning poor governance practices in the Panaya acquisition as well as the outsize severance package to CFO Rajiv Bansal. It was only when his concerns

Fig. 6.3 Degree of activism (*Source* Jhunjhunwala [2018])

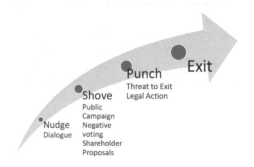

became public and caught media attention it created enough stir that both the Chairman and CEO had to leave the company. Public campaigns can be costly but successful when other shareholders join the cause. Well-publicized activism can allow shareholders to achieve the desired corporate decions.

Shareholder Proposals: Investors may even decide to introduce proposal. As already discussed most countries permit investors with a minimum of 5% shareholding to add an agenda in the general meeting. The minimum shareholding requirement may be as high as 10% in countries such as India and Mexico but as low as 1% in some jurisdictions such as USA provided that the shares have been held for at least one year. Changes in board structure, shareholder voting rights and executive pay are some of the more frequently proposed resolutions by shareholders. The number of shareholder proposals has been increasing over the years in USA. With increase in the total proportion of shares held by institutional investors, shareholder proposals are proving to be an effective way to balance control.

The Feud Over Rights

Ashok Kapur and Rana Kapoor founded YES Bank in 2004. In 2008 Kapur was shot dead in a restaurant during the 26/11 terror attacks in Mumbai. His 12% percent shares are now held by his wife Madhu Kapur. Rana Kapoor who owns about 14% percent of the shares is the Managing Director & CEO (Kapoor vs Kapur: How 26/11 blew open a succession battle at Yes Bank). In 2009 Madhu requested that her husband's board seat be given to her. The board in their wisdom did not accept her proposal as she was a housewife and did not have any experience justifying a board seat.

In May 2013, Madhu learned that according to the articles of association of the company, she and Rana jointly had the right to nominate three directors on the YES Bank board. The bank had decided to appoint three new directors in the forthcoming Annual General meeting (AGM) scheduled for June 8, 2013 (PTI, 2013). Two of them, Chopra and Srinivasan, were Rana's nominees. Madhu wrote to the board members that she had the right to nominated at least one director and proposed her daughter Shagun's name. Shagun, who is a double major in economics and biology from Tufts University and an MBA from the Indian School of Business, Hyderabad. She did a three-year stint with private equity fund ICICI Ventures where she was a part of the team that closed five deals with equity investment of around $100 million. She had experience in mergers and acquisitions and private equity placements and founded her own investment firm Tuscan Ventures in 2007 (Chakraborty, 2013).

In response to her letter Rana informed that the matter would be raised in the next board meeting. On June 6, Madhu and her two children filed a petition in the Bombay High Court to stay the AGM where the three new directors were going to be appointed as their rights as co-promoter were violated. (Chakraborti, 2013) The court did not accept her petition. At the AGM, Madhu objected to the appointment of three directors but it was put to vote. They got elected by 80% votes (PTI, 2013). Several small shareholders were of the opinion that as a promoter she had a right to a board seat. In the next board meeting in July, the board did not nominated Shagun as a Board Member.

Points to ponder: Is Madhu's expectation of a board seat correct? What steps can she take to appoint Shagun as a board member?

Legal Recourse: If all else fails, shareholders may **punch** management with a law suit. Resorting to legal recourse may be the only option with minority shareholders when they are being oppressed by those with majority control. Minimum 10% or 100 members in Indian companies may file a suit with the National Company Law Tribunal if company is being grossly mismanagement or conducted in a manner prejudicial to minority's interests (Sec 241–244, Companies Act, 2013). Law suits are difficult and long-drawn and subject share prices to speculation that could hurt majority interest. Rather than initiating proposals, shareholders may prefer judicial action as it helps in fixing criminal liability as well as claim compensation and damage from the management. Individually, it may be difficult and costly to take legal action but Class Action Suit allows small number of shareholders to get together and jointly sue the management. We saw how US investors who filed a class action suit against Satyam were awarded $150 million.

Institutional Activism

Shareholders can reduce the imbalances in power through activism. The success of activism depends on the credentials, financial strength, professional competency and investment size of the activist. Institutional investors are in a unique position to influence management. If they withdraw their investments, the share prices will definitely fall. A public display of dissent would affect the reputation of the company and influence other shareholders. Hence, they can successfully address their concerns through private negotiations. Together institutional investors hold a large block of shares sometimes majority shares and can impact proposal outcomes. In the matter of Life Insurance Corporation (LIC) v. Escorts Ltd.;1 1986 AIR 1370, the Supreme Court held that being a shareholder LIC can exercise all shareholder rights including the requisition of an Extra-Ordinary General Meeting. The holders of the majority of shares in a company can replace the board. This is the essence of corporate democracy.

As small shareholders find it difficult to impact corporate decisions, institutional investors must use their financial muscle and professional expertise to protect the interest of shareholders. Institutional investors have great potential to influence and make the investee company set high standards of corporate governance. Stewardship codes have been introduced to encourage them to be more accountable. The stewardship codes require institutional investors to be transparent about their investment processes, engage with investee companies and vote at shareholders' meetings. Stewardship includes voting as well as monitoring and engaging with companies on matters such as strategy, performance, risk, capital structure and corporate governance. UK introduced the concept in 2012. The UK Stewardship Code, 2020 that replaces it is based on 'apply and explain' principles (see Table 6.3). The Stewardship responsibilities for institutional investors implemented by SEBI in 2020 is similarly based on six principles (Table 6.4).

The revised European Union Shareholder Rights Directive ("SRD II") is a legally binding regulatory act to enhance the rights of shareholders by imposing certain minimum standards on the exercise of shareholder voting rights at EU-listed companies. It imposes certain disclosure requirements for EU-based asset managers and asset owners on engagement and investment strategies as investors in European Economic Area ("EEA") companies (Glass Lewis, 2019). The European Fund and Asset Management Association (EFAMA) Stewardship Code highlights how, through stewardship, asset managers can encourage best business and management practices in companies on environmental, governance, human rights and social challenges. Stewardship is part of an asset manager's fiduciary duty to protect and enhance clients' assets, but also encourage long-term value creation and long-term sustainability (Rust, 2018).

Table 6.3 Principles: The UK stewardship code, 2020

Purpose and governance	Investment approach	Engagement	Exercising rights and responsibilities
• Purpose, strategy and culture • Governance, resources and incentives • Conflicts of interest • Promoting well-functioning markets • Review and assurance	• Client and beneficiary needs • Stewardship, investment and ESG integration • Monitoring managers and service providers	• Engagement • Collaboration • Escalation	• Exercising rights and responsibilities

Source Adopted from THE UK Stewardship Code, 2020, https://www.frc.org.uk/getattachment/5aae591d-d9d3-4cf4-814a-d14e156a1d87/Stewardship-Code_Final2.pdf. Accessed April 10, 2021

Table 6.4 Stewardship code of India

Principle 1: Institutional Investors should formulate a comprehensive policy on the discharge of their stewardship responsibilities, publicly disclose it, review and update it periodically

Principle 2: Institutional investors should have a clear policy on how they manage conflicts of interest in fulfilling their stewardship responsibilities and publicly disclose it

Principle 3: Institutional investors should monitor their investee companies

Principle 4: Institutional investors should have a clear policy on intervention in their investee companies. Institutional investors should also have a clear policy for collaboration with other institutional investors where required, to preserve the interests of the ultimate investors, which should be disclosed

Principle 5: Institutional investors should have a clear policy on voting and disclosure of voting activity

Principle 6: Institutional investors should report periodically on their stewardship activities

Source SEBI, Stewardship Code for all Mutual Funds and all categories of AIFs, December 2019. https://www.sebi.gov.in/legal/circulars/dec-2019/stewardship-code-for-all-mutual-funds-and-all-categories-of-aifs-in-relation-to-their-investment-in-listed-equities_45451.html. Accessed April 11, 2021

Proxy Advisory Firms Abetting Activism

A proxy firm provides services to shareholders related to voting at shareholder meetings including voting recommendations on shareholder resolutions of listed companies. Institutional Investor Advisory Services India Limited, an Indian proxy advisory firm analyses shareholder resolutions to be addressed at AGMs, EGMs, postal ballots and court convened meetings of nearly 300 companies listed on the Bombay Stock Exchange and National Stock Exchange of India, and provides voting recommendations on these resolutions to shareholders. This helps small investors in exercising their voting powers.

Shareholders' (proxy) advisory firms through traditional and social media are wielding enough influence across a large number of small shareholders to effect change. Companies in India that seek to pay the executive directors more than 5% of a company's net profit are required by law to seek minority shareholders' approval (Companies Act, 2013). Due to awareness created by the advisory firms, Tata Motors, India's largest auto maker's proposal of excessive pay to executives after underperformance was turned down by 64% of institutional investors and 30% of other small shareholders (Mohile & Laskar, 2014).

REFERENCES

Chakraborti. (2013, July 2). Madhu Kapur might challenge board appointment of 3 executive directors. https://www.business-standard.com/article/companies/madhu-kapur-might-challenge-board-appointment-of-3-executive-directors-113070100949_1.html. Accessed November 30, 2022.

Chakraborty, S. (2013). The inside story of the YES Bank feud. https://www.rediff.com/business/slide-show/slide-show-1-special-the-inside-story-of-the-yes-bank-feud/20130617.htm#8. Accessed April 11, 2021.

Companies Act. (2013). India.

Glass Lewis. (2019). EU SRD II—An Overview. https://www.glasslewis.com/wp-content/uploads/2019/11/SRD-Europe-Final.pdf. Accessed April 11, 2021.

Jhunjhunwala, S. (2018). Control conflicts, costs and activism. *IUP Journal of Corporate Governance*.

Kapoor vs Kapur. How 26/11 blew open a succession battle at Yes Bank, November 27, 2016. Moneycontrol News. https://www.moneycontrol.com/news/printpage/3219621/. Accessed November 30, 2022.

Mohile, S. S., & Laskar, A. (2014). Tata Motors shareholders reject proposals executive pay. https://www.livemint.com/Companies/r2bfqMfLmzHLPQz OsJXQwJ/Tata-Motors-shareholders-reject-remuneration-proposals-for-t. html. Livemint.

PTI. (2013, June 11). Yes Bank gets shareholders' approval for appointment of three new directors. https://www.thehindu.com/business/Industry/yes-bank-gets-shareholders-approval-for-appointment-of-three-new-directors/art icle4800736.ece. Accessed November 30, 2022.

Rust. (2018, May 31). EFAMA adopts stewardship code to align with EU laws. https://www.ipe.com/efama-adopts-stewardship-code-to-align-with-eu-laws/10024971.article. Accessed April 11, 2021.

SEBI. (2019, December). Stewardship Code for all Mutual Funds and all categories of AIFs. https://www.sebi.gov.in/legal/circulars/dec-2019/ste wardship-code-for-all-mutual-funds-and-all-categories-of-aifs-in-relation-to-their-investment-in-listed-equities_45451.html. Accessed April 11, 2021.

THE UK Stewardship Code. (2020). https://www.frc.org.uk/getattachment/ 5aae591d-d9d3-4cf4-814a-d14e156a1d87/Stewardship-Code_Final2.pdf. Accessed April 10, 2021.

CHAPTER 7

Corporate Social Responsibility

Making a Difference

Maggi Noodle

Maggi; present in every household, at all times. Not many could fathom why India's favourable instant noodles ceased to exit. 'No added MSG (monosodium glutamate)', claimed a bright-yellow packet of Nestle Maggi Noodles. In a routine test check a food inspector sent the product for testing. The results read: "MSG: Present and Lead: 17.2 ppm (parts per million)". The amount of lead found was over 1,000 times more than what Nestle India Ltd had claimed (Mitra, 2017). On receiving notice from the food safety commissioner Nestle responded with documents that necessary quality checks were in place but did not take any further action.

From an 'insignificant' news article published in a local Hindi newspapers of Uttar Pradesh, the incident soon become a hot controversy in main stream media. Mothers' stopped allowing their kids to eat their ever favourite Maggi. Nestle failed to react. Little did Nestle realize that such a trivial news would cost them "an estimated half a billion-dollar loss (including erosion of brand value) that would shake the Swiss multinational" (Mitra, 2017).

When Nestle was forced to recall Maggi noodles, the company's global chief executive Paul Bulcke finally had to address the issue. He claimed that Maggi was "absolutely safe .....We do not add MSG in Maggi noodles... We apply the same quality standards everywhere." (PTI, 2015), But it was

S. Jhunjhunwala, *Corporate Governance*,
https://doi.org/10.1007/978-981-99-2707-4_7

too little too late. As a result of the withdrawal order Nestle collected 38,000 tonnes of Maggi noodles from retail stores and destroyed them taking a massive "hit of Rs. 450 crores" (Bhushan, 2016). The ban caused the company to report a loss to the tune of "Rs. 64 crore" for its June quarter—The first in over 30 years (Bhushan, 2016).

The impact of the incident was such, that UK food regulators too decided to test check the product as a safety measure. The uproar caused Maggi's market share to fall by more than 30%. The instant noodle industry was introduced to India by Nestle and it controlled more than three-fourth of the market. In the year that followed, in the absence of Maggi, the category itself shrunk by almost half from 3800 to 2000 crores (Dutta, 2016). The loss was not just to the company, as stated by the Chairman of Nestle India Suresh Narayanan "the impact of the Maggi crisis extended to not just factories and employees but also partners, suppliers, farmers, retailers and customers" (Bhushan, 2016).

The relaunch of Maggi post clearances from regulators began with a mega media campaign reassuring customers that Maggi was safe to eat. As Buckley himself put it "Our main focus is to win the trust of customer" (PTI, 2015). At 60% market share as of Aug 2018 after almost three years Maggi still has a long way to catch up its pre-crisis volumes (Madhukalya, 2018).

Points to Ponder

1. Who are the stakeholders here? Does perception of stakeholders matter?
2. Did Nestle address the concerns of the stakeholders appropriately?
3. If you were the India head of Nestle in 2015, would you have done anything differently?

THE STAKEHOLDER APPROACH

Traditionally and particularly in the Anglo-Saxon approach it was assumed as Milton Friedman (1970) puts it "the business of business is business ... the social responsibility of business is to increase its profits". The objective of companies was to generate profits and consequently returns for shareholders on their investment. Wealth maximization of shareholders was the fundamental goal of firms. The shift to being sensitive to the needs of all stakeholders has hardly been proactive or voluntary. Instead, it is a reactive response compelled by regulation and public outcry. The consumer boycott faced by Nike in the late 1990s in the USA over abusive labour practices of sub-contractors in Indonesia, which forced Nike to take corrective action, is a case in point (Jhunjhunwala, 2014). It became apparent that for the long-term survival, a company must run its business transparently and ethically and weigh the interest of all stakeholders while taking decisions (Fig. 7.1).

Stakeholder theory (Refer Chapters 1 and 3 for stakeholders and theory respectively) emphasizes that a company's real success lies in satisfying all its stakeholders. Primary stakeholders such as directors and shareholders have the largest stake in the company and are directly involved in decisions and actions of the company. Secondary stakeholders have a business interest in the company giving them economic power, the ability to impact business decisions (say, price of product). Tertiary stakeholders hold a social or political interest in the company and influence its behaviour. Regulators for instance can demand better disclosures. The problem of governing the corporation in today's world must be viewed in

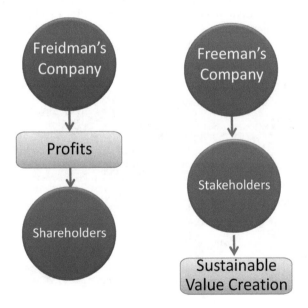

Fig. 7.1 Shift from shareholder approach to stakeholder approach (*Source* Developed by Author)

terms of the entire grid of stakeholders and their power base (Freeman & Reed, 1988) (Fig. 7.2).

The Maggi Noodle incident reflects the impact of the behaviour of all three sets of stakeholders on the company. The power of food regulators (Tertiary) to ban for non-compliance of standards, the boycott buy customers (secondary) on the mere perception of poor quality and the delay by management (primary) in addressing the concerns.

Corporations, as citizens, have a responsibility to the society and/or country in which they operate. As a society, we depend on companies to achieve economic goals such as employment opportunities for all, higher per capita income and self-sufficiency of basic needs of the country; and for social needs by taking care of employees, protecting environment and supporting local communities. With the growing concern for environmental issues and development of all sections of society, governments are increasingly expecting corporates to shoulder their share of responsibility. Corporate Social responsibility (CSR) has been aptly defined as "the continuing commitment by business to behave ethically and contribute to economic development while improving the quality of life of the workforce and their families as well as of the local community and society at large" (World Business Council for Sustainable Development).

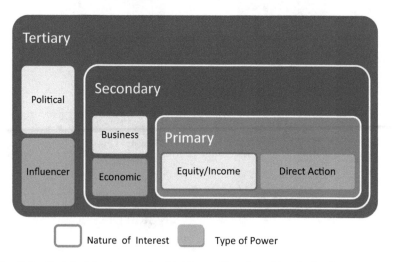

Fig. 7.2 Stakeholders' control grid (*Source* Developed by Author)

In this chapter we will focus on companies' responsibility to society and in the following chapter we will address its role in protecting the environment.

CORPORATE SOCIAL RESPONSIBILITY

CSR is a continuum approach which includes the elements (what is CSR); the principles (the purpose of CSR); the process of responsiveness (how CSR is to be done); the corporate social performance (the outcome of CSR); and its impact on stakeholders (Fig. 7.3).

Elements

Carroll's CSR Pyramid, a seminal research work in this domain, describes the elements of CSR. Carroll's four part definition of CSR states: "Corporate social responsibility encompasses the economic, legal, ethical, and discretionary (philanthropic) expectations that society has of organizations at a given point in time" (Carroll, 1979, 1991) (See Fig. 7.4).

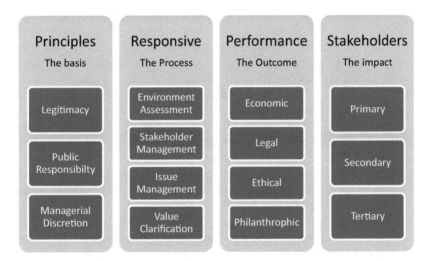

Fig. 7.3 CSR continuum (*Source* Developed by Author)

Fig. 7.4 Carroll's CSR pyramid of responsibilities (*Source* Adopted from Carroll, 1991)

Economic: The reason society permits companies to exist is because they need them for generating economic activity. The only way businesses can survive is by being profitable. Profits are necessary both to reward investors/owners, else why would they finance a business and also for reinvesting so that companies may expand. Profits are generated only when they create value by providing goods and services. Unless a firm meets its economic responsibility, it cannot achieve any other objective.

Legal: Society establishes the rules and regulations under which businesses are expected to operate and function. Businesses are required to comply with these laws and regulations. Laws ensure that businesses are run fairly and stakeholders are protected from unjust or fraudulent corporate behaviour. Enforceability of contracts, minimum wages or safety standards for edibles are all established to this end.

Ethical: In addition to what is required by laws and regulations, society expects businesses to operate and conduct their affairs in an ethical manner. Companies should consider the "spirit" of the law, not just the 'letter' of the law. Businesses are expected to adopt fair business practices even where the law is silent. Facebook and various other companies were pulled up for misusing personal data of their users for business gains. When they failed to me the expectation of society of maintaining individual's privacy, laws were enacted.

Philanthropy: Company use resources of society (labour, raw material, etc.) to profit and thus must return something back to society. The public has a desire that businesses will 'give back'. This social contract between business and society creates expectation that corporates as good citizens fulfil their philanthropic responsibilities of giving. Philanthropy may be a voluntary or discretionary action, but it generates goodwill for the company and builds relationship with the communities.

Economic responsibility is necessary, Legal compliance is required, Ethical behaviour is expected and Philanthropy is desired from a company. Carroll's CSR pyramid assumes a stage-wise approach, where companies first become economically sound, then legally compliant, thereafter ethical and over a period of time develop a sense of charity. When the first step is achieved efficiently one moves to the next. Does that mean it's okay for a start-up that is yet to break even to act unlawfully, say by bribing an officer to get a permit or licence? Naturally not. Further research and experiences have pointed out that for a company to be a good corporate citizen, it must simultaneously do all four.

Principles

Wood (1991) summarized the three principles of CSR, one at each level- institutional, organisational and individual. As expected, the first principle is derived from the institution-level legitimacy theory. The Principle of Legitimacy is about the company's obligation to society, because it is society that allows companies to exist in the first place. The second principle is applicable at the organizational level. The Principle of Public Responsibility is with reference to behaviour in its interaction with society as part of its operations. The third, Principle of Managerial Discretion puts onus on individual managers to choose socially responsible options in their decision-making process.

Process of Responsiveness

Responsiveness to CSR refers to a company's inclination to respond to stakeholder's concern, about the impact of their business. Carroll (1979) suggests four possible responses that a firm may choose. Reaction—business denies any responsibility for social issues and prefers to do nothing; Defence—company is resistant to take responsibility and does the minimum that is required; Accommodation—Organization accepts responsibility and does what is demanded by the stakeholder and Proactive—the firm goes over and beyond what was expected. The process that companies adopt to respond towards their social responsibility involves four steps (Ackerman, 1975; Wood, 1991).

Environmental Assessment: The first stage is 'awareness' of their social obligations and how their business may be effecting society. A company must scan the external environment to know how stakeholders perceive their actions and whether any social risk is brewing.

Stakeholder Management: The next is the 'planning' stage, where the company analyses the problem and identifies an approach to deal with the issue. It involves developing the policy or programmes for stakeholder management.

Issue Management: The company then 'implements' the solution to address the problem. It is the action that the company takes.

Value clarification: The final step is continuous 'evaluation' to determine whether stakeholder's concerns have been addressed or any further intervention is needed.

The online streaming music platform Spotify has made music available for free to music lovers around the world. However music artists say they are being exploited and paid negligible compensation, Spotify's failure to be responsive to artist has led musicians such as pop star Taylor Swift to temporarily withdraw from the platform. A company's Responsiveness to CSR may be considered as a measure of its commitment to being a good corporate citizen.

Corporate Social Performance

Corporate Social performance measures the outcomes of CSR. It aims to measure how a company is doing on the four elements of CSR. This is dependent on the degree to which a firm is driven by the principles of CSR and its responsiveness to stakeholder expectation. Corporate social performance is concerned with what the company ultimately does and how its actions or inactions impact stakeholders.

CSR Crusade

The evolution of CSR movement to its present state can be traced from company's complete rejection of the notion of CSR, to an altruistic motive of philanthropy, to realizing CSR as a value proposition, to finally strategically integrating it into business.

Corporate Charity—The Philanthropic Approach

Through the profit-driven focused businesses' initial reaction to CSR was denial, over time social pressure gained momentum. After all large companies have huge amount of resources at their disposal. The budgets of some of the global giants is considerable much bigger than those of small countries. As good citizens, the 'right thing' or the 'moral thing' would be to share their seemingly huge wealth with the poor and weaker sections of society. In the name of ethical and social behaviour, philanthropy became a corporate obligation. 'Charity' is the new mantra for CSR.

Albert J. Dunlap, a famous corporate restructuring and turnaround specialist of the 1990s was very vocal in his views that CEOs have no business giving away shareholder's money to Charity. According to him, "Corporate charity exists so that CEOs can collect awards, plaques and honors, so they can sit on a dais and be adored" (Collins, 1996). But CEOs are not paid for that. He argued that if they spend a lot of time on social activities, the company would not reach its full potential.

Implementing CSR activities was considered distinct from the business and an additional burden and cost to the firm. It is a humanitarian act with no direct benefit expected. The nature and amount of CSR would be influenced by the CEO's social and religious background. One can question the right of a board to give corporate funds to charity, which rightfully belong to shareholders and could have been given as dividends or reinvested into the business to create more wealth for them.

CSR—Value Creation Approach

Since organizations are an integral part of society, they are expected to operate responsibly. Over-emphasis on the objective of maximizing market value of shares has led management to indulge in unethical practices, often resulting in corporate scams finally destroying shareholder value. Dunlap considered a corporate reconstructing guru famous for successfully turning around several companies emphasized on enhancing shareholder value. He was heavily criticized for ignoring other stakeholders and is often cited as an example of bad leadership. After all 'to serve the shareholders well you have to serve the other stakeholders first'. Spending on CSR benefits the company in the form of strengthened public relations, improved reputation, reduced risks, licence to operate and an opportunity for cause marketing.

Reputational Capital is based on the company's relationship and trust with its external stakeholders—customers, suppliers, creditors and investors, and is reflected through its goodwill, image, brand equity and customer loyalty. A strong reputational capital is what differentiates winning companies from their competitors. Companies known for responsible behaviour are able to create value by establishing a more open and trusting relationship with their stakeholders (Jhunjhunwala, 2014). They become the choice for stakeholders (Table 7.1).

CSR activities help to strengthen public relations and win the trust of society. It creates a more positive image of a company if it is doing something to make the world better. As seen in the case of Maggi, even the perception of unethical practices and lack of concerns for all stakeholders can put the company at risk. Managing Social risk has become more important in the modern world. Social risk is caused by business actions that affect communities around it such as poor labour standards, human rights violation and corruption. When stakeholders challenge these actions, a social risk emerges. Globalization, information explosion and social media have empowered stakeholders. Social activism can be brutal to companies that misbehave. Even seemingly sound business decisions such as outsourcing services from a developing country which will

Table 7.1 Creating value for stakeholders

Stakeholder	Choice for
Customer	Provider of products/services
Employees	Employment
Shareholder	Investment
Suppliers	Partnership
Government	Complier
Community	Social contract to do business

Source Adopted from Shital Jhunjhunwala, Intertwining CSR with strategy—the way ahead, Corporate Governance, Vol. 14 No. 2 (2014), pp. 211–212

mean cost saving can become a social risk as the local community sees it as jobs lost. Effective stakeholder engagement can reduce social risk. Maggi officials clearly failed to engage with the stakeholders. Social risk if not dealt timely and appropriately gains attention of media and activists and becomes a major risk effecting business operations (Kytle & Rugge, 2005).

CSR—Strategic Approach

(S. Jhunjhunwala, 2014)
Society and businesses are interdependent. Companies want healthy, well qualified and skilled workforce. This calls for education and health care for the people. Efficient and effective use of resources—land, water, energy and other natural resources—increases productivity and lowers the cost of production. Resource utilization must be optimal and not exploitative so as to maximize operational efficiency and not impair future operations. Safe products at reasonable prices attract customers and generate revenue. Unfair business practices can unleash backlash from activists or even government action. Societies that are imbalanced and unhappy create disturbances causing disruptions and losses to business. Political or economic instability in the society can be detrimental to businesses. Strong societies, that provide equal opportunities and a good standard of living, are the ones with considerable demand for products and services that companies provide. A company's success and long-term continuity is dependent on its ability to meet society's expectation of legitimacy, public responsibility and accountable managerial discretion.

The response to demands for responsible behaviour by companies has mostly been cosmetic. While firms have realized the need to run their business responsibly, they are not sure how to go about it. They have reacted by framing fancy codes of conduct for their employees, setting up large number of board committees and giving money for philanthropic work. These are showcased in CSR reports and media campaigns.

Firm's need to appreciate that CSR can be integrated into the companies' strategy right from the beginning to create winning models. The Amul success story is one such glaring example. (see box) CSR, as an integral part of corporate strategy, fulfils stakeholder expectations and creates sustainable business.

Amul: The Taste of India
Of the farmer, by the farmer, and for the farmer
50 years after it was first launched, Amul's sale figures have jumped from few lakhs a year in1966 to over. US$5.3 Billion million a year in 2020–2021. No other brand comes even close to it. Everyday Amul collects more than 24 million litres of milk from 3.6 million farmers (many illiterate), converts the milk into branded, packaged products, and delivers goods to over 10,00,000 retail outlets across the country. (http://www.amul.com/m/organisation) "Amul," from the Sanskrit Amoolya, meaning precious or priceless is a brand name managed by an apex cooperative organization, Gujarat Co-operative Milk Marketing Federation, (GCMMF), a dairy cooperative in India. One of India's largest food products marketing organizations it provides quality products at reasonable prices on one hand and protects the interest of the farmers and offers them remunerative returns on the other hand. It has contributed in making India the largest producer of milk and milk products in the world. Amul is the biggest brand in the pouched milk sector in the world. Amul's range of products includes milk, ghee, milk powders, curd, ice cream, paneer, cream, chocolate, cheese, butter, and shrikhand. Amul exports its products to roughly 37 countries including USA, Australia, Mauritius, China, Hong Kong, Singapore, UAE, and Bangladesh.

It all started in the small town named Anand (in Kaira District of Gujarat, India) in December1946 with a group of farmers keen to free themselves from the exploitation of intermediaries, gain access to markets and thereby ensure maximum returns for their efforts established the Kaira District Co-operative Milk Producers' Union. Milk is collected twice a day from each cow/buffalo. Producers had to travel long distances, physically carrying individual containers to deliver milk to the only dairy, the Polson Dairy (monopoly rights given by government). The milk would often get sour, particularly in summer. As milk is perishable, they were forced to sell at whatever price the agents gave.

Angered by the unfair and manipulative trade practices, the farmers established the Kaira District Cooperative to collect, process and supply milk. It began with two village cooperatives and 250 litres of milk per day. Milk collection was decentralized, as most of the producers were marginal farmers who were in a position to deliver only 1–2 litres of milk per day. Village level cooperatives were established to coordinate the marginal milk producers in each of these villages.

The success of the dairy co-operative movement spread rapidly in Gujarat. Within a short span five other district unions—Mehsana,

Banaskantha, Baroda, Sabarkantha and Suratwere formed a cooperative. In order to combine forces and expand the market while saving on advertising and avoid a situation where milk cooperatives would compete against each other it was decided to set up an apex marketing body of dairy cooperative unions in Gujarat.

Thus, in 1973, the Gujarat Co-operative Milk Marketing Federation was established. The Kaira District Co-operative Milk Producers' Union Ltd. which had established the brand name Amul in 1955 decided to hand over the brand name to GCMMF (AMUL). The Amul Model is a three-tier cooperative structure. This structure consists of a Dairy Cooperative Society at the village level affiliated to a Milk Union at the District level which in turn is further consolidated into GCMMF at the State level.

Primitive market conditions and poor infrastructure proved to be an obstacle for marketing milk and its products. The cooperative started supplying high quality buffalo semen. Through village society workers, artificial insemination service was made available to the rural animal population. They started mobile veterinary services to render animal health care at the farmers' doorstep. Improvements in animal husbandry and veterinary services saw production multiply, leaving farmers with surplus milk. Thus indigenously developed plants and processes were set up for producing milk powder and butter and later for condensed milk and cheese. Beginning with liquid milk, GCMMF enhanced the product mix through the progressive addition of higher value products while maintaining the desired growth in existing products.

With consumers in India, in those days, having limited purchasing power and modest consumption levels of milk and other dairy products, Amul adopted a low-cost price strategy to make its products affordable and attractive to consumers by guaranteeing them value for money. Managing the supply chain efficiently is critical as GCMMF's competitive position is driven by low consumer prices supported by a low cost system.

Today Amul's supply chain involves collecting milk from over 3 million farmers spread across 18,000 villages and delivering milk and dairy products across the world. Amul has come a long way from the time when farmers had to walk long distances to sell the milk. Through the process of door to door collection and electronic automatic collection system across its multiple collection centres that weighs the milk and measures the fat at time of deliver itself it has built an efficient collection channel. Price is calculated and payment is made to farmers, there and then. Chilling units have been set up at the village cooperative society levels to prevent the milk from turning sour. Once the milk is processes it is sent from warehouses to wholesalers, who distribute to retail outlets and home delivery contractors.

A movement in dairy corporative, its success has established it as a uniquely appropriate model for rural development. Everyone in the villages, rich and poor, educated and illiterate came together for a mutually beneficial cause creating means of livelihood for millions in thousands of villages. By delivering quality products of international standards to customers at affordable prices its turnover has multiplied several times from Rs. 11,140 ($ 355) million in 1994–1995 to Rs. 392,480 ($ 5300) million in 2020–2021 (http://www.amul.com/m/organisation).

Point to Ponder:

Do you think the title 'Of the farmer, by the farmer, and for the farmer' is appropriate? How far was it responsible for the success of Amul?

Adopted from Shital Jhunjhunwala, Intertwining CSR with strategy—the way ahead, Corporate Governance, Vol. 14 No. 2 (2014), pp. 211–212.

Cutting-edge innovation and competitive advantage can result from redesigning business strategy to mitigate social risk. Social and environmental causes can in fact be converted into business opportunities. Amul did just that. C.K. Prahalad (2010) in the Fortune at Bottom of the Pyramid suggests that the poor people (which are about 4 billion globally) can be a great source of new business providing a huge customer base. Firms by involving NGOs, civil society organizations and local governments can benefit the weaker sections and create new business models of success. Prahalad suggests 12 principles of innovation for converting necessaries at the Bottom of the Pyramid into fortunes for companies. These include appropriate pricing, scalability of operations across cultures and languages, eco-friendly products that reduce resource exploitation and distribution methods suitable for both urban and rural markets.

Framework for Integrating CSR into Business

As firms understand the need to integrate CSR activities into business strategy, they must develop a strategic framework that makes CSR an integral part of the business model. Integrating CSR into business strategy requires firms to (see Fig. 7.5):

Fig. 7.5 Integrating CSR into corporate strategy (*Source* Developed by Author)

Identify overlapping areas: The company should identify the point of interaction between business and the community. For example, wages and working conditions define the living standards of the labourers. Common interests are to be identified. The digital sector requires skilled workforce. Computer engineering students on the other hand desire jobs.

Determine its competitive advantage: Companies should determine what their competitive advantage is going to be and how they want to achieve it. There are millions of social and environmental issues that a firm can undertake. Companies must select those issues which interlock with their business interests and create a competitive advantage for the firm. Skilled computer and software engineers are the forte of a digital business. Employability of fresh engineers is questionable. The firm should identify alternatives to close this gap between business and society needs.

Decide CSR activities: From the alternates, appropriate CSR activities are to be selected. CSR activity chosen should minimize social risks and strengthen community bonds. In our example, the company may choose to support a few software engineering colleges. It could get involved in designing curricula, providing summer internships and imparting practical inputs. The company would then be able to source its fresh recruit, from these colleges, who would naturally suit the company's requirements. This would save time and cost in training new recruits as they would be productive employees for the company from day one. And the young graduates would get a good start to their career.

Integrate CSR activities into business: Once an activity has been selected, it must be rendered an integral part of the business model. The digital firm should provide internships, have their employees involved in teaching and facilitate mentoring these students.

Make it a corporate social agenda: The CSR activity should become a constituent of the firms' vision and mission. Supporting the selected activity should be embodied into the culture of the organization and an essential responsibility of all employees. For instance, employees may be asked to dedicate certain time from their normal work hours to the CSR activity.

A potent illustration of integrating CSR into corporate strategy is the 'e-Choupal' launched by ITC Ltd. ITC is one of India's foremost FMCG company rated among the "World's most reputable companies" by Forbes magazine. ITC is one of India's largest exporters of agricultural goods. ITC "conceived e-Choupal as a more efficient supply chain aimed at delivering value to its customers around the world on a sustainable basis. The e-Choupal model has been specifically designed to tackle the challenges posed by the unique features of Indian agriculture, characterized by fragmented farms, weak infrastructure and their involvement of numerous intermediaries, among others" (Source: ITC, 2013).

With the use of internet, small and marginal farmers (mostly below poverty line) are provided with farming know-how and services, timely and relevant weather information, transparent price discovery and access to wider markets. E-Choupal has enabled farmers to strengthen their bargaining power, enhance productivity, get higher prices for their product and reduce risks. By directly sourcing the crop from farmers, ITC benefits from reduced purchasing cost, (higher crop price but much lower transaction costs by eliminating middle man and multiple handling), assured supply of inputs, and quality raw material that meets food safety norms. By addressing the issues of farmers, the company gets its raw material at the 'right price, quality and quantity' (Jhunjhunwala, 2014).

Intertwining CSR in Strategy solves a problem profitably. Creating shared value between company and community requires innovation in "reconceiving products and markets, redefining productivity in the value chain, and building supportive industry clusters at the company's locations" (Porter & Kramer, 2011). This in turn provides a competitive advantage and new streams of revenue. Purpose-driven firms by embedding shared value in business strategy have a sustainable lasting impact.

Mandating CSR in India—The Push

There are mandatory CSR reporting requirements in several countries, including Sweden, Norway, the Netherlands, Denmark, France and Australia. However, India is the only country to legislate requiring companies to undertake CSR. Every company having a net worth of Rs. five hundred crore or more, or a turnover of Rs. one thousand crore or more, or a net profit of Rs. five crore or more is to use at least 2% of average net profits made during the three immediately preceding financial years towards CSR (Section 135, Companies Act, 2013). The company is to constitute a CSR Committee consisting of three or more directors. Further, if it is a listed company, then at least one director should be independent. The committee will determine the company's CSR policy and amount it will spend and the same is to be disclosed in the board's report.

If a company does not spend 2% by the end of the year, then the unspent amount on ongoing projects is to be deposited in an Unspent Corporate Social Responsibility Account that can be opened in any scheduled bank within a period of thirty days from the end of the financial year and this amount is to be utilized within a period of three years. The remaining unspent amount is to be deposited to any of the fund specified in Schedule VII, within a period of six months of the expiry of the financial year. If a company fails to do so, the company and concerned officers will be penalized [Companies (Corporate Social Responsibility Policy) Rules 2014].

Schedule VII of the Companies Act, 2013 lays down the activities that may be undertaken by companies for CSR (Table 7.2). India has adopted a philanthropic approach of CSR where companies are to share the government's responsibility of economic and social upliftment of the poor and underprivileged. As the list shows government agenda such as "Swacch Bharat" (clean India) is promoted through this. Companies may simply donate to such funds to comply with their CSR requirements.

Even though it is mandatory, the amount spent on CSR is considered as appropriation of profit not a business expenditure. Thus, the expenditure on CSR activities is non-deductible for tax purposes unless

Table 7.2 CSR activities under schedule VII

(i) eradicating hunger, poverty and malnutrition; promoting health care including preventive health care and sanitation including contribution to the 'Swachh Bharat Kosh' set-up by the Central Government for the promotion of sanitation and making available safe drinking water;

(ii) Promoting education, including special education and employment enhancing vocational skills especially among children, women, elderly, and the differently abled and livelihood enhancement projects;

(iii) promoting gender equality and empowering women, setting up homes and hostels for women and orphans; setting up old age homes, day care centers and such other facilities for senior citizens and measures for reducing inequalities faced by socially and economically backward groups;

(iv) ensuring environmental sustainability, ecological balance, protection of flora and fauna, animal welfare, agro forestry, conservation of natural resources and maintaining quality of soil, air and water including contribution to the 'Clean Ganga Fund' set-up by the Central Government for rejuvenation of river Ganga;

(v) Protection of national heritage, art and culture including restoration of building and sites of historical importance and works of art; setting up public libraries; promotion and development of traditional arts and handicrafts;

(vi) measures for the benefit of armed forces veterans, war widows and their dependents;

(vii) training to promote rural sports, nationally recognized sports, Paralympic sports and Olympic sports;

(viii) contribution to the Prime Minister's National Relief Fund or any other fund set up by the Central Government for socio-economic development and relief and welfare of the Scheduled Castes, the Scheduled Tribes, other backward classes, minorities and women;

(ix) Contributions or funds provided to technology incubators located within academic institutions which are approved by the Central Government;

(x) Rural development projects

(xi) Slum area development

Source Companies (Corporate Social Responsibility Policy) Rules 2014

falling within certain specific provisions such as expenditure for scientific research and rural development. This acts as a deterrent. Detailed CSR rules have been painstakingly framed with the hope that companies contribute to social development of India and do not use the funds for any personal gains. Administrative cost for conducting the CSR activities such as salary of person employed to coordinate the CSR activities is restricted to 5% of the total funds allotted to CSR. Donations to political parties and activities for the exclusive benefits of employees of the company are not considered as CSR. CSR project is to be undertaken in India only, preferably in and around the areas where the company operates.

Nevertheless, the CSR policy of a company will depend on one side on the expectations made by society and on the other hand the commitment of the company. Companies have been doing lip service, when it comes to CSR, which does not really make any lasting impact. A huge amount of CSR funds have been channelized towards building schools in rural areas of India with the hope to make at least primary education available to children. However access to quality education is still a far cry. Most schools lack adequate number of teachers. It is estimate 'd that about 10% schools are a one teacher school. The few teachers that are available lack commitment, adequate qualification and required experience. Poverty and ignorance of the importance of education keeps children away from schools. Those that come have limited or no access to books or other learning tools. Like any public policy, CSR policy should undergo a two-stage social impact assessment process (OECD) to evaluate the impact of CSR initiatives on the communities they are intended to serve. This will help the companies to understand the extent to which their social investments are achieving the targeted social goal.

Ex ante impact analysis: The first step is to conduct a base line survey of the social and economic conditions of the community to do a need analysis. Once a gap has been identified, suitable activities can be planned along with a potential impact assessment of the proposed CSR initiative.

Ex post impact assessment: It involves evaluating the effect of the intervention and the extent to which it has filled the identified gap. Both positive or negative effects must be examined and measures must be taken to mitigate any negative effects. The outcome of the CSR initiative should preferably be measurable in quantifiable terms. 'How many children are getting education'. It is equally important to have a continuous monitoring process. This will help identify additional interventions required to bring a meaningful change. In the beginning may be only a handful of children started coming to school, but actual impact will happen if the number of children keep rising each year. Awareness creation among parents to send their kids to school may be the follow-up CSR programme.

India has mandated that companies on completing CSR projects above rupee one crore are to conduct an impact assessment to determine whether it had the desired impact on target beneficiaries. This will compel companies to choose their CSR initiatives carefully and give it considerable thought, at least a small percentage of what they give to corporate strategy. They will also then probably align their CSR policy with the overall strategy creating long-term value for everyone. The entire process must involve all the key stakeholders. The success of any CSR policy is dependent on three factors: the presence of stakeholders as directors, a dedicated CSR committee with stakeholder representation and the commitment of the board as a whole.

CSR AND CRISIS

The global pandemic of 2020–2021 heightened and highlighted the need of corporates to be socially responsible. During extreme turbulent conditions such as the financial crisis of 2008 and the COVID-19 epidemic businesses are wheeling under extreme economic pressure. Their own survival is in question. Then, which set of stakeholders should be given priority. Shareholders' and investors' money should be protected, employees' pay and job, suppliers' payments or the general society?

Carroll (2021) argues that even in crisis, all four elements of CSR are equally important. During the financial crisis, several companies in the financial sector were shut down and others resorted to massive layoffs to just survive. Worldwide businesses were completely destroyed during the pandemic by periods of lockdown necessitated to save human lives. If the firm does not exist, there will be no production, no jobs and no income. The GDP of even the developed nations saw a huge dip. Unemployment rose to unprecedented levels. The economic responsibility of the companies during the crisis becomes not to make good returns but to survive, to be financially sustainable.

The financial crisis resulted in legislation of additional rules. The Dodd-Frank Wall Street Reform and Consumer Protection Act of USA was enacted to regulate irresponsible behaviour of the financial industry that perpetuated the catastrophe of 2007–2008. New rules were introduced during the COVID-19 outbreak such as wearing mask and maintaining a social distance between people. To comply companies had to reorganize their factory set up and workplace practices. 'Work from home' became the new norm in industries such as information technology and education. Restrictions on travel ushered in an era of 'online meetings' and 'webinars'. These changes weren't all bad. Travel time and cost dipped benefiting companies.

Ethical responsibility suffers the most during a crisis. Employees are laid off. Payments to suppliers delayed. Health workers and police forces had to work tirelessly for long hours, putting themselves and their families at risk during the COVID-19 pandemic. A surge in mental health issues was observed. In Delhi, the capital of India, during the peak of the 2nd phase of COVID-19, several schools and universities that were operating online made a conscious choice to close down for a few days. Large number of teachers and students fell ill or their family members were. Many encountered deaths in their families. The mental and emotional environment were not conducive for learning. Companies took the ethical responsibility to facilitate vaccination of employees and their families. This directly benefited companies as employees were at less risk of falling ill. Customers in retail stores and restaurants displayed less reluctance to enter the premise if all employees were vaccinated, thereby reviving business.

The financial crisis witnessed a downfall in CSR activities as CSR projects were stalled, postponed and even cancelled, particularly those not in the limelight for more 'important' corporate actions. Absence of integration of CSR with main stream strategy made it easy to cut the expenditure on discretionary CSR activities (https://link.springer.com/article/10.1007/s13520-022-00). The weakest sections of society such as daily labourers and small unorganized businesses were most affected in the pandemic. Is this not the time for companies to act with philanthropic responsibility? CSR spending which had been steadily rising in India since mandated in 2013 initially saw a drastic fall at the beginning of the COVID-19 crisis as companies themselves were struggling. But then, there was a surge in CSR initiatives not just in India but all over the world. Large companies, and in particular family businesses, that had the resources come forward. It is not clear whether corporate leaders were moved by the sufferings of the vulnerable in society or they saw it as an opportunity to showcase their altruism. Masks were manufactured and supplied for free, food was distributed to the needy and salaries were paid to the employees even though they were not working. Research suggests that CSR acts as insurance for companies in times of crisis by building trust with the stakeholders. Lins et al. (2017) found that companies that had higher CSR experienced better sales, profitability and stock returns during the financial crisis than those with lower CSR. Stakeholders are more likely to stand by firms they trust during the times of crisis. Similarly companies that go the extra mile during crisis win stakeholders' confidence that reaps future benefits.

Jacob (2012) while examining the impact of financial crisis found that employees are the most affected followed by shareholders. Massive layoffs meant extra world load for the remaining employees. When business started bouncing back, companies found themselves lacking adequate competencies and rebuilding competence takes time. During the pandemic, 'work from home' threw the work life balance completely out of gear. Domestic violence surged. Female employees were worst hit with lack of childcare facilities and becoming the de facto school teacher. During lockdown, India witnessed the domestic migrant workers crisis. Left jobless and no means to survive workers in cities wanted to return to their families in villages. With no travel means they were left stranded with no place to stay and no food to eat. Thousands were seen walking on railway tracks and highways desperate to somehow reach home. Investors' interest is the next most affected in a crisis. Both times, profits plummeted and share prices nose-dived. Small retailer investors saw their entire savings wiped out.

Corporate boards need to appreciate that business and society are more inseparable than ever. Most companies and governments were completely unprepared to deal with the crisis. Lack of medical resources and infrastructure handicapped our ability to save lives. Companies need to be more prepared. Crisis management must be given more priority. In 2020 when India was faced with an acute shortage of ventilators, several small and large companies revamped their manufacturing setups to make affordable ventilators. The Mahindra Group of companies modified their car manufacturing unit to make ventilators. Noccarc Robotics pivoted from making robots to making ventilators in just 90 days. This was possible with the IIT Kanpur Ventilator Consortium a team of experts in design, manufacturing, certification and relationship with doctors. Biodesign Innovation Labs made RespirAid—"a portable mechanical ventilation device—which can even be used inside ambulances when a patient is being taken to a hospital" (Banerjee, 2021). It got support from various government agencies and used the facilities of an ophthalmology devices manufacturer to produce the ventilators. These affordable ventilators have create huge export opportunities for these companies. The government of India funded and coordinated the manufacture of ventilators and even made available experts to help start up these production facilities. The distribution process sought to provide hospitals all over the country with ventilators and task force was set up to tackle any technical issues in real time (https://network.exemplars.health/india-covid-19-sos/b/best-practices/posts/made-in-india-the-government-s-role-in-supporting-industries-to-tackle-the-ventilator-crisis).

Organizations' capabilities are tested in times of crisis. Public expectation from companies to act responsibly increases. Social risks magnitude manifold. Mismanagement during calamities can do irreplaceable damage to reputational capital. Crisis of such gigantic magnitudes requires collaboration from authorities, companies, NGOs and community members. All stakeholders must come together. Investors should agree not to take dividend; senior executives should accept a cut in their pay; suppliers should be willing to restructure the supply chain network and revise payment schedules. An ecosystem has to be built which uses companies' business acumen to create shared value which solves the world's urgent problems and provides new economic benefits to firms.

REFERENCES

Ackerman, R. W. (1975). *The social challenge to business*. Harvard University Press.

Banerjee. (2021). Covid-19 ventilators, made in—and for—India. *Forbes*. https://www.forbesindia.com/article/healthtech-special/covid19-ventilators-made-inand-forindia/69329/1. Accessed March 31, 2023.

Bhushan, (2016, February 24). Maggi ban impact: Nestle India may take 3 years to recover. *The Economic Times*. Accessed from https://economictimes.indiatimes.com/industry/cons-products/food/maggi-ban-impact-nestle-india-may-take-3-years-to-recover/articleshow/51114562.cms, on September 6, 2018.

Carroll, A. B. (1979). A three-dimensional conceptual model of corporate social performance. *Academy of Management Review, 4*, 497–505.

Carroll, A. B. (1991). The pyramid of corporate social responsibility: Toward the moral management of organizational stakeholders. *Business Horizons, 34*(4), 39–48.

Carroll, A. B. (2021). Corporate social responsibility (CSR) and the COVID-19 pandemic: Organizational and managerial implications. *Journal of Strategy and Management, 14* (3), 315–330.

Companies (Corporate Social Responsibility Policy) Rules. (2014).

Companies Act. (2013). India.

Dunlap, A. J. (1996). Mean Business: How I Save Bad Companies and Make Good Companies Great, revived *For a Struggling Sunbeam, Shock Therapy*, by Glenn Collinsaug. Accessed from https://www.nytimes.com/1996/08/11/business/for-a-struggling-sunbeam-shock-therapy.html, on September 30, 2018.

Dutta, A. (2016, February 22) Post-ban, Maggi noodles still No.1 despite ceding large market share. *Business Standard*. Accessed from https://www.business-standard.com/article/companies/post-ban-maggi-noodles-still-no-1-despite-ceding-large-market-share-116022200412_1.html, on August 13, 2022.

Freeman, R. E., & Reed, D. L. (1988). Stockholders and stakeholders: A new perspective on corporate governance. *California Management Review, 25*(3), 88–106.

Friedman, M. (1970, September 13). The social responsibility of business is to increase its profits. *New York Times Magazine*.

http://www.amul.com/m/organisation

ITC. (2013). "e-choupal." www.itcportal.com/itc-business/agri-business/e-choupal.aspx (Accessed 2013).

Jacob, C. K. (2012). The Impact of financial crisis on corporate social responsibility and its implications for reputation risk management. *Journal of Management and Sustainability, 2*(2).

Jhunjhunwala, S. (2014). Intertwining CSR with strategy—the way ahead. *Corporate Governance, 14*(2).

Kytle & Rugge. (2005). Corporate social responsibility as risk management. *A Model of Risk Management*. https://www.hks.harvard.edu/sites/default/files/centers/mrcbg/programs/cri/files/workingpaper_10_kytle_ruggie.pdf

Lins, K. V., Servaes, H., & Tamayo, A. (2017). Social capital, trust, and firm performance: The value of corporate social responsibility during the financial crisis. *The Journal of Finance, 72*(4), 1785–1824.

Made in India: The government's role in supporting industries to tackle the ventilator crisis. https://network.exemplars.health/india-covid-19-sos/b/best-practices/posts/made-in-india-the-government-s-role-in-supporting-industries-to-tackle-the-ventilator-crisis. Accessed March 31, 2023.

Madhukalya, A. (2018). Nestle's Maggi back on top with 60 per cent market share. *BusinessToday*. In August 7, 2018, https://www.businesstoday.in/latest/corporate/story/nestle-maggi-back-on-top-with-60-per-cent-market-share-109550-2018-08-07. Accessed August 13, 2022.

Mitra, S. (2017, February 16). The Maggi ban: How India's favourite two-minute noodles lost 80% market share. Accessed from https://www.livemint.com/Companies/1JKHsutTXLWtTcVwdIDg0H/The-Maggi-ban-How-Indias-favourite-twominute-noodles-lost.html, on September 6, 2018.

OECD. What is impact assessment?

Porter & Kramer. (2011). Creating shared value. *Harvard Business Review*. https://hbr.org/2011/01/the-big-idea-creating-shared-value

Prahalad, C. K. (2010). Fortune at bottom of the pyramid. Wharton School Publishing.

PTI. (2015, February). We do not add MSG in Maggi noodles: Nestle's Global CEO Paul Bulcke. *Financial Express*. https://www.financialexpress.com/ind ustry/maggi-noodles-are-safe-for-consumption-says-nestles-global-ceo-paul-bulcke/80673/. Accessed August 13, 2022.

Wood, D. J. (1991). Corporate social responsibility revisited. *Academy of Management Review, 16*, 691–718.

CHAPTER 8

Sustainable Development for Corporate Sustainability

Live and Let Live

Odd–Even

'Emergency Plan for Delhi Air Pollution to Come into Action Tomorrow' - read the headlines on a cold winter morning.

Under the emergency plan called Graded Response Action Plan (GRAP), stringent actions are implemented based on the Delhi air quality. The overall air quality index (AQI) recorded at 4 pm on Saturday stood at 300 which falls in the poor category and is just one point from being 'very poor', according to Centre-run System of Air Quality and Weather Forecasting and Research (SAFAR). An AQI between 0–50 is considered 'good', 51–100 'satisfactory', 101–200 'moderate', 201–300 'poor', 301–400 'very poor', and 401–500 'severe (NDTV, 2018).

Air pollution in Delhi			
Source	Contribution in %		
	PM2.5	SO2	NOx
Transport	17	2	53
Gen sets	6	4	25
Brick kilns	15	11	2
Industry	14	23	11
Construction	5	–	1
Waste burning	8	1	1
Road dust	6	–	–
Power plants	16	55	7
Domestic	12	6	1

Source   https://www.business-standard.com/article/opinion/dinesh-mohan-dea ling-with-pollution-in-our-cities-115040400713_1.html

Pollution levels in New Delhi the Capital of India is the worst in world, according to the World Health Organization report of 2018, causing major concerns for human health include effects on breathing and respiratory systems, damage to lung tissue, cancer and premature death. Elderly persons, children and people with chronic lung disease, influenza or asthma are especially sensitive to the effects.

Former President of USA Obama lost about 6 hours of his expected life expectancy after spending three days in India's capital when he visited it as the chief guest at Republic Day in 2015 as he breathe "unhealthy and hazardous" air during his stay according to a Bloomberg report.

To address the situation the Chief Minister Kejriwal introduced the odd even scheme where vehicles with odd and even number licence plates are allowed to ply on alternate days. Its impact has been questionable.

Point to Ponder: Should we continue to develop at the cost of human Life? Or should we go back to stone ages?

CORPORATIONS AND SUSTAINABLE DEVELOPMENT

"Sustainable development is development that meets the needs of the present without compromising the ability of future generations to meet their own needs" (World Commission on Environment and Development, 1987). Population explosion with increased demands led by industrialization and advanced technology has caused scarcity of resources. As we have seen in the previous chapter, companies must 'do well and do good'. Besides being financially rewarding, it must take care of society and the environment. Business uses and impacts the resources of the earth—water, air, trees minerals, etc. If the air gets so polluted that we all die, to whom are these companies going to sell and become rich off? Thus companies must play their part in protecting the environment.

In September 2015, all 193 Member States of the United Nations adopted the 17 Sustainable Development goals (SDG)—a plan for achieving a better future for all. Companies can advance the SDG agenda by incorporating the 'Ten principles of the UN Global Compact' into their corporate strategies and business practices (https://www.unglobalc ompact.org/sdgs/about). (Table 8.1) In fact it's a business opportunity. By innovating new products and services that tackle issues such as hunger, health and climate change, businesses can grow their revenues faster. Just imagine the market potential for new innovations that deliver on clean water and sanitation or ensure healthy lives for all.

Table 8.1 Ten principles of the UN Global Compact

UN Global Compact -2000	
Human Rights **Principle 1**: Businesses should support and respect the protection of internationally proclaimed human rights; and **Principle 2**: make sure that they are not complicit in human rights abuses	**Labour** **Principle 3**: Businesses should uphold the freedom of association and the effective recognition of the right to collective bargaining; **Principle 4**: the elimination of all forms of forced and compulsory labour; **Principle 5**: the effective abolition of child labour; and **Principle 6**: the elimination of discrimination in respect of employment and occupation
Environment **Principle 7**: Businesses should support a precautionary approach to environmental challenges; **Principle 8**: undertake initiatives to promote greater environmental responsibility; and **Principle 9**: encourage the development and diffusion of environmentally friendly technologies	**Anti-Corruption** **Principle 10**: Businesses should work against corruption in all its forms, including extortion and bribery

Source adopted from https://www.unglobalcompact.org/what-is-gc/mission/principles

SUSTAINABILITY REPORTING

A Sustainable Report presents the social and environment impacts of the company's business and activities. It showcases the commitment level of an organization towards CSR and Sustainable Development. Several frameworks have evolved over the years to measure a company's contribution towards sustainable development. Notable among them are:

The Communication on Progress (COP)

The COP requires participating companies to annually publicly commit support to the Ten Principles into their strategies and operations and monitors their progress in five broad areas—governance, human rights, labour, environment, anti-corruption (https://www.unglobalcompact.org/participation/report/cop).

Triple Bottom Line

The Triple Bottom Line (TBL) is an accounting framework that incorporates three elements of performance: social, environmental and economic (Elkington, 1997). It is a broader approach than traditional reporting frameworks that focus only on financial aspects. As a sustainable framework, it expands the traditional accounting framework to include two other performance areas: the social and environmental impacts of a company. The phrase triple bottom line was introduced in 1994 by John Elkington. The TBL dimensions are also commonly called the three Ps: people, planet and profits (Fig. 8.1).

People: People addresses the impact company has on society. It measures the way a company benefits society. These include better labour practices, safe products and 'giving back' to society.

Planet: This dimension measures environmental performance. It indicates that businesses are to reduce their ecological footprint as much as possible. These efforts can include reducing waste, investing in renewable energy and managing natural resources more efficiently. Global warming and its effects are clear indication that if something is not done soon, there will be no business to do at all.

Profit: A company has to be financially viable, otherwise it cannot survive. Thus the three dimensions must be integrated. For instance

Fig. 8.1 Triple Bottom Line (*Source* Adopted Elkington, 1997)

improving energy efficiency reduces cost for the company while saving natural resources.

A key challenge with the triple bottom line, according to Elkington (1997), is the difficulty of measuring the social and environmental bottom lines.

Global Reporting Initiative (GRI)

The GRI framework initiated in 1997 is the first global standards on sustainable reporting. The sustainability reporting framework attempts to make the Triple Bottom Line operational. On one side it allows companies to report how they contribute to sustainable development and on the other acts as a reference point for regulators, investors and other stakeholders. The GRI standards are a modular system of interconnected standards that allow organizations to identify on all issues it considers material and report on its impacts and how it manages these material topics. As a sustainable framework, it aims to provide a comprehensive picture of an organization's most significant impacts on the economy, environment and people (https://www.globalreporting.org/standards/).

ESG Reporting

The purpose of ESG reporting is to help investors better understand the firm's future value by disclosing information on Environment (E), Social (S) and Governance(G) performance of company. It communicates the quality of the company's governance, how it behaves with its stakeholders and society, and its impact on environment. Legislation in Europe and various other parts of the world insist that companies through financial and non-financial data report on ESG activities.

The three pillars of ESG are detailed for a better understanding.

Environment: It includes the impact the firm's business has on the environment such as depletion of natural resources, greenhouse gas emissions, biodiversity, pollution and climate change.

Social: It encompasses the relationship the firm has with its stakeholders, how it treats its employees and its attitude towards the community including its philanthropic activities. It requires reporting on issues such as product quality, health and safety standards, supply chain, community outreach, human capital, child labour, diversity and inclusion.

Governance: It refers to the company's governance structure and the extent to which it is meeting stakeholder expectations. Disclosure requirements comprise of board structure, board diversity, executive compensation, ownership structure, internal control and risk management systems, reporting frameworks and transparency.

Business Responsibility and Sustainability Reporting

Several companies globally report using the GRI framework. Its implementation however is not easy. Therefore, countries based on their governance frameworks and business condition have customized the format desired for sustainable reporting by organizations. SEBI regulation requires top 1000 companies by market capitalization in India to publish a Business Responsibility and Sustainability Report (BRSR). This is in addition to the Corporate Governance Report and CSR report. It is based on nine principles encompassing the major stakeholders and is aligned with the 17 SDGs. It covers the Environmental, Social and Governance (ESG) aspects. Principle 1 based on governance states, 'Businesses should conduct and govern themselves with integrity, and in a manner that is Ethical, Transparent and Accountable'. Principle 6 states that 'Businesses should respect and make efforts to protect and restore the environment'. Companies have to report on their energy consumption, water consumption and emission as well as steps taken towards waste management and renewable energy. Principle 5 addresses social concerns of human rights and Principle 8 is about promoting inclusive growth and equitable development and requires details of Social Impact sAssessments (SIA) of projects undertaken by the company. It is expected that these reports will help stakeholders compare performance of companies on all three parameters (SEBI, 2021).

Integrated Reporting[1]

As defined by value reporting foundation, *"The integrated report communicates how an organization's strategy, governance, performance and prospects, in the context of its external environment, create preserve or erode value in the short, medium and long term"* (https://www.integratedre porting.org/wp-content/uploads/2022/08/Transition-to-integrated-reporting_A-Getting-Started-Guide.pdf). Integrated Reporting combines financial and non-financial measurements into a single report to showcase how a company maximizes value by serving the interest of not just the suppliers of finance, but all stakeholders such as employees, suppliers, customers, government and local communities.

The framework is based on the notion that value creation of a business is contingent on how the organization applies its capital (resources and relationships) and interacts with the external environment. Its activities and resulting outcomes increase, decrease or transform capital. Value generation occurs when the firm creates value for other stakeholders. For instance, suppliers' willingness to do business depends on benefits they gain in return. All such activities, interactions and relationships that create value must form part of the integrated report.

Capitals

The framework includes six categories of capitals. The extent of relevance of each form of capital may vary in different industries.

---

[1] (for more details see S Jhunjhunwala, Beyond financial reporting-international integrated reporting framework, Indian journal of corporate governance 7(1), 73–80).

Financial Capital: Financial Capital consists of all the funds with the firm either internally generated or externally obtained (debt, equity, grants) by the firm.

Manufactured Capital: These include tangible assets that are considered manmade such as buildings, equipment and infrastructure (roads, ports) that are used to produce goods or provide services.

Natural Capital: Consists of all renewal and non-renewal environmental resources such as land, water, air and minerals that are depleted by the organization.

Intellectual Capital: Intangible assets comprising of organizational capital such as systems and processes and intellectual property such as patents and copyrights constitute intellectual capital.

Human Capital: Human capital refers to combined knowledge, skills capabilities and competencies of the managers and employees. Leadership, ability to adopt to change and innovativeness of its human capital directly influence firms' ability to create value.

Social and Relationship Capital: It includes both relationships within the entity and external relationships that grant implicit licence to operate and includes supply chain networks, brands and reputation it has built.

Content Elements

As per the IIRC framework, the process of value transformation increase or decrease in capital is based on eight elements of the company that are not mutually exclusive but fundamentally linked to each other (Fig. 8.2). The elements are.

Organizational Overview and External Environment: The economic, political, social and technological climate under which the firm operates.

Governance: The governance structure and systems that enable the business to create value in the short, medium and long term.

Risks and Opportunities: Scanning the external environment for identifying risk and opportunities and incorporating them into the firm's business model and strategy.

Business Model: The business model involves choosing the inputs and converting them into outputs (products and services).

Strategy and Resource Allocation: The strategic objectives to create value by aptly allocating resources and mitigating risks.

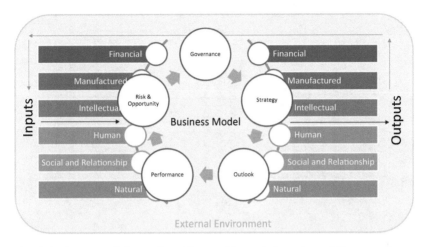

Fig. 8.2 Integrated Reporting (*Source* Adopted from http://integratedrepor ting.org/what-the-tool-for-better-reporting/get-to-grips-with-the-six-capitals/, accessed Oct 21, 2018)

Performance: Building a performance management system to measure the outcomes of the business model in terms of impact on the capitals applied by it.

Outlook: Future prospects and improvements to be made in the other elements to augment the value creation process.

Basis of Presentation: The basis of determining what matters to include in the integrated report and how the information is to be quantified or evaluated.

The report depicts the past, present and future activities, performance and outcomes to provide a holistic view of the firm's value creating process. The effect on manufactured and financial capital are easy to measure using traditional accounting. Suitable indicators are to be developed for measuring changes in other forms of capital (see Table 8.2).

Guiding Principles

IIRC has laid down certain underlying principles that form the basis for developing the integrated report. It helps to determine the information it should contain and how it should be presented. These are:

Table 8.2 Indicators for measurement

Financial	Financial & Non-Financial	Non-Financial
Human Capital		
Training expenses	Market value/employee	Leadership index (%)
Total employee expenses	Income/employee	Motivation index (%)
Training expense/total expenses	Value-added/employee	Empowerment index (responsibility/authority)
Training expense/administrative expenses (%)	Fixed assets/employee	Employee satisfaction index
Training expenses/total employee expense	Training expenses/employee	Efficiency: output/employee (units)
		Average working hours
Social & Relationship Capital		
Sales from top five customer	Services expenses/customer	Number of accounts
Sales from top five customer/total sales	Sales/new customers	No. of repeat customers
Sales/marketing expenses	Sales/front-line employees	Customer satisfaction index
Investment in developing new markets	Marketing expenses /customer	Market share
Investment in strategic partnership development	Marketing expenses/product	
Intellectual Property		
Income from new business operations	New Product/Investment in R&D	Percentage of new products reaching market
Return on net assets from a new business operation	New Patents/ Investment in R&D	No. of new patents
Revenue from new patents	No of patent Applications/ Training Expenses	New products in development
Investment in R&D		Average estimated age of products
Revenue/ R&D expenses		No. of patent applications

Source Developed by Author

Strategic Focus and Future Orientation: An integrated report should reflect on how the firm's strategy is going to employ its capitals to create value.

Connectivity of Information: The report should show a holistic view by interconnecting all the factors that influence the company's ability to create value in short, medium and long term.

Stakeholder Relationships: An integrated report describes the nature and quality of the firm's relationships with its key stakeholders and how it is addressing their interests.

Materiality: The report should disclose all qualitative and quantitative information that significantly affect the value creation process of the company.

Conciseness: An integrated report should be concise including only relevant and sufficient information to understand the past, present and future performance of the company.

Reliability and Completeness: An integrated report should include all material information, both positive and negative. It should be a material error-free, faithful representation of information provided by a vigorous internal control and reporting system and verified by internal and independent external audit.

Consistency and Comparability: The information in an integrated report should be presented in a consistent manner that allows intra firm comparison of performance over time as well as inter-firm to the extent applicable.

Integrating Reporting by integrating six forms of capital and eight elements through financial, quantitative and qualitative information embraces performance evaluation on all four parameters—Financial, Governance, Social and Environment, of a company. It gives a holistic view of the firm's past, present and future prospects.

THE INVESTMENT GOAL

The goal of a company could range from generating large returns on its investments to being a non-profit organization that focuses on creating social value (Fig. 8.3). Public demand and regulatory pressure are encouraging companies to be responsible. Growing awareness towards social and environmental concerns can be witnessed following the rise in the number of social-driven businesses that also aim to be profitable. Accordingly, different forms of investment strategies have emerged.

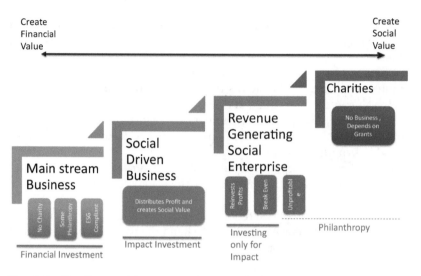

Fig. 8.3 The Range of Investment (*Source* Developed by Author)

Responsible Investment

Responsible investment is an investment strategy which seeks to generate both financial and sustainable value. Responsible investment is an approach to investing that aims to incorporate environmental, social and governance (ESG) factors into investment decisions (https://www.unpri.org/an-introduction-to-responsible-investment/what-is-responsible-investment/4780.article), to better manage risk and generate sustainable, long-term returns. If investors adopt responsible investment and prefer companies that are high on the ESG scores, it will force companies to adopt a sustainable approach to growth.

Principles for Responsible Investment (PRI), a United Nations initiative, has identified six fundamental principles, to which signatory companies must assent to. These six principles require companies to (1) include ESG factors into their investment analysis and decision-making (2) consider ESG issues in their ownership policies and practices (3) demand ESG-related disclosures from firms in which they invest (4) promote these principles (5)work towards effective implementation of the principles and (6) report on their activities and progress in regard to the principles (https://www.unpri.org/pri/what-are-the-principles-for-responsible-investment).

The PRI acts in the long-term interests of its signatories and of the financial markets and economies in which they operate and ultimately of the environment and society as a whole.

MSCI, Standard and Poor, CRISIL and other ESG ratings and indexes are available for the reference of investors and companies. Each element of ESG is composed of several sub-parameters. Environment measures factors such as companies' contribution to climate change, reduction in carbon emission and energy consumption. Social factors address issues such as diversity, human rights and philanthropy. Quality of corporate governance is considered based on aspects such as board independence, treatment of minority shareholders and disclosures.

Where the Poor Can Bank on

Grameen Bank pioneered the concept of micro-finance in Bangladesh way back in 1976. It all began when Muhammad Yunus, Head of the Rural Economics Program at the University of Chittagong, witnessed poor villagers starving to death as the country faced a famine. During his visit to the nearby village Jobra, he came across Sufia Khatun a widow with two daughters who crafted beautiful stools but earned only 2 cents a day. She borrowed money from the village moneylender who in return forced her to sell all her finished stools only to him at a miniscule price. Yunus "couldn't accept why anybody should make only two cents for such a beautiful skill" (https://www.gdrc.org/icm/grameen-art icle3.html). Professor Yunus with the help of a student identified 42 such villagers who needed a grand total of $27 to pay off the moneylender, buy their raw materials and sell their finished products in the open market. That's right; all they needed was an average of 68 cents each. With her loan of less than $1 the stool-maker's profits soared from 2 cents a day to $1.25 a day (Jhunjhunwala, 2010).

The bank thus took roots "to help poor people escape from poverty by providing loans on terms suitable to them and by teaching them a few sound financial principles so they could help themselves" https://www.nobelprize.org/prizes/peace/2006/yunus/biographical/). With its success it expanded to other parts of Bangladesh and soon got replicated in different parts of the world. Since its humble beginnings, half a century ago, it has helped to empower 10.22 million (as of Oct 2022) marginalized poor in Bangladesh through micro-credit borrowers, 97% of them being women (https://grameenbank.org/). 90% of the Bank is owned by the rural poor, mostly women who borrow from the bank. It works exclusively for them. The remaining 10% shares is owned by the government. The Grameen bank has shown the world that financial inclusion not only helps in socio-economic development of a region but makes good business sense.

Through its struggling members program Grameen Bank offers interest-free loans to help beggars build financial capacity so that they don't have to beg anymore. Already 21,383 members have given up begging and become self-sufficient. As of October 22, it has 2,568 branches working in 81,678 villages covering more than 94% of the total villages in Bangladesh (https://grameenbank.org/). The bank shares the profits (US$ 35,350.14) (https://grameenbank.org/) with its borrowers by declaring huge dividends each year.

Points to Ponder

1. Was the Grameen Bank project CSR or Business model?
2. Are there areas of meeting points between Grameen Bank and villages of Bangladesh?
3. How did the bank integrate them into their business strategy?

Socially Responsible Investing

Socially responsible investing (SRI) goes one step further than ESG by screening investments to exclude businesses that conflict with the investor's values. Investors may avoid investing in "sin stocks" that generated profits through undesirable products or services—alcohol, tobacco, weapons or gambling. SRI uses ESG factors to apply negative or positive screens. An investor may prefer to invest in companies with high gender diversity. A company may have a high ESG score and still be unacceptable to an investor. ITC, the leading tobacco manufacturer of India, "is rated AA by MSCI on ESG, the highest among global tobacco players and better than most Indian FMCG companies. This is backed by its strong credentials—ITC has been carbon positive for 15 years, water positive for 18 years and solid waste recycling positive for 13 years" (Mirchandani, 2020). An investor may however prefer not to invest in a tobacco (sin) company and choose a more 'ethical' company with a lower rating.

Impact Investment

Impact investing refers to actively making investments that create measurable, beneficial social or environment impact while also providing a financial return. Investment in renewable energy, micro-finance and education to weaker sections of society are examples of impact investment. Unlike Social Enterprises that are not-for-profit businesses with social good as their focal point; "socially driven" businesses describe their primary business goals as "results" or "profits". Simultaneously, the investors necessarily intend to create a social or environmental impact; it is not a by-product of the business. It is different from social responsible investing which considers both positive and negative screening. Targeted positive impact is quintessential for considering it Impact Investment.

REFERENCES

Shital Jhunjhunwala, Unit 14, Ethics, Governance and CSR In Practice/Case Studies, MS-495 [Ethics and Corporate governance] of MBA (Banking and Finance), IGNOU.

http://www.grameen-info.org/. Accessed on December 7, 2022.

Sanam Mirchandani. (2020, December 10). ITC is best in class on ESG, says Jefferi, https://economictimes.indiatimes.com/markets/stocks/news/itc-is-best-in-class-on-esg-says-jefferies/articleshow/79640393.cms?utm_source=contentofinterest&utm_medium=text&utm_campaign=cppst. Accessed April 2021.

https://www.unpri.org/pri/what-are-the-principles-for-responsible-investment. Accessed April 2021.

http://integratedreporting.org/what-the-tool-for-better-reporting/get-to-grips-with-the-six-capitals/. Accessed October 21, 2018.

John Elkington. (1997). Cannibals with Forks: The Triple Bottom Line of 21st Century Business.

G4, Sustainable Reporting Guidelines, Global Reporting Initiative.

S Jhunjhunwala, Beyond financial reporting-international integrated reporting framework, *Indian Journal of Corporate Governance*, 7(1), (73–80).

World Commission on Environment and Development (WCED), (1987). *Our common future*, Oxford: Oxford University Press, (p. 43).

NDTV (2018), Delhi's Air Quality Deteriorates, May Get Worse Today https://www.ndtv.com/delhi-news/delhis-air-quality-deteriorates-may-get-worse-today-1931759 and Emergency plan for Delhi air pollution to come into action tomorrow, https://www.ndtv.com/delhi-news/delhi-air-pollution-emergency-plan-for-delhi-air-pollution-to-come-into-action-tomorrow-1931878

https://www.nobelprize.org/prizes/peace/2006/yunus/biographical/. Accessed December 7, 2022.

https://www.gdrc.org/icm/grameen-article3.html.   Accessed   December   7, 2022.

SEBI. (2021, May). Business responsibility and sustainability reporting by listed entities, sebi.gov.in/sebi_data/commondocs/may-2021/Business%20respons ibility%20and%20sustainability%20reporting%20by%20listed%20entitiesAnnex ure1_p.PDF

CHAPTER 9

Managing Conflict—Measures and Mechanism

Going the extra mile

GOVERNANCE MECHANISMS TO MANAGE CONFLICT

Good governance is about 'taking care of all stakeholders'. As we discussed earlier, each stakeholder has their own set of conflicting expectations. To minimize conflicts among different stakeholders, various measures have been put in place, such as auditors to prevent misrepresentation of financial statements and independent directors to minimize abuse of powers by inside directors. Committees such as audit, nomination and remuneration committee have been formed to improve the governance mechanism. We have already discussed the role of auditors, independence directors and committees in different chapters. However as the scams over the years brought out various other problems caused by conflicts, to address them several measures have been taken such as establishing a Code of Ethics, prohibition of Insider Trading, implementing a Whistle-Blower Policy and monitoring of Related Party Transactions.

INSIDER TRADING

Insider trading involves trading in a company's shares by someone who has non-public, material information about that stock for any reason. Insider trading involves three elements—Insider, Trading and Unpublished price sensitive information (UPSI).

© The Author(s), under exclusive license to Springer Nature
Singapore Pte Ltd. 2023
S. Jhunjhunwala, *Corporate Governance*,
https://doi.org/10.1007/978-981-99-2707-4_9

Insider: is any connected person such as director or key managerial personnel or any other officer of a company in possession of or is reasonably expected to have access to any non-public price sensitive information in respect of a security.

Trading: means and includes subscribing, buying, selling, dealing or agreeing to subscribe, buy, sell or deal in any securities in any form.

Unpublished price sensitive information (UPSI): refers to any information, relating to a company or its securities that is not presently available to public, which upon becoming published is likely to materially affect the price of the securities.

Insider Trading means an act of subscribing, buying, selling, dealing or agreeing to subscribe, buy, sell or deal in any securities by any person closely associated with the company such as director, key managerial personnel or any other officer of a company who has or is reasonably expected to have access to any non-public price sensitive information in respect of securities of company.

Rajat Gupta a former corporate head of McKinsey & Company and a member on board of several large US companies provided insider information to Galleon hedge-fund founder Raj Rajaratnam about a $5 billion Berkshire Hathaway investment in Goldman Sachs. He was convicted of insider trading only because he disclosed an UPSI. The US Securities and Exchange Commission (SEC) defines illegal insider trading as: *"The buying or selling a security, in breach of a fiduciary duty or other relationship of trust and confidence, on the basis of material, non-public information about the security"*. It thus involves breaking trust that the company has in the person. Communicating or helping in acquiring unpublished price sensitive information is also a breach of trust and consider as insider trading. If a company officer shares UPSI to an outsider, who then traders on it, the officer will be considered guilty of insider trading. In 2020 SEC charged an Amazon Manager and her family with Insider Trading. Laksha Bohra worked as a senior manager in Amazon's tax department, through which she allegedly acquired, and tipped her husband Viky Bohra with highly confidential information about Amazon's financial performance. Viky Bohra and his father, Gotham Bohra, traded on this confidential information reaping illicit profits of approximately $1.4 million (SEC, 2020).

Prohibition of Insider Trading

Most countries have regulations that prohibit or restrict insider trading such as Prohibition of Insider Trading Regulations, 2015 issued by SEBI in India. It is deemed illegal and can attract fine and prison sentence. Giving a "tip" can land you in trouble. The objective of prohibiting insider trading is to disallow insiders to make unfair gains due to the private information they have. In several scams such as Enron and Satyam, it was noticed that those in control, falsified accounts to show a rosy financial picture to boost share prices and make a quick buck before the firm collapsed. There is a need to have some restriction on trading activities by insiders to maintain efficiency of financial markets.

However, genuine investors who are risking their money, even if they are insiders must be given a chance to buy and sell shares after taking adequate precautions. One way this is done is to allow insiders to trade provided they disclosed their trading plan in advance.

WHISTLE-BLOWING

The act (often by an employee or former employee) of disclosing an action which he/she believes to be unethical, immoral, illegal, corrupt, fraudulent, harmful, undesirable or against public interest to higher authority or external agency is referred to as whistle-blowing. Whistle-blowers are the persons who blow the whistle, that is, raise their voice and inform the public or the concerned person about any inappropriate or undesirable activity going on inside the organization.

Whistle-blowers may be of different kinds. If the person appears on national television and blows the whistle on corruption in a government then it is a form of open, external and freewill whistle-blowing. The identity of the individual is known and hence open; it is done outside the organization hence external, and not out of any compulsion hence freewill. If he had instead used a fake account on social media or used a platform such as Wikileaks, he could have remained anonymous. Manjunath, a fresh management graduate was working as a sales officer for the Indian Oil Corporation. When he tried to report the practice of adulteration in a petrol station to his superiors, he was burnt alive by the owners of the said petrol station. Manjunath was just doing his duty and informing the matter within the organization, hence internal and dutiful (Table 9.1).

Table 9.1
Whistleblowers'
Typology

Types of Whistle-Blowers	
Internal	External
Open	Anonymous
Dutiful	Freewill
Manjunath	Fake Twitter Account

Source Developed by Author

Whistle-Blower Policy

Companies are required to have a Whistle-Blower Policy to encourage reporting of any wrongdoings and protect the whistle-blower from being victimized. Many scams both in the corporates and in governments have come to light due to whistle-blowers. The board is responsible for laying down a clear policy and ensuring the operation of an effective whistle-blowing or vigil mechanism. With this objective in mind, the process must be overseen by an independent director such as the chairman of the audit committee or an outside ombudsman. The policy should clearly spell out the persons who can complain, the process, the authority to whom complain is to be made, the redressal procedure and measures for protecting the whistle-blower. The formal structure of the policy would depend on the relevant regulations the company is subject to.

Benefits of Whistle-Blower Policy

The effective protection of whistle-blowers and confidential handling of the disclosures made, are central to promoting integrity and preventing corruption. Whistle-blowers can play a significant role in revealing information that would otherwise go undetected, leading to improvements in the prevention, detection, investigation and prosecution of fraud or corruption. The risk of corruption is heightened in environments where reporting is not facilitated nor whistle blowers protected (G20 High-Level Principles for the Effective Protection of Whistleblowers, 2019).

A Whistle-Blower Policy

- Is effective in exposing and preventing corruption, fraud and other types of wrongdoing in the public and private sectors.

- Provides Whistle-blowers protection, shields them from retaliation or awards compensation
- Increases corporate accountability—encourages companies towards safer products, cleaner environment, etc. (see Box Uber).

The Uber Roller Coaster Ride

In 2009 Kalanick and Camp conceived the idea of a smartphone app that could be used to order rides from private drivers on demand after the two experienced difficulty catching cab rides in San Francisco. Thus, was born Uber Technologies Ltd and the ride sharing industry. However 4 months into operations it faced regulatory objections as it did not comply with cab operating relations. But this didn't deter CEO Kalanick from embarking on an aggressive campaign to dominate the ride-sharing industry, expanding first across the U.S. and then internationally. By 2014—less than four years after launching its app—Uber was operating in more than 250 cities in 53 countries.....Revenue, which was $125 million in 2013, rose to $6.5 billion three years later. In the words of an early employee, Kalanick's focus was "growth above all else." This mindset was reflected in the company's 14 cultural values, which encouraged behaviors such as 'always be hustling,' 'make magic,' and "toe-stepping" (Larcker & Tayan, 2017). In each city across the world they faced resistance from regulators and taxi drivers. However they build a huge base of customers and drivers by offering incredulously low prices to passengers and unbelievably high returns to Uber drivers making it impossible for authorities to shut them down.

Their aggressive strategies and disregard for laws and rules caused them problems in London, Paris, Johannesburg, China and South Korea. Meanwhile drivers were complaining of falling revenues as incentives that had made it so attractive suddenly stopped, making it difficult for them to pay the loan instalments on the car they had bought. "Reports of bullying, sexism and sexual harassment within the company surfaced with alarming regularity."(Lownsbrough, 2017). Richard Jacobs a former employee in a letter claimed Uber's Marketplace Analytics team obtained through illegal and fraudulent means confidential information and trade secrets from competitors. Encrypted, ephemeral chat app Wickr, secret servers and devices that couldn't be traced back to Uber was used for this purpose (Zaveri, 2017). Uber ultimately reached a $4.5 million dollar settlement with Jacobs, and paid an additional $3 million to his lawyers (Conger, 2017). On Ubers' claim that the whistleblower was extorting the company,

Judge Alsup argued that Uber would not have made such a massive payment to Jacobs if there was no merit to his claims. "You said it was a fantastic BS letter, nothing to it. And yet you paid $4.5 million dollars" (Conger, 2017). In 2017, after scandals of unethical conduct spread from the offices of San Francisco to incidents of sexual harassment of women passengers by drivers in Delhi, the board finally fired co-founder and CEO Kalanick.

Points to Ponder:

1. What was the impact of whistle-blowing on the company?
2. What form of whistle-blowing was this?
3. Would you consider the company ethical? What made it so?

Legal Framework

Necessary legal framework has been established in many countries to encourage and protect whistle-blowers. The Whistleblower Protection Act was made into federal law in the USA in 1989. The Sarbanes Oxley Act also provides for whistle-blowing mechanism and Dodd-Frank Act of 2010 gave it more teeth by rewarding whistle-blowers with 10–30% of the money recovered due to the information received. In France, the rights and remedies for whistle-blowers have been covered under the French Labour Code. Japan's Whistleblower Protection Act (WPA) came into effect on 1 April 2006. Protection for whistle-blowers in the UK is provided under the Public Interest Disclosure Act 1998 (PIDA), which amends the Employment Rights Act 1996. Canada established the Public Servants Disclosure Protection Act in 2005. Both Companies Act and LODR require Indian Companies to set up adequate whistle-blower mechanism.

The G20 High-Level Principle for the Effective Protection of Whistle-blower adopted by the G20 countries can be used as a basis for creating an effective framework. The High-Level Principles focus on five core pillars: (1) legal framework, (2) scope of protected disclosures, (3) procedure for protected disclosures, (4) remedies and effective protection against retaliation and (5) effective enforcement and self-evaluation of the legal framework (see Table 9.2).

Table 9.2 G20 High-Level Principle for the Effective Protection of Whistle-blower

Legal Framework	Principle 1: Establish and implement clear laws and policies for the protection of whistleblowers
Scope Of Protected Disclosures	Principle 2: The scope of protected disclosures should be broadly but clearly defined
	Principle 3: Protection should be available to the broadest possible range of reporting persons
Procedure For Protected Disclosures	Principle 4: Provide for visible reporting channels and adequate support to whistleblowers
	Principle 5: Ensure confidentiality for whistleblowers
Remedies And Effective Protection Against Retaliation	Principle 6: Define retaliation against whistleblowers in a comprehensive way
	Principle 7: Ensuring robust and comprehensive protection for whistleblowers
	Principle 8: Provide for effective, proportionate and dissuasive sanctions for those who retaliate
	Principle 9: Ensure that whistleblowers cannot be held liable in connection with protected disclosures
Effective Enforcement and Evaluation of the Legal Framework	Principle 10: Conduct training, capacity-building and awareness-raising activities
	Principle 11: Monitor and assess the effectiveness and implementation of the framework
	Principle 12: Lead the way on the protection of whistleblowers

Adopted from The G20 Anti-Corruption Working Group, G20 High-Level Principle for the Effective Protection of Whistleblower, 2019

CODE OF ETHICS

A code of ethics document may outline the mission and values of the business or organization, how employees are supposed to approach problems, the ethical principles based on the organization's core values, and the standards to which the company representatives are held. Ethical codes are adopted by organizations to assist members in understanding the difference between right and wrong and in applying that understanding to their decisions. While many laws exist to set basic ethical standards, it is largely up to the company to develop their code of ethics based on the ethical principles that govern decisions and behaviour at the company. They should provide general outlines of how employees should behave, as well as specific guidance for handling issues such as harassment, safety and bribery.

A separate code of conduct may be laid down for directors and senior management of the company. These may address additional issues such as insider trading and conflict of interest. Schedule IV of Companies Act 2013 lays down a separate code for Independent Directors. The code focuses on the directors acting objectively and ensuring they exercise independent judgement at all time.

RELATED PARTY TRANSACTIONS

A company, as part of its activities enters into deals with different parties, some of who may be related party. Related party transaction are a normal aspect of business.

A related party transaction (RPT) is an agreement to buy, sell, exchange or transfer assets, goods, services or obligations between the company and a related party. It is irrelevant whether consideration has been paid or not and whether that consideration is adequate. A related party is a person or entity that has a pre-existing connection with the company.

Related Person: A person or a close member of that person's family is related if that person exercises control, or significant influence over the company, the directors or its key management personnel. Directors and Senior executives exercise control over the company and are thus related party. Their immediate family—parents, spouse, children, siblings also are treated as related persons.

Related Entity: An entity is related to the company if, it is a parent, subsidiary, fellow subsidiary, associate or in a joint venture with the company or it is controlled, jointly controlled or significantly influenced or managed by a person who is a related party. If two companies have the same director, they are considered related party to each other.

Because of this relationship, companies may enter into transactions with related party on terms that would have been different if they were outside parties. A company may rent out an apartment it owns to its CEO at a rate far below fair market price. This is not illegal. The question that needs to be asked is, is it in the interest of the company or not. This may be a perquisite negotiated with CEO to recruit him and not necessarily disadvantageous to the company.

While entering into a contract or arrangement, the company may give favourable treatment to related party in terms of pricing, or credit period, or some other condition which unfavourably impacts the company. Although related party transactions are themselves legal, they may create situations of conflict of interest. Suppose the board of a company awards a contract to one of the director's brother for purchasing machinery. The said director is supposed to protect the interest of the company, but as a sibling he is also to promote his brother's interest. Thus arises a conflict of interest.

The proposed deal between Satyam Computers and Maytas is a classic example of conflict of interest occurring in related party transactions. (Refer The Satyam Scandal in Chapter 5). RPTs may not always be of disadvantage to a company. The problem arises when the power drawn from this relationship is abused. RPTs can very easily be used to divert resources or siphon funds. Monitoring and transparency of these transactions is essential.

Monitoring Related Party Transactions

Regulatory frameworks use a combination of measures to monitor and restrict RPTs (Fig. 9.1).

Restriction of RPTs: Some RPTs may be restricted by law. Brazil, Estonia, France, Hungary, India, Korea, Portugal, Turkey and the USA prohibit companies from giving loans to Directors (OECD, 2021). The collapse of World.com one of the largest telecommunication companies of its time can be traced to the loan given to the CEO. As a result the SOX disallowed personal loans to directors in 2002 itself. In India executive directors may be allowed to avail loans on the same terms as granted to all employees of the company if duly approved in a shareholder meeting by at least 75% of the members present.

Board Approval: Board approval of majority members is required in most countries for at least non-routine material RPTs. Related /interested directors are not to participate in the process. RPTs that are entered into by the company is in ordinary course of business and on an arm's length basis do not require approval. Arm's length implies that the terms of

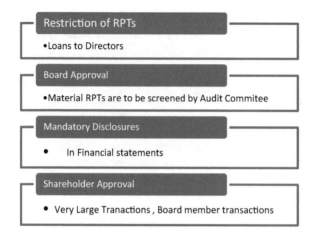

Fig. 9.1   Monitoring RPTs (*Source* Developed By Author)

transaction are same as they would be if they were unrelated. If a company sells its product for $100 to all customers and also sells it to the related party for $100, the transaction is considered at arm's length. If customers are required to make payment on the spot and the related party is given a credit period of three months, the transactions cannot be considered as at arm's length, as all terms of conditions are not same.

In addition several counties insist that the RPT be reviewed by the audit committee or independent director(s) to examine the terms of the agreement, to determine whether it can be considered at arm's length, and if not, whether the terms are in any way unfavourable to the company. Canada, France and few other countries even require that an independent expert evaluate the RPT. In India all RPTs are to be approved by the audit committee. The Audit Committee may make omnibus approval for a period of one year for RPTs that are routine and repetitive in nature such as purchase of raw material on a regular basis. It may specify the conditions of approval, such as the price range for the deal.

Shareholders' Approval: In addition to board approval consent from shareholders may be required for certain transactions. When a company enters into large Related Party Transaction, exceeding a certain percentage (5–10%) of its assets or turnover, approval by way of resolution from the shareholders of the Company is to be taken in India, China, Russia, Spain and the UK. Canada, New Zealand, South Africa require shareholder's approval if the transaction value is above a specified proportion of its market capitalization. Greece, Indonesia and New Zealand seek approval for RPTs in which board of directors are interested. Austria, Brazil, Denmark and Japan do not have requirement of shareholder approval (OECD, 2021). In France, while shareholder voting on RPTs are required, those that are not approved by shareholders can nevertheless be entered into. In such cases, the interested party can be held liable for any detrimental consequences that the transaction may have had on the company. The rules as can be seen are quite varied across nations. Shareholders who are the related party in a transaction are generally not permitted to vote on such resolutions.

Disclosures: Transparency of RPTs is essential to ensure that the transactions are in the interest of the stakeholders. International accounting standards mandate extensive disclosures with regard to RPTs in the financial statements. Most important are appropriate disclosures of RPTs with board members, key managerial personnel and controlling or large shareholders as they have the opportunity to misuse company assets and misappropriate funds. EU's Shareholder Rights Directive II (SRD II) require its Member States to provide immediate disclosure of material related party transactions.

From 'Icon' to 'Bars'

Shares of ICICI bank, largest private bank in India lost 28% market value in three months ending March 2018. The profits of March quarter were half of what it was the previous year. This was due to a sharp rise in provision for bad loans. To add to the bank woes was the 'conflict of interest' scandal against their CEO Chanda Kochhar. At the heart of it was a 3250 crore ($456 Million) loan sanctioned by her to Videocon Group allegedly for a quid pro quo (Mukherjee, 2019). The loan soon became a non-performing asset. Her husband Deepak Kochhar had set up a joint venture 'Nupower Renewables' with Videocon promoter Venugopal Dhoot. Using complex web of transactions large amounts of money was transferred to it. Dhoot later transferred his stake in the firm to Kochhar (ET Online).

Once Central Bureau of Investigation (CBI) stated examining the case share prices of ICICI started falling further. Though the board of ICICI bank initially gave their CEO a clean chit, on mounting pressure they were forced to remove her (Mukherjee, 2019). Chanda Kocchar should have recused herself from the credit committee that sanctioned the loan.

Her failure to do so led to her finally being fired from the bank. Chanda Kocchar had joined ICICI bank as a management trainee and in a short period of 25 years became MD and CEO of the company (ET online). Once an Icon for millions of women, an inspiration as someone who broke the corporate glass ceiling in conservative India, today she is behind bars.

Conflict of Interest

Conflict of Interest as we saw earlier is a situation in which a person is in a position to derive personal benefit from actions or decisions made in their official capacity and serving one could involve working against the other. The directors have a fiduciary duty towards the company. If at any time a conflict of interest arises in any decision being taken by the board, it is necessary for a director to give full disclosure of his interest and refrain from participating in it. There may be situations which don't strictly fall under the related party transactions but all still conflict of interest. For instance if a director or his family member works or provides consultancy to a major competitor. Rajat Gupta starting his own consultancy while still working for McKinsey was a conflict of interest. Chanda Kocchar apparently abused her power as MD & CEO at the bank by authorising loans rife with 'conflict of interest' for personal gains (see Box from Icon to Bars).

REFERENCES

Bloomber, ICICI Board must answer for the scandal around Chanda Kochhar, *The Economic Times*, January 31, 2019. https://economictimes.indiat imes.com/industry/banking/finance/banking/icici-board-must-answer-for-the-scandal-around-chanda-kochhar/articleshow/67769515.cms?utm_sou rce=contentofinterest&utm_medium=text&utm_campaign=cppst. Aaccessed Sepember 4 , 2021.

Andy Mukerjee , ICICI Board must answer for the scandal around Chanda Kochhar, *The Economic Times*, January 31, 2019. https://economictimes.ind iatimes.com/industry/banking/finance/banking/icici-board-must-answer-for-the-scandal-around-chanda-kochhar/articleshow/67769515.cms?utm_sou rce=contentofinterest&utm_medium=text&utm_campaign=cppst. Aaccessed September 4 , 2021.

Conger, K. (2017, November 29). Uber says whistleblower was extorting the compan. https://gizmodo.com

ET online , The fall of a star banker: Why Chanda Kochhar quit, https://eco nomictimes.indiatimes.com/industry/banking/finance/banking/the-fall-of-a-star-banker-what-did-chanda-kochhar-in/articleshow/66070721.cms?utm_source=contentofinterest&utm_medium=text&utm_campaign=cppst accessed April 14, 2022.

Larcker, D. F. & Tayan, B. (2017, December). Governance gone wild: Epic misbehavior at Uber technologies. https://www.gsb.stanford.edu

Lownsbrough, H. (2017, July 13). Uber's practices are morally unacceptable – but a boycott won't help. *The Guardian*. https://www.theguardian.com

OECD, (2021). OECD Corporate Governance Factbook.

Paayal Zaveri. (2017). Unsealed letter in Uber-Waymo case details how Uber employees allegedly stole trade secrets, CNBC, December 15 2017 , https://www.cnbc.com/2017/12/15/jacobs-letter-in-uber-waymo-case-says-uber-staff-stole-trade-secrets.html

SEBI. (2015). Prohibition of Insider Trading Regulations, India.

Rawat, S. R., Raj, V., Manoharan, A., & Vineet, S. (2013). Rajat Gupta: An American Dream Upturned, *Indian Journal of Corporate Governance*, 6(2), 42–51.

The G20 Anti-Corruption Working Group. (2019). G20 High-Level Principle for the Effective Protection of Whistleblower.

US Securities and Exchange Commission. (2020, September 28) SEC Charges Amazon Finance Manager and Family With Insider Trading, https://www.sec.gov/news/press-release/2020-228

CHAPTER 10

Building Dynamic Boards

If Everyone Thinks Alike What's the Use of a Board

Creating Value-Adding Boards[1]

A board may prove to be one of the following: a board that creates negative value (deteriorates the company from its earlier position); a board that creates no value (ensures compliance and maintains status quo) or; a board that creates value (through vision, strategic guidance and monitoring). Every board desires and strives to be a 'value creator'. They want to live up to the expectations made from them. They want to build great companies. Great companies are not just 'tracked by history', they 'create history'. A far-sighted board with a strong character and the ability to do things differently can do just that. It calls for a board with a vibrant personality, a 360 degree view capable of taking complex decisions in trying situations and making sure that those decisions are implemented, yet, quickly changing these very decisions taken by them, if circumstances change. Such a board needs to be made of heterogeneous members in terms of personality, gender, age, race, nationality, educational and experience background to bring diversity in views, capabilities and approach.

The company's success and long-term survival is dependent on board decisions. Their decisions impact shareholder, employees, customers and all other stakeholders. Being a top performer in a highly complex

---

[1] (adopted Mishra and Jhunjhunwala, Diversity and the Effective board, 2013).

© The Author(s), under exclusive license to Springer Nature Singapore Pte Ltd. 2023
S. Jhunjhunwala, *Corporate Governance*,
https://doi.org/10.1007/978-981-99-2707-4_10

and competitive environment requires a dynamic board. One that can comprehend the global environment, political and economic conditions in different countries, industry's competitiveness and nuances, market situation, financial and legal aspects, latest technology and has the ability to innovate and overcome challenges faced in turbulent times. The board must thus possess a wide range of knowledge, competencies and perspective. Such "completeness" is possible if the directors come from different backgrounds in terms of education, experience, country and time periods. Successful boards are those that choose the right combination of heterogeneous directors and by correctly managing the complexities of diversity, leverage those differences to their advantage.

BOARD DIVERSITY[2]

Board diversity refers to the heterogeneous composition of the board in terms of gender, age, race, education, experience, nationality, lifestyle, culture, religion and many other facets that make each of us unique as individuals. A well-performing board needs diversity of knowledge, skills and perspectives. If everybody thinks in the same way what is the need of a board? It may as well be a one man show. Diversity for its own sake, however, is not an improvement in governance; what matters is the combination of complementary talent and experiences of members that enables boards to steer the company towards success and long-term stability.

There are two categories of diversity—Surface-level and deep-level diversity. Surface level consists of observable and non-observable diversity. Deep-level diversity is concerned with personality—Cognitive features such as perceptions, values and personal characteristics.

Observable diversity: Attributes of directors that are easily determinable or *visible* fall under this category. *Demographic* factors such as race/ethnic background, nationality, gender and age are examples of observable features.

Gender Diversity: Gender diversity refers to the proportion of females to males. Men and women behave differently. Women are believed to be more intuitive in decision-making, have the ability to multi-task and

[2] (adopted from Mishra and Jhunjhunwala, Diversity and the Effective board, 2013).

are better at relation-building. Men tend to be more task-focused and decisions are based on information and procedures.

Age Diversity: Age diversity indicates the mix of members of different ages. Younger people are perceived to be more flexible with high energetic levels, willing to take risk, conversant with and capable of easily adapting new technology. They have the ability to grasp complex mathematical models and a deep understanding of the ability, reach and limitations of online platforms and social media. The board may on the other hand benefit with the wide experience of the senior members. Senior members often have strong networks and clout which the company can leverage.

Regional Diversity: Regional Diversity implies board has members of different nationalities. In a globalized world, having a board that understands how different countries operate, their business environment and people is a necessity. Foreign directors bring with them rich experience. Further people from different countries have different lifestyles, cultural and upbringing that bring alternate perspectives and solutions to the table. Foreign directors can be expected to act more independently.

Tenure Diversity: It measures the balance between new and old directors. Having esteemed directors on boards for a long length of time improves corporate reputation. Directors who have been on the board for long, develop a good understanding of the company enabling them to take quick and appropriate decisions. This also causes the risk of directors becoming complacent and unwilling to change past strategic decisions and practices in accordance with current business conditions. Long association with management can impact their independence. A fresh pair of eyes always brings with it a new perspective. Having a mix of old and new directors would be beneficial by adding "new blood to the board" while providing continuity.

Race/Ethnic/Community/Caste/Religion Diversity: Literature mostly discusses race and ethnic diversity in boards given the social structure of countries such as USA, Singapore and Malaysia. It suggests that people of all race and ethnic groups should be represented on the board. The idea may be extended to include any social stratification such as religion, community or caste. Majority members may stigmatize minority making it difficult for them to perform to their potential. An open and conducive environment should be created. It is important that the minorities are selected not just as a token but are competent people who are treated as peers so that they can effectively contribute to board activities.

Non-Observable diversity: It relates to attributes that are less visible such as educational qualification, expertise and experience.

Multi-disciplinary: Multi-disciplinary boards are expected to be useful in decisions that are high in complexity and have many interdependent subtasks. Members with complementary education, knowledge and skills can take a more comprehensive approach to problem solving. Research indicates that teams that are multi-disciplinary are likely to be more innovative.

Cross-Functional: Members with varied experience—functional, industry-specific, specialized skills—look at problems differently and focus on different aspects of issue under consideration. This leads to creative problem solving and innovative decision-making.

Personality Diversity: The personality of an individual is framed by his or her attitudes, attributes, social endowment and skills. People differ not only in their interest and skill but also in the way they perceive, their reactions, values, motivations and the way they arrive at conclusions. While some characteristics may be desirable for all board members, such as confidence, accountability, self-motivated, honesty and integrity, having boards with diverse personal traits will help board members take up different responsibilities and play various roles (visionary, executor) in the decision process.

Rationale for Board Diversity

Great ideas come from differences. Differences can be created by diversifying the board. 'Homogeneity at the top of a company is believed to result in a narrow perspective while diverse top managers take a broader view. The result of diversity at the top is a better understanding of the complexities of the environment and more astute decisions' (Carter, 2003). Heterogeneous boards with dissimilar opinions and approaches foster critical thinking and creative problem solving to effect better decision-making, allow active monitoring and boost strategic direction. All the components are essential for corporate success.

Innovation and Creativity Problem Solving: People from different backgrounds and with different life experiences are likely to approach similar problems in different ways. Evidence indicates that more diverse groups foster creativity and produce a greater range of perspectives and solutions to problems. That is, diverse groups are less likely to suffer from *groupthink*.

Talent Acquiring and employee relationship: Companies are facing a talent crunch that goes right up to the top. Hiring women, minority and people from different parts of the world can increase the talent pool of corporate boards. A diverse board facilitates a more inclusive hiring and is better equipped at managing diverse employees.

Understanding of Business Market Place: Firms exposure to a wide variety of cultures, ideas and views at every level of the organization, including the board is needed to meet the demands of increasingly diverse customers and clients. A heterogeneous board will have a better understanding of the market place, increasing sales performance and thereby profitability. Together with a diverse employee base, they will be able to customize products and services to the specific needs of multiple communities and penetrate new markets.

Access to resources and networks: A primary responsibility of the board is to build external linkages and acquire resources for the firm (refer Resource Dependency theory). By selecting directors with different characteristics, firms may gain access to different resources. For instance, directors with financial industry experience can help firms to gain access to specific investors. Directors with political connections may help firms deal with regulators or win government contracts. Dissimilar group members may also contribute to by acquiring information through a more diverse set of sources. A minority members' networks is likely to give them access to a completely alternate set of information.

Reputation Enhancer: Including women, minorities (ethnic, religious, etc.) and stakeholders' representatives (employees, suppliers or minority shareholders) on board helps firms to enhance their reputation as being socially responsible. They are perceived as companies that protect the interest of all stakeholders gaining respect in the eyes of media, government and public at large.

Diversity, it is argued, enhances the effectiveness of corporate leadership. While the above provide business justification for board diversity, there is also a social argument. Appointment of women, minority race and lower caste on boards will be an affirmative action for social and economic upliftment.

Constraints of Board Diversity

Though diversity for enhancing board performance is logical and intuitively sound and has become a widely accepted view, empirical findings have not been that convincing. Creating a diverse board can be a challenge in terms of finding competent people. Diverse board like any heterogeneous team face the problem of mutual trust and understanding among members.

Group Conflict: Diversity may increase friction among sub groups and create communication bottlenecks that interfere with board functioning. Effective communicating among a team who do not share a common technical language or perspective can be challenging. Foreign directors may have difficulty even following the language. Often the question of status or superiority among members creates conflict.

Limited Talent: The proportion of women, lower caste or minority race with adequate qualification and experience needed for board-level appointment are few. Those who meet these requirements can be expected to hold multiple directorships. Thus no one company gains a competitive edge by hiring them. Increased workload may also reduce their efficiency. Finding suitable candidate may be difficult.

Tokenism: It is important not to appoint directors just on the criteria of diversity. There is no point appointing a 'woman' who does not have the necessary skill or experience to participate in board deliberations. Those in minority are ever so often unable to have their views heard. Instead of new ideas and views, it may lead to stifled voices and dominance by few.

Making Diversity Work

To reap the fruits, boards must successfully manage diversity. Instead of shunning diversity, boards need to minimize the conflict that diversity often introduces and learn to respect and work with colleagues who are selected because they are 'different'. Coordination efforts are required to increase group cohesiveness and improve flow of communication. Conflicts can be avoided by clearly defining process, roles and expectations and building mutual trust with each other.

Communication is another critical factor that influences the boards' effectiveness. Body language, tone of voice and face expression are as important as words. While constructive arguments are an integral part of decision-making process, it should not become a personal battle. Board discussions should take place in a conducive environment where members talk to each other, not against each other, or to the chairman.

The chairperson by involving everyone in discussions and quickly resolve conflicts can set the tone for synchronization. *The feeling of unity in diversity is essential.* Spirit of oneness among directors and willingness to work together in the interest of the company's stakeholders will create a dynamic board where members' co-create strategy to create value for the company. A winning board is one that can *leverage the diversity*.

BOARD SELECTION[3]

As we have seen again and again layers of regulation does not stop companies from poor governance. Value creation will occur when there is a significant improvement in the quality and functioning of directors serving on the board. The board members meet four times a year, may be eight times in some of the more active boards. They have to take decisions with whatever information is available and within a limited time. No resources are allotted to them. It is the CEO and his team that run the show. Yet it is the board that is answerable to stakeholders. They are to build long-lasting companies. Naturally, selection of the right members is critical.

Board should be formed of luminous individuals with varied skills who are geared up to face today's challenging and ever-changing business environment. The board should map its competency with the requirements of the company and accordingly select new member and replace those that have outlived their utilities.

Selecting of Board members must be based on a set of appropriate criteria, performance review of director and talent gap analysis (Table 10.1). What skills and traits are needed but lacking in the current board? Are all the members above 60 years? Is a young and energetic person needed? What functional experience is required? Are we planning several acquisitions? Should the board have a lawyer with expertise in mergers and acquisitions? Is the company planning to expand to the Middle East? Will it be useful to have someone who understands that market? Such questions need to be answered before considering appointing members to board.

---

[3] (adopted Mishra and Jhunjhunwala, Diversity and the Effective board, 2013).

Table 10.1 Choosing board members

Age	•	Young
	•	Old
Gender	•	Male
	•	Female
Tenure	•	Existing member
	•	New member
Nation	•	Which location
	•	India, South America, Middle East etc
Education	•	What level of edicatuction is required
	•	Which stream-Finance, Marketing Law, Arts, etc
Experience	•	Functional-Accounts, Human Resource, Operations, ...
	•	Industry-Steel, Software, Pharma, Real estate, ...
	•	Specialized-Branding, IPR, Designing ......
	•	Company Profile-small or big, new or mature, ...
Personality	•	What blend of Characteristics is required
	•	Organized Logical Thinker with an analytical bend or a Spontaneous lateral thinker with a collobrative approach

Source Mishra and Jhunjhunwala, Diversity and the Effective board, 2013

Suppose if the results of the analysis indicates that the board needs a member who has the traits, skills and competencies as shown in the Fig. 10.1, then efforts may be made to find a member who fits the bill. The selection process should be structured and involve all stakeholders. While it may not be possible to find the exact fit, the best possible candidate must be selected.

Ultimately what is important is unique contribution each potential broad member will bring to the table. The aim must be to have a broad talent base. There is no ideal mix of directors. It depends on the needs of the company and its business. It is important to understand the talent and skill need in future and plan accordingly. Just like employee management, board talent must be strategically managed to build a competent board with diverse perspectives and abilities. Not just CEO succession planning but a dynamic Board Succession Planning must be put in place

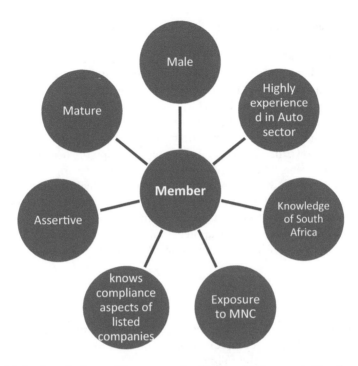

Fig. 10.1 Required candidate example (*Source* Mishra and Jhunjhunwala, Diversity and the Effective board, 2013)

where through an aggressive recruitment process, top-quality members are selected based on the current and future needs.

BOARD EVALUATION

It is important for boards to continually assess how effectively they are performing their roles against the objectives and the goals they have set for themselves. Board evaluations have becoming widely established as a critical structural tool for assessing Board success. Board Evaluation is the most effective way to ensure Board members to understand their duties and adopt effective good governance practices. To be effective, board-room appraisals need to have specific, clearly defined steps and processes, and a special commitment from the Board. Explicit guidelines and expectations are to be set at the beginning. Company cannot turn around and blame someone for not achieving an objective they did not know existed. The board as a whole, the different committees and the contribution of individual directors should be evaluated on a periodical basis.

The function of board evaluation is to understand if the board has executed their role (as unfolded in the different chapters). Have they met the expectations of different stakeholder? The broad parameters for evaluation are shown in Fig. 10.2. The outcome helps to identify and take measures to strengthen any areas of concern. It provides inputs where the competency of the board needs augmentation. Individual directors can take a stake of their own performance. Directors with continuous unsatisfactory performance should not be reappointed. The board should report the manner in which formal annual evaluation has been made by the board of its own performance and that of its committees and individual directors.

CEO Oversight

A major parameter of board success is effective monitoring of CEO and his team. Boards have repeatedly failed to do so. The board responsibility in this regard includes the following:

Selection: When it comes to selecting a new CEO, prudence really matters. Making the right choice is not easy. Before Steve Job returned and took over as CEO, Apple has two CEOs in a short span of four years. Share prices were at an all-time low. The choice can make or break a company. It is not relevant where the CEO come from inside or outside the firm. What counts is whether he/she has the right abilities. The nomination committee must judiciously identify possible candidates. CEOs must have a specific set of skill to implement the company's strategy. If the strategy changes, the skill set required from the CEO may change. In 2019 Nike board appointed veteran Tech John Donahoe, formerly CEO of eBay, to oversee a big push into ecommerce and prepare for the future; a well-forecasted move, given the growth in digital business precipitated by the COVID-19 crisis. The board must also identify areas where the CEO is weak and either adequately coach him or appoint team members that can complement him.

Compensation: CEO compensation is a function of the CEO's competency and past performance. CEOs that have a track record of enhancing shareholder wealth are rewarded with huge pay packages and perquisites. The remuneration committee has to take a call between cash incentives or stock option plans. As discussed earlier, stock options increase long-term commitment and alignment with shareholders' interest but encourage focus on short-term profits and even accounting manipulations to raise share prices. Reputed CEOs may insist on a big severance package, especially if they are being made to sign a non-compete agreement. The board should consider this with caution. The severance package should not be so attractive, as to reduce the CEO's inclination to put in his best. Boeing's former CEO, Dennis Muilenburg, was ousted in December 2019 after two fatal crashes of the company's bestselling plane, but he departed with stock and pension awards worth more than US$60 million (Smyth, 2020). On the other hand, Boeing's shareholders took a significant beating with the shares losing value.

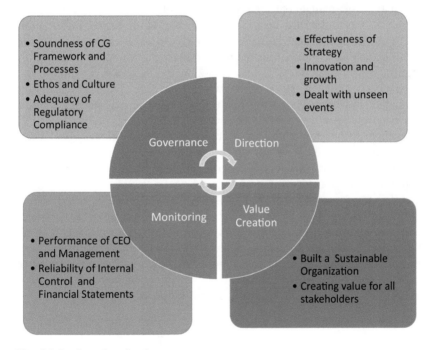

Fig. 10.2 Board evaluation

Board Relationship: The most complex aspect is the relationship between board and CEO. Board must foster a relationship of trust with the CEO. They have to determine the extent of hand holding and monitoring required. Boards should take care of successful CEOs by engaging with them and compensating them well. At the same time, successful long-serving CEOs tend to dominate boards. They may use entrenchment strategies to remain relevant. Independent directors must not get complacent, just because the company has been doing well. They must remain vigilant.

Performance Evaluation: A CEO is eager to succeed not only to increase expected compensation in the current period but also to impress the board and retain his position. The financial performance and stock market returns are commonly used to evaluate CEO performance. Results of short-term projects can enable the board to assess the new CEO's skills early in his tenure. This would however give a distorted view of the CEO's leadership and managerial abilities. Sustainable value creation is important. CEOs should thus be evaluable on their long-term performance. Factors other than financial returns should also be considered. Does the CEO behave in a transparent manner and share adequate relevant information with board. How is his relation with stakeholders—employees, customers, suppliers? How do they perceive him? What has been his contribution towards innovation and penetration of new markets? There has been a significant rise in the share of CEOs who were forced out of their positions for ethical lapses rather than financial struggles. Uber CEO was forced to leave on sexual harassment cases but McDonald's CEO Steve Easterbrook was forced to step down only on admitting to a consensual relationship with an employee.

CEO Succession: CEO turnover has been on an upward trend. When high profile CEOs leave a firm either on retirement or for greener pastures, investor react negatively. New CEOs may find it difficult to fill the shoes of their predecessors. When a CEO fails, the board should take responsibility, do a rigorous due diligence of their actions or absence of it, so as to avoid future mistakes. Proper CEO succession planning and building a pipeline for CEOs must be on the board's agenda.

REFERENCES

Carter, D. A., Simkins, B. J., & Simpson, W. G. (2003). Corporate governance, board diversity and firm value, *The Financial Review*, *38*(1), 33–53.

Mishra and Jhunjhunwala. (2013). *Diversity and the effective board*. Academic Press.

Lisa Smyth. (2020). Adapt or die': Why being a CEO is more challenging than ever, theceomagazine.com/business/management-leadership/ceo-turnover

CHAPTER 11

Corporate Governance in Family Businesses

It's all in the Family

Castle in the Air- Liquor Baron on the Rocks

Mallya, 63—a former Rajya Sabha member of parliament in India, currently living in a £11.5-million mansion near London—is fighting multiple lawsuits after defaulting on bank loans worth about Rs 9,000 crore that he had borrowed to run the now-defunct Kingfisher Airlines. Disputes over the loans led to civil lawsuits in India and the UK as well as criminal fraud charges. Indian Government is in the process of extraditing the fugitive.

The son of businessman, Vijay Mallya is the ex-chairman of United Spirits, the largest spirits company in India and United Breweries Group home of India's favourite beer—Kingfisher. Known for the lavish parties on his yachts the playboy sported Rolls Royce Ghost one of the rarest cars, and other race cars such as Jaguar XJR15 and Ferrai 1965 California Spyder ("From Yachts to Villas", n.d.). Once called the "King of Good Times" due to his extravagant lifestyle, Mallya fled from India on March 2, 2016 to his beautiful palatial house at "the most cherished addresses" in London overlooking Regent's Park, that has all the worldly luxurious things one can imagine, one of which is a golden toilet (Wiggins, K., 2018).

Founded in 2003, Kingfisher Airlines Maiden flight took off in May 2005 close to his son Sidhartha Mallya's birthday. "Urban legend has it

---

© The Author(s), under exclusive license to Springer Nature Singapore Pte Ltd. 2023
S. Jhunjhunwala, *Corporate Governance*,
https://doi.org/10.1007/978-981-99-2707-4_11

that the airline was a gift for the son……. In the evening function at the Air India hangar in Mumbai, which was attended by a whole galaxy of stars and the high and mighty from Indian politics (across party lines), Mallya, who was then a member of Parliament, spelt out his dream of creating India's largest airline" (Sanjai, P.R. & Shukla, T., 2016). In 2007 he expanded operations by acquiring crisis-laden no frill Air Deccan. The aircraft and service reflected the Kingfisher 'fly the good times' lifestyle and experience. Models were hand-picked by Mallya to be in-flight hostesses. They wore a stylish red skirt and coat (as against Sarees in Air India), underwent voice training and elocution lessons, and were taught to do their own make-up and hair. Equivalent to a finishing school, skills were built to treat passengers as guests. At its peak, Kingfisher Airlines was flying 66 planes to 68 locations, including eight international destinations, with 374 flights a day, and accounted for 20% of the market (Bandyopadhyay, T., 2013). As expected, the who's who of India served on the board of Kingfisher Airlines. It saw distinguished people such as heart surgeon Dr Naresh Trehan, tennis great Vijay Amritra, former chairman of LIC and SEBI G N Bajpai, ex-finance secretary Piyush Mankad, Rediff India founder Diwan Arun Nanda and bankers of repute serving as its independent directors (Sinha, S., 2016).

However, the airlines never made profits. By 2011 it was not able to pay airport dues and service taxes. During July—August 2012 pilots went on strike against non-payment of several months' salary. Following this its licence was suspended in October by the Directorate General of Civil Aviation (DGCA), India's aviation regulator, the airline's operating licence has since expired (Bandyopadhyay, T., 2013).

Identified as a "wilful defaulter" over Kingfisher Air, Mallya is also accused of fraudulently obtaining these loans and of laundering the money to shell companies in seven countries, including the US, France, Ireland and even to British companies (Sharma, M., 2018). A consortium of 17 banks lead by State Bank of India, the largest bank in India had lend Rs. 6000 crores to the airlines. The banks received a corporate guarantee from United Breweries Holdings Ltd, the holding company of the group, and a personal guarantee from Mallya. Finally, they also took as collateral the Kingfisher brand, valued at ₹ 3,000 crore by audit firm Grant Thornton India. An indication of the kind of sway Mallya once exerted over the bankers, he had the banks pay him ₹ 98 crore for offering his personal guarantee (Bandyopadhyay, T., 2013).

Points to Ponder:

1. Why was Kingfisher Airlines set up? Should a liquor group have diversified into this industry?
2. Where did you think the company draw its philosophy from?
3. Did Mallya create the company to fraud money out of bank?

FAMILY BUSINESS

About 80% of companies worldwide and 40% of Fortune 500 companies are family businesses. (https://www.ifc.org/wps/wcm/connect/top ics_ext_content/ifc_external_corporate_site/ifc+cg/regional_advisory_ programs/middle+east+and+north+africa). Walmart, Volkswagen, Ford, Facebook are all family firms. While there is no universal definition, a business may be considered a family business, a family firm or a family-managed company when the founder either individually or along with family members, or their descendants own majority stake or control decision-making. Family-owned businesses may be the oldest form of business organization. Farms are probably the earliest kind of family business where all members of the family are involved in farming activity. Family life and business get intertwined. Family structure defines organization structure. Key positions are kept in the family.

In patriarchal societies of Asia, the senior most male member who is the head of the family will be the Chairman cum Managing Director of the company. As there is now a need to separate these positions, the younger brother or son will be made CEO. Several members of the board will be family members. In addition, many extended family members or relatives are employees of the company. Hence owners, board of directors, senior management and even employees are all family members. 49.3% of the shares of Bajaj Auto Ltd, the primary company of the Bajaj group, are owned by 23 family members and other family-owned organizations of which Bajaj Holdings and Investment Ltd controls 32%. After 75 years of operations, still almost half the directors of the board are family members and all three top positions chairman, vice chairman and managing director are within the family. Similarly, Facebook founder Mark Zuckerberg owns less than 18% shares but controls nearly 60% voting rights as his class B shares have 10 votes per share while the Class A shares that trade have only one vote per share. In India the founding family (or descendants) are commonly referred to as promoters of the company.

GOVERNANCE THROUGH STAGES OF GROWTH

Family businesses have a multifaceted governance system. Ownership, management and governance structure change as the business grows and expands. As organizational complexities increase, the governance issues also shift. The ownership structure and governance institutions need to evolve to meet new governance challenges that emerge as business progresses across family generations (Table 11.1).

Table 11.1   Business stages and governance institutions at Family-owned Businesses

Stages	Ownership Structure	Family Governance Institution	Governance factors
1st Generation	Founders	None	One man Show Business and family funds become non-distinguishable
2nd Generation	Sibling Partnership	Family Meetings—Informal	Leadership and team work Succession Planning Business and Family reputation become one
3rd Generation	Cousin Confederation	Family Assembly – Formal Family Council – may be formal or informal	Allocation of Responsibilities Conflict between family aspirations and business requirements Cross Ownership Maintaining family ownership
4th Generation	Family Dynasty	Family Constitution/ Charter- formal Family Council – formal	Survival Moving to professional managers Distribution of Profits Demergers

Source Developed by Author

First Generation

The initial phase belongs to the founders. The founder starts the business and focuses on making it a success. The business is owned and managed by the founder. He exercises complete control and takes all major decisions. The success or failure of the business depends on the entrepreneurship skills of the founder. Often the individual or spouse's funds are used for starting the business and their assets (jewellery/house) used as collateral to borrow. Thus, begins the intermingling of business and family funds. The founder's personality is embedded in the company's culture. Dhirubhai Ambani's Reliance is known for risky aggressive strategies and bending rules, JRD's Tata companies for being ethical and Vijay Mallya's flamboyance can be seen in the (in)famous Kingfisher Calendars (See Box).

Second Generation

In this stage, the children of the founder start taking charge of the business. Traditionally only male members were brought into the business and the elder sibling given the senior post and groomed to take over the family business. Continued success of the business depends on the teamwork of the siblings. Decisions are generally made at dinner table. As the business grows, the wealth and reputation of the family multiplies. Mukesh Ambani is the richest man in India (Forbes, 2018) and holds immense influence across spectrums thanks to his business group being the second largest in India. Business collapse will similarly cause a spiral downfall for the family as witnessed in the case of Kingfisher and Vijay Mallya.

Third Generation

The family tree expands faster with the addition of the third generation. There are several small families coming together to form a joint family. Three generations are now involved simultaneously. While the first generation is typically an entrepreneur who has an idea and starts a business, the second generation, in contrast, grows under the shadow of the patriarch, learning tricks of the trade and understanding the business values. By the third generation, each member has his own aspiration, business ideas and style of operation. "The values and virtues of the founder are diluted over time and business growth fails to match with the growth of the family tree. Third generation family members occupy positions and areas they are not much excited about. Frustration starts to build" (Much-hala, 2020). If proper succession planning has not been carried out in the earlier phase, this can lead to conflicts and splits. Hardly three out of 100 Indian family businesses make it to the third generation (Piramal, 2000). In the case of Ambani's, the absence of the towering personality of their father led to the conflict between Mukesh and Anil (second generation only) and split of Reliance.

As the business group expands, it is likely that the family will need to go public to raise money or liquidate value. As outside shareholders come into picture and regulation compliance kicks in; there is need for greater transparency, induction of independent directors and balancing the needs of family and shareholder expectation. Governance becomes complex, a formal governance structure needs to be introduced. A formal family assembly or forum could be put in place similar to a shareholders meeting where all members of the family get together and are informed about roles and responsibilities of different members, major business develop-ments and any proposed changes. A family council representing a board of directors may formally or informally set in where few key members get together to decide direction and strategy of the company.

Fourth Generation

The family is now very huge. There are several sub-families and number of members could be as high as 100, especially as female members are also claiming their place. It is not possible for everyone to be part of the business. Some members may not be interested, others may not have adequate business acumen. As the family size increases and managing it becomes difficult, a family charter or constitution may be a good idea to define the relationship between family and business, ownership pattern, governance structure, selection of leadership and communication mech-anism. A formal family council with elected members helps the family to maintain control while creating shareholder wealth. Professionals may be brought in to manage the business. It took the Burmans of Darbur Ltd in their fifth generation 18 months and several family get together to finalize their charter. Over the last two decades, it has helped professionalize the business to enable rapid growth while keeping the family united.

THE FAMILY EDGE

The greatest part of the world wealth lies with family-owned businesses. Several studies show that family firms constantly outperform non-family firms. Indian family businesses have earned 14 per cent annualized returns between January 2017 and January 2020 on the stock exchanges. In the same period, professionally run companies gained 12 per cent (Shinde, 2020). The success of family firms is even more prominent during economic downturns and crises. This is because family firms are not looking at making a give buck. They are in it for the long haul. The reputation and wealth of the family is tied to the performance of the company. They are creating wealth for their future generations. Family firms are free from the principal agent conflict that besieges professional companies. Knowledge of the business that is passed through the generations is a major asset. The founders binding with the company, their commitment and passion, focus towards steady growth and a long-term horizon encourage them to invest in innovation and build sustainable business models. Family values, stakeholder relationships build on mutual trust and a hands-on approach forms the basis of success.

Yet, a little more than 30% of all family-owned businesses make the transition into the second generation. 12% will still be viable into the third generation, with only 3% of all family businesses operating at the fourth-generation level and beyond (Family Business Alliance). Those that do, however, tend to perform well over time comparably.

GOVERNANCE INTRICACIES OF FAMILY-RUN BUSINESSES

The structure of family business is such that points of conflict are built into it. The interdependence between family, ownership, board and management and overlapping interest groups that arise create contradicting roles. The primary stakeholders can be broken into two groups—family members and non-family members. Each can play the role of one or more stakeholder (Fig. 11.1). Fifteen sub groups are formed. In addition, there are various other stakeholders in the company. Naturally balancing the interest of all these increase governance complexities manifold.

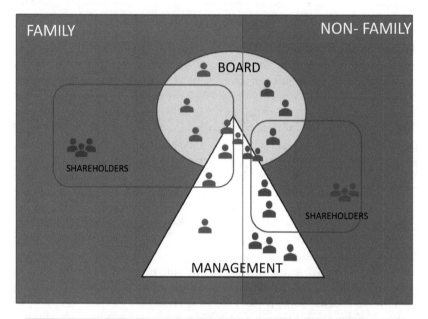

Stakeholder	Family	Non-Family
One role	Family member with no involvement with company	Outside Shareholder
		Outside Non-Executive Director
		Employee
Two Roles	Family Ownership (Family member + Shareholder)	Executive Director
	Family Non-Executive Director	Employee-Ownership
	Family and Employee	Shareholder and Non-Executive director (ex: Nominee of Institutional Investor)
Three Roles	Family Ownership and Non-Executive Director	Executive director with ownership
	Family Ownership and Employee	
Four Roles	Family Ownership and Executive Director (including may be CEO)	
Five Roles	Family ownership , executive Chairman and CEO	

Source: Developed by Author

Fig. 11.1 Governance structure and multiple interest groups

Father Son Battle

Mr. Vijaypat Singhania transformed a small fabric company into a world renowned brand—Raymond, the largest integrated manufacturer of fabric in the world. In 2015 he gifted his 37% ownership in the company to his only son Gautam Singhania. Gautam joined the family business in 1986 while still in his early 20s and took over the reins of Raymond Limited as Chairman & Managing Director in September 2000 ("List of Board Directors," n.d.). Shares of Raymond have jumped 50% since he got the controlling stake, grossly outperforming the benchmark BSE Sensex that gained just 12% during the same period (Mandavia & Kalesh, 2017).

However, father and son are in a bitter battle with the father regretting his decision to transfer the shares, accusing his son of cheating him out of an exclusive apartment and of unceremoniously kicking him out of the company offices. Gautam holds that the change of ownership had been a family understanding for 30 years (Mandavia & Kalesh, 2017).

Under a 2007 agreement the company was to sell an apartment in the Singhania family's 36-storey JK House in the upmarket Malabar Hill area of Mumbai, India's financial capital to Vijaypat Singhania at a price far below its market value. Gautam advised the Raymond board and shareholders against selling it. As the feud escalated, the board also took away Mr Vijaypat's 'chairman emeritus' title ("Gautam Singhania battles with father," 2019).

Points to ponder:

1. Should family understanding decide who runs the company?
2. Is Gautam right in not allowing the company to sell a property at a price far below market price? Is he doing right as a son?

Family Dynamics

Family dynamics spill into corporate decisions. Founders are revered and their personality is embedded in the company's culture. They single-handedly take all decisions. The dominate member in the family controls the business. Unqualified family members are placed into leadership positions simply because it is a birth right promoting a culture of nepotism. Primogeniture succession could leave it in the hands of an incompetent. Family feuds can lead to splits in a company (Reliance group being a point in case) and even its downfall.

Family vs. Company

Family managers tend to take decisions that balance the interest of the family and company. Emotions and sentiment seep into the decision-making process. Appointment to key managerial posts are kept within the family, and ancestral outdated factories are held on to because a great grandfather built them, or because they've been in the family for generations. Family is a social enterprise where decisions are based to protect the family. Directors, as agents and trustees, are expected to protect the interest of all shareholders. These two sets of expectations are contrary to each other (See Table. 11.2). Gautam Singhania (see box Father and Son) has a responsibility to generate maximum value for Raymond's shareholders. He is also to care for the well-being of his father.

Table 11.2   Paradox in family-controlled business

	Family needs	*Company needs*
*Objective	Mutual Growth of Family Members	Maximizing Stakeholder Wealth
Motivation for Participants	Love and care, Power and Control	Remuneration and Status
*Focus	Inward	Outward
Membership	Birth or marriage	Funds (Shareholders /Financers) or Capability and best fit (managers/employees)
*Returns/ Rewards	Equally between members, based on family understanding	Performance based
Leadership	Hereditary	Competence
*Decision making	Informal, Intuitive	Formal, Structured
Basis for Decision	Emotional, Family Dynamics	Rational, Professional
Speed of Decision	Quick	Requires due process
Organization Structure	Authoritarian	Democratic
Control	Direct Control	Delegation

* Adopted from Jain (2006), Chains that Liberate, Governance of family firms

Unwillingness to Relinquish Control

Traditionally, family businesses have always been run by a member of the family. In recent years, companies are coming around to the idea of having their businesses run by professional managers. To every father, no man is good enough for his daughter, and there is always a power struggle between the mother and the wife to exercise dominance over the man they both love. Simply put, it's very difficult for a parent to let go of their baby, even if he or she is all grown up and ready for a life of his or her own. Businesses are the babies of the promoter, raised with their blood and sweat. Promoters want to continue having a say in major decisions. Seeing someone else now deciding the future of the company is very difficult for them, particularly if it is being taken in a different direction (Jhunjhunwala, 2020). They are apprehensive about their legacy being destroyed. Founding member Narayana Murthy and other promoters had suggested that major decisions that Infosys plans to take should be run through them before being finalized. How can some shareholders be given privacy to information before others. This goes against the basic governance principal of equal treatment of shareholders.

Insider vs. Outsider

(Jhunjhunwala, 2020).
Family firms often face challenge in attracting professionals to management positions and even more so in retaining them. Successful and experience managers seek autonomy and decision-making power. The family have difficulty in accepting outsiders leading the business. All decisions in a family-run business are taken with a view of the long-term benefits of the family. They are not only interested in tomorrow or even next year, but in the growth, success and survival for generations to come. Professional managers need to prove their performance through quarterly and annual results, their appointment and remuneration being tied to them. Thus, they tend to hold a short-term view. As stewards, it is their duty to steer the company in a way that best achieves its goal not the family. This can lead to family interests being hurt, and thus the promoter being unhappy with the chosen non-family business leader. The difference

in strategy and leadership style between promoter Ratan Tata and erst-while outside Chairman Cyrus Mistry of Tata Sons could stem from this. Ratan Tata did not have to prove his mettle or justify his appointment in the short run.

(See Tata Sons and the Mystery of Mistry, Chapter 12).

Inadequate Succession Planning

Just like in the days of royals, training of the prince would begin from early childhood so that when the time came, he would become a great king and rule his kingdom well, business families such as the Birlas start grooming their children from a young age in a manner that instils in them a business acumen enabling them to successfully take charge of the business empire. However, the problem arises when there is no child or the child is not up to the task—or perhaps is not willing (Jhunjhunwala, 2020). Vijay Mallya's son did not wish to join the booming brewery business of his father which led him to unchartered waters. Many family heads delay retirement as they struggle to accept—as well as begin—the process of letting go. This delay often means their succession planning strategies are reactionary, rather than carefully and thoughtfully planned out. If say an unexpected illness occurs, then all hell breaks loose. In fighting among successors or an ill-equipped inheritor soon bring the company down.

Independent Directors' Dilemma

Family businesses bring in 'friends of the family' in the name of independent directors. A rubber stamp board is present to meet regulatory compliance. Even if experts and professionals with calibre are appointed as Independent directors, they remain vulnerable as they serve at the pleasure of the promoter. Both appointment and continuation of independent directors is at the mercy of the majority shareholder, putting their independence into question. When the CEO is a very charismatic founder, independent directors are wary about asking questions.

Independent directors don't owe allegiance to major shareholders. Their fiduciary duty is to promote the interest of all shareholders. The Code of Independent Directors enshrined in the Companies Act states that an independent director must "exercise his responsibilities in a bona fide manner in the interest of the company; refrain from any action that would lead to loss of his independence; assist the company in implementing the best corporate governance practices, safeguard the interests of all stakeholders, particularly the minority shareholders and balance the conflicting interests of the stakeholders". In family-controlled businesses, the whole purpose of independent directors is to protect the interest of the minority. However, their role is limited. As seen in the case of Kingfisher, when trouble brews, they resign and flee. In fact, independent directors suddenly resigning is a sure signal to investors that company is distress. In the battle between Ratan Tata and Cyrus Mistry, Independent directors were warned against supporting Mistry and those that did were removed.

Inactive Non-Promoter Shareholders

The lack of active participation by institutional shareholders and small shareholders gives promoters unchallenged power. In the case of Satyam for years, the Raju brothers did whatever they liked without any involvement by other shareholders. By the time institutional investors expressed disapproval at their actions, it was too late.

Board Processes

Board processes are very loosely structured and deliberations and decision-making processes can tend to take on an informal turn. The promoter dominates the board and is able to control and steer discussions in his favour. In the case of Satyam even the absence of the Raju brothers in the decision process did not in no way reduce their influence and the board unanimously approved the purchase of Mayatas.

Rotating Chair

At Apollo hospitals the four daughters of Dr. Reddy have been involved in the family business from the beginning, where as young girls they spend weekends interacting with patients collecting feedback on measures to improve the hospital. Each sister has a clear role depending on their interest and talent. Shobana the eldest designs and executes new projects, Suneeta the second daughter handles finance, Sangita a people person heads human resources and Preeta the youngest manages the hospitals. Each one of them brings their individual and distinct acumen

---

to the growth of the company. Sangita likes to put it this way: "It's always nice to check out a financial idea with Suneeta, talk about something entrepreneurial with Shobana, and look up to Preetha to build on those" (Dhamija, 2017). To prevent any conflict, the chairmanship of the company is rotated between the sisters. This way the group benefits from the strengths of each of them. However, for third generation it's not so simple. The family corporate board (family council) of Apollo group consisting of five family members and three independent directors evaluate family members to ensure that entry to the business is on merit. The presence of independence directors encourages a professional unbiased process.

Points to Ponder:

1. Are there any merits and demerits of induction at an early age into family business?
2. What do you think of the practice of rotating chairmanship at Apollo?
3. Do family businesses need to professionalize with time?

MAKING IT WORK - THE FAMILY ENTERPRISE

Business families can be considered as an enterprise in their own right. "A family enterprise is the collection of a family's meaningful activities and economic interests that help to identify, support and unite the family. These activities need to be well led, managed and governed so that .....enterprise is productive, meets the goals of the family and can be continued into the next generation" (https://johndavis.com/family-enterprise/). Managing family business successfully across generations is tricky if not impossible. Only a small percentage of family businesses survive and grow beyond second and third generations. "Once families define their family enterprise, they begin to understand their family mission as extending beyond the family business" (https://johndavis.com/family-enterprise/).

Family Bond: Family Value and Mutual Trust

Large family businesses that survive for many generations, make sure to nurture family values and impart a sense of pride in the company's contribution to society to their offsprings. Think how children of royal families easily handle their regal duties, and the inability of those who marry into it. All members share a common purpose and vision for the family. 'Family is more important than me' is imbibed from the start. Mutual trust among members is important. FMCG giant Emami, whose products are available in over 4 million outlets across India was founded by two friends. Not only has the company grown so has their friendship. Their children are also part of the business. Two families, two generations. The success can be credited to the concept of 'relationship of equality' etched in the minds of all family members. The shareholding in Emami and other ventures is equally split among the Agarwal and Goenka families, and both are equally represented on the board, with four members each. The Emamis (not Agarwals and Goenkas) meet every fortnight to discuss business matters. Besides, the entire family (even spouses not involved in business) has to go on a holiday together every year. This process helps them to strengthen communication and trust and instils a sense of bonding.

Family businesses are built on networks. Relationship with stakeholders and 'keeping one's word' taking priority over business. Studies show that employee turnover is much lower in family-owned businesses. Employees are not easily fired. Loyalty is rewarded. Similarly long-term relationships are fostered with suppliers and customers. Remember how 'mom and pop' neighbourhood shop or 'Kirana store' owners knew all about your family. You couldn't possibly leave without a chat.

Ownership

To keep control, family retain majority ownership. Sale of shares to outsiders is restricted. Family shareholders who want to sell must offer to the other family members with right of first refusal. In 2004, Priyamvada Devi Birla bequeathed her entire estate worth Rs 5,000 crore to her chartered accountant R.S. Lodha, stunning the Birla family and India Inc. (Rahman, 2012). The Birla family has been united in their fight against the Lodhas over the will. Since then business families have become very cautious. The pricing formula and other terms of sale or transfer are clearly spelled out in family charters.

Relations between the family owners and non-family investors can suffer from principal—principal conflict. The need for enhanced activism by institutional and retail investors is all the more pronounced in family businesses—not only to act as a check and balance on the powers of the board, but more importantly, to control the promoter's supremacy.

Institutional investors can significantly influence and improve corporate governance in family firms.

Well-Defined Roles

Most business houses, typically, work through a network of companies that are connected through cross holdings and interlocking of directors with each other. To avoid confusion and conflict, the roles of each member should be clearly stated. The Bajaj Group that was founded by Jamnalal Bajaj is divided into several companies that are now primarily managed by the fourth generation. Each company of the Bajaj group is chaired by a different family member of the third generation—Bajaj Auto by Rahul Bajaj, Bajaj Hindustan by his brother Shisir Bajaj and his cousins Shekhar and Niraj Bajaj chair Bajaj Electricals and Mukund Ltd, respectively. Their sons are the second in command. This helps each member have control of some part of the business with ownership remaining with all members. Clear division of roles and responsibility prevents conflict while joint ownership helps to create a sense of oneness. Rahul Bajaj demerged the finance division from the auto business arguing that it would release shareholder value, but the primary purpose was to give each of his sons a separate business to manage. Rajiv heads the auto business and Sanjeev the finance, yet both are on each other's board. This gives them managerial independence and a sense of togetherness. The line of succession is also set in motion.

Professional Management

As the company expands, to continue building on past success and creating value for future generations, outside professionals must be taken into the fold. The relationship between family managers and non-family professionals must be carefully crafted to maintain a well-functioning management team and minimize ambiguity about their areas of control. Professional managers should be given adequate autonomy if they are to give desired results. This does not mean they shouldn't be monitoring, but they should not be micro managed. As the family grows in size and business expands, both increase in complexities. Family members may give up their day-to-day operational roles and professional CEO brought in. As Amit Burman, vice chairman, Dabur puts it: "We realised that for Dabur to grow rapidly there was a need to professionalise the management, and to attract the best managerial talent it was important to keep the top slot vacant" (Madhavan, 2017).

Strategic Boards

Strong boards are the backbone of any successful company. Choosing the right independent directors could go a long way towards this. As companies grow—knowledge needs increase—not only in terms of depth but also in width (Jain, 2005). Independent directors can provide expertise in areas that the family lacks. They can objectively help to assess the family managers and accordingly help to structure leadership roles and in succession planning. Another key role that independent directors can play is, reduce if not completely eliminate, promotion of family aspirations and needs at the cost of business and outside shareholders. They act as a sounding board to bounce off ideas and provide advice and insight when companies are facing challenging times.

The expectations of outside stakeholders from independent directors should be limited. If Independent directors object too much, they will be removed. When the family have significant control, some are of the opinion that independent directors 'serve no purpose'. In family-managed business, the monitoring role of independent directors is secondary and the advisory role is primary. Not allowing promoter/majority shareholder to vote in the appointment or removal of independent directors could be a possible measure to strengthen their position. Successful family firms make use of the expertise available. They value the opinion of independent directors. Instead of mere 'sounding boards', they choose to build 'strategic boards' (see Fig. 11.2).

Fig. 11.2 Evolution of boards in well-governed family managed business (*Source* Developed by author)

Succession Planning

For many family-run companies, succession planning implies choosing an heir from the next generation to take over the business. A well thought-out succession plan is necessary for seamless and hassle-free transition of power. It is not about just naming someone. It is a long-term process involving mentoring and grooming the successor to smoothly navigate through business nuances. Inadequate succession planning has been the cause of many family business failures. Internal power struggles are the main source of disputes. The collapse of joint family system in India which was a binding agent has increased the rivalry among younger members. Often the next generation just does not have the adequate leadership and entrepreneurship skills required for the business. Splitting the business into verticals to create more leadership positions such as Bajaj Group or professionalizing management such as in Dabur are some options. Faultless succession planning is essential to ensure business continuity for multiple generations.

Wealth Management

As the family business grows, so does the wealth. An important aspect of family governance is wealth management. How will profits be distributed? How much will be distributed? Under what circumstances can a family member withdraw money? Cash flow and distribution policies are to be established. The proportion of liquid and semi-liquid assets is to be maintained for emergencies and future must be determined. As families become large, appropriate financial planning for each sub-family needs to be considered. Equitable distribution strengthens family ties. Estate planning is probably the most important aspect to avoid family disputes and legal battles in the future.

Governance Framework

With appropriate governance mechanisms and timely actions, both families and their businesses can not only preserve but prosper. Formal family governance system should develop over time. The transition from the successful founding entrepreneurs 'benevolent dictatorship' to the sibling partnership is extremely difficult for most companies. Similar values arising from common upbringing, mutual trust and sibling bond form the basis of their relationship. Power struggles can still erupt. The roles, responsibilities and share in business of each should be specified. As the family grows over time, formal and informal structures and agreements need to be put in place.

The three components of family governance are the family council, family assembly and the family charter (Fig. 11.3).

Family Council: The family council is similar to a board of directors. Members may be elected by the family assembly. It provides leadership, develops the family creed to be followed and formalize business vision. The family creed is the values and philosophy of the family and can be akin to a code of conduct. The council is entrusted with strategic decisions. All family members who are part of the Emami business constitute the family council. They must attend its meeting every alternate Friday. All participants can express their views and concerns. Though unwritten, based on their values, Emami's family creed includes not entering into the alcohol business.

The Family Assembly or Forum: The family forum can draw parallels to a shareholders meeting where all family members are invited to participate. Family members can meet and discuss business matters such

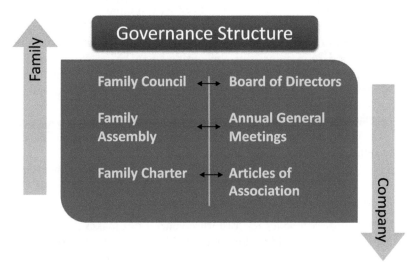

Fig. 11.3 Family governance (*Source* Developed by Author)

as ownership, share in profits and roles of different members. Any major business change, significant restructuring, or crisis should be brought to the notice of the assembly. Regular family get togethers help to reinforce family bonds. Mr Vellayan Subbiah of the Murugappa Group—emphasizes the importance of having regular family meetings to thrash out any differences. Periodical meetings create a sense of inclusion in business decisions. Members understand their roles and rights and act responsibly. Free flow of communication builds mutual trust among members and achieves consensus in decision-making.

Family Charter or Constitution: As the family becomes large, similar to the articles of association a family charter or constitution should be drafted. "Whatever the nomenclature, the document serves as a mechanism to enforce family governance" (Madhvan, 2017). It formalizes the business relationships between family members and provides the approach for sale of ownership interests, the process for succession planning, dividend and distribution policies, qualifications/conditions for members to work in the organization or take senior positions and their remuneration policies.

"There is much that family-led businesses can learn from the experience and journey of the over Rs 36,000-crore Murugappa Group that is currently run by the fifth generation of its founding family" (Sharma, 2020). The family has a constitution that lays down the roles, responsibilities, codes of conduct and guiding principles for acts of succession, entry, exit and retirement. But the business can be passed on only to male heirs in the family. Arunachalam, the eldest daughter of former executive chairman M V Murugappan has been battling to be recognized as her father's successor on the board. As she puts it: "The question remains why a female heir with a doctorate degree, 24 years work experience in Fortune 500 multinational companies, and numerous patents and publications to her name, cannot be inducted into the board........." (Narasimhan, 2020). As business, family and society change with time, some parts of the document may become dated. Every few years they should be reviewed and appropriately revised.

The need to create a legacy for future generations makes family-owned businesses focus on building long sustainable businesses. It should come as no surprise that many family businesses make it to the coveted Fortune 500 company. In a world full of uncertainties, only business houses that have mastered the art of family enterprise have survived many years. Others have just gone down without a trace.

REFERENCES

Ajay, M. (2014). Kushagra Bajaj now betting big on the power sector to expand. *Business India*. https://www.businesstoday.in/magazine/features/story/sugar-producer-kushagra-bajaj-betting-big-on-power-sector-138245-2014-07-14.

Anderson, R. C., & Reeb, D. M. (2003). Founding-family ownership and firm performance. *The Journal of Finance, 58*(3), 1301–1328.

Bajaj Group. https://www.bajajgroup.company/bajaj-group/bajaj-group-tree/

Bandyopadhyay, T. (2013, January 14). Kingfisher Airlines: The beginning of the endgame? https://www.livemint.com.

Dhamija. (2017). How Dr Prathap Reddy avoids ambiguity on succession and structure at Apollo Hospitals. *Forbes India*. https://www.forbesindia.com/article/indias-family-businesses/how-dr-prathap-reddy-avoids-ambiguity-on-succession-and-structure-at-apollo-hospitals/46379/1.

Family Business Alliance. Retrieved June 2014. http://www.fbagr.org/index.php?option=com_content&view=article&id=117&Itemid=75

From yachts to villas: Vijay Mallya will lose these 6 properties in India. (n.d). *Business Today*. https://www.businesstoday.in.

Forbes India, India Rich List (2018). https://www.forbesindia.com/lists/india-rich-list-2018/1731/1

Gautam Singhania battles with father for billion-dollar Raymond Group (2019, January 2). *The New Indian Express.*

Jain, (2005). *Chains that Liberate*. Macmillan Publishers India.

Jhunjhunwala, S. (2020). Vikalpa: The Journal for Decision Papers, *45*(3), 170–182.

List of Board Directors. (n.d.). Retrieved March 22, 2019. http://www.raymond.in/boarddirectors?subcat=359.

Madhvan, N. (2017). A family constitution can bridge the gap between family and business values. www.forbesindia.com/article/indias-family-businesses/a-family-constitution-can-bridge-the-gap-between-family-and-business-values/46417/1

Mandavia, M. & Kalesh, B. (2017, August 29). Gautam Singhania bluntly dismisses father's sob story, says he's the victim, not Vijaypat .*The Economic Times*. https://economictimes.indiatimes.com.

Muchhala, H. (2020). How to tackle a split in the family business. *Forbes India*. https://www.forbesindia.com/article/family-business/how-to-tackle-a-split-in-the-family-business/62871/1 accessed October 5 2021.

Narasimhan (2020). Murugappa family votes to keep Valli Arunachalam out of holding co board. *Business Standard*. https://www.business-standard.com/article/companies/murugappa-family-votes-to-keep-valli-arunachalam-out-of-holding-co-board-120092201030_1.htm.

Piramal, G. (2000). *Business Maharajas*. Penguin Books.

Rahman (2012). Battle for Billions: Birlas vs Lodhas. *India Today*. https://www.indiatoday.in/magazine/the-big-story/story/20120305-battle-for-m.p.-birla-fortune-icai-indicts-lodhas-757506-2012-02-25.

Sanjai, P. R. & Shukla, T. (2016, February 27). How Kingfisher Airlines floored Vijay Mallya. https://www.livemint.com.

Sharma, M. (2018, August 10). Fugitive businessman Vijay Mallya's London mansion has a golden toilet. *Business Today*. https://www.businesstoday.in.

Sharma. (2020). Murugappa group family feud: It's time for more women to join family businesses. *Business India*. https://www.businesstoday.in/latest/corporate/story/murugappa-group-family-feud-time-more-women-join-family-businesses-242389-2020-01-18.

Shinde (2020, February 13). Family businesses are doing better than rest of India Inc. *Economic Times*. https://economictimes.indiatimes.com/markets/stocks/news/family-businesses-are-doing-better-than-rest-of-india-inc/articleshow/74109424.cms?utm_source=contentofinterest&utm_medium=text&utm_campaign=cppst accessed October 5, 2021.

Sinha, S. (2016, March 16). Who's who of India served on Kingfisher Airlines' board. *Times of India*. https://timesofindia.indiatimes.com.

Wiggins, K. (2018, October 10). Vijay Mallya fights to save plush London home from bank takeover. https://www.ndtv.com.

https://www.ifc.org/wps/wcm/connect/topics_ext_content/ifc_external_corporate_site/ifc+cg/regional_advisory_programs/middle+east+and+north+africa accessed October 5 2021.

CHAPTER 12

Corporate Governance—Beyond Borders

Navigating the Seven Seas

MULTINATIONAL COMPANIES

A multinational company is a business that operates in many different countries at the same time. In other words, it's a company that has business activities in more than one country. Multinationals in comparison to a company operating in a single country are in a better position to exploit growth opportunities, expand markets, increase profitability, reduce costs of operation and source cheaper capital. The various entities in the enterprise are interconnected through ownership or control of one or more units over the others and they influence each other's activities by sharing knowledge, resources and responsibilities. Large multinational companies generally operate by creating a 'corporate group'.

CORPORATE GROUP

A corporate group or group of companies is a collection of holding and subsidiary corporations that function as a single economic entity through a common source of control. Google for instance is part of a corporate group that all work under the umbrella of the parent company Alphabet. Alphabet has several subsidiaries. Each of these separate business entities all perform unique operations that add value to Alphabet (see Fig. 12.1). Big businesses groups such as the Bajaj Group (discussed in previous

© The Author(s), under exclusive license to Springer Nature Singapore Pte Ltd. 2023
S. Jhunjhunwala, *Corporate Governance*,
https://doi.org/10.1007/978-981-99-2707-4_12

chapter), Tata Group, Sony and Berkshire Hathaway operate through a group of companies.

Controlling a company means having the power to appoint the majority of its directors or significantly influence its decisions. According to Sec 12.2(27) of the Companies Act 2013, "control shall include the right to appoint majority of the directors or to control the management or policy decisions exercisable by a person or persons acting individually or in concert, directly or indirectly, including by virtue of their shareholding or management rights or shareholders agreements or voting agreements or in any other manner". The group may have a single holding company or be a network of companies through cross holdings. The control of company S by company H may be direct, i.e. company H directly holds the majority of voting rights of company S or indirect, i.e. H controls intermediate companies A, B, C, etc., which it can ask to vote the same way as the board of H, thereby obtaining a majority of rights in S. H becomes the holding company and S its subsidiary company.

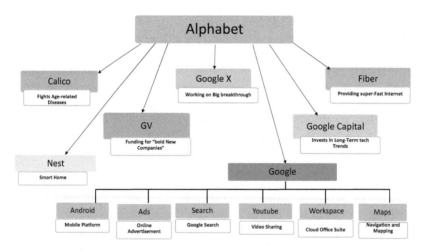

Fig. 12.1 Corporate group of an MNC (*Note* May not be an exhaustive list. *Sources* Complied from different sources)

Holding or Parent Company

A parent or holding company is a company that owns enough voting shares in another company to control its policies and management. According to s.1162 of the Companies Act 2006, UK an undertaking is a parent undertaking in relation to another undertaking, a subsidiary undertaking, if:

- it holds a majority of the voting rights in the undertaking, or
- it is a member of the undertaking and has the right to appoint or remove a majority of its board of directors, or
- it has the right to exercise a dominant influence over the undertaking by virtue of provisions contained in the undertaking's articles, or by virtue of a control contract, or
- it is a member of the undertaking and controls alone, pursuant to an agreement with other shareholders or members, a majority of the voting rights in the undertaking, or
- it has the power to exercise, or actually exercises, dominant influence or control over it, or
- it and the subsidiary undertaking are managed on a unified basis.

A holding company may have several subsidiaries and not carry on any business or operation on its own, its purpose being to own other companies to form a corporate group. In Fig. 12.1, Alphabet is the parent company and Google its Subsidiary.

Subsidiary

A company becomes a subsidiary when more than 50% shares are controlled by another company, referred to as the parent company or the holding company. According to Sec 12.2(87) of the Companies Act, Subsidiary company' or 'subsidiary', in relation to any other company (that is to say the holding company), means a company in which the holding company—

i. controls the composition of the Board of Directors; i.e. at its discretion can appoint or remove all or majority of the directors

ii. exercises or controls more than one-half of the total share capital either at its own or together with one or more of its subsidiary companies:

If a company in any manner is able to exercise dominant control over another, the former becomes a parent company and the latter its subsidiary. It may be noted that the holding company may be a private company or unlisted and the subsidiary a listed company, or the subsidiary may be unlisted and holding a listed company. The holding and subsidiary may be in different countries. Since 1919, Coca-Cola Inc an American Multinational has been trading on the New York Stock Exchange. Its Indian subsidiary, whole owned by Coca-Cola is a private company.

Layers of Subsidiary: Google is a subsidiary of Alphabet. At the same time You Tube is a subsidiary of Google. Thus theirs can be layers of subsidiaries. Google is the 1st tier subsidiary of Alphabet. You Tube is the 1st tier subsidiary of Google but the 2nd tier subsidiary of Alphabet (Fig. 12.1).

Wholly Owned Subsidiary: A wholly owned subsidiary is a company whose shares are 100% owned by the holding company. This gives them complete control. Other subsidiaries where ownership is more than 50% and less than 100% are sometimes referred to as partly owned subsidiaries.

Material Subsidiary: A subsidiary is considered material if it has a considerable role in the overall performance of the holding company or the group as a whole. Material subsidiary is a subsidiary, whose income or net worth exceeds ten per cent {10%} of the consolidated income or net worth respectively, of the listed company and its subsidiaries in the immediately preceding accounting year [Listing Obligation and Disclosure requirements, 2015]. If the subsidiary is sold off the holding companies' financial status will significantly change.

Associate Company

Companies within a group which do not have a holding–subsidiary relationship are known as associate companies. For instance two subsidiaries of the same holding company will be considered as an associate company. "Associate company, in relation to another company, means a company in which that other company has a significant influence, but which is not a subsidiary company of the company having such influence and includes a joint venture company" (Sec 12.2(6) of Companies Act, India).

Legal Position

Holding and subsidiary are separate and distinct legal entities. The employees of the subsidiary are not employees of the holding company. The holding company is not liable for the dues of the subsidiary. However a holding, subsidiary or an associate company will be treated as a related party of a company [Sec 12.2(76)]. Foreign Subsidiary must follow the laws of the country where it is incorporated and operates.

Reasons for Forming Corporate Groups

The most common reason to create separate companies is segregate the business structure with distinct entities and separate management. For example Berkshire Hathaway's different verticals are managed by different companies (see Fig. 12.2).

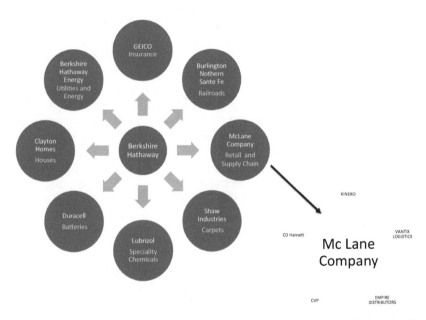

Fig. 12.2 Example of some Berkshire Hathaway Companies and their businesses (*Source* Based on information available at https://www.berkshirehathaway.com/subs/sublinks.html, accessed September 14, 2021)

This enables the value of different businesses or brands to be captured separately. It facilitates buying and selling of an individual business. An investor can acquire shares of the individual company they are interested in. Reliance Industries Limited's plan to demerger its financial services business and list it separately on the stock exchanges under Jio Financial Services is expected to create more value for both units separately.

As the parent company and its subsidiary are separate legal entities, it limits the risk exposure of the holding company. Subsidiaries may be formed for a specific reason such as for tax advantages. By creating a new company, it may obtain some tax breaks available for new ventures or in international operations to take advantage of tax treaties. During buyout keeping the new acquisition as a separate subsidiary may reduce tax and regulatory compliances that a merger would require.

Subsidiaries are used to enter new geographical markets. Some countries may require business be done through a domestic company only. If they are restrictions of direct foreign investment in the country, the company may partner with a local company. Sometimes they may enter into joint venture because that company can bring strategic advantage to the business. Starbucks had tried to enter India unsuccessfully earlier. Entering into a joint venture with Tata Global Beverages, one of the many subsidiaries of the Tata Group gave them a unique advantage. Tata Coffee Limited a subsidiary of Tata Global Beverages supplies roast coffee to Tata Starbucks Private Limited. With a more than 100% import duty on coffee—the coffee is sourced and roasted locally. A local partner with a close business relationship with a major supplier gave them access to crucial resources and local knowledge and the expertise to deal with an unknown institutional environment (Fig. 12.3) (Fischer & Roy, 2019). In Tatas, they found a business partner with a big brand, access to networks and someone to 'help them navigate through the complexities of India' (Fischer & Roy, 2019).

GOVERNANCE OF CORPORATE GROUP

Corporate groups create a complex organizational structure resulting in a complicated governance environment. Boards have a fiduciary duty to work in the best interest of the company. For the board of a holding company, the question is to what extent should it be involved in the governance of its subsidiaries? To properly carry out its fiduciary role, the subsidiary board must act independently and objectively. The parent

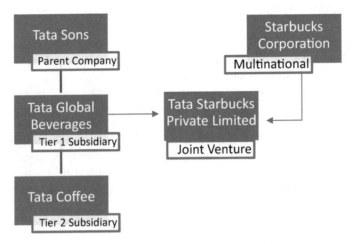

Fig. 12.3 Complex structures of MNC: Example of Tata Starbuck Pvt Ltd (*Source* Developed by Author)

company often nominates its director or officers as directors on the subsidiary company. It is difficult for the board of the subsidiary to act in its own interest alone. If directors of subsidiaries act against wishes of the controlling authority, they risk being removed from the board. As a result, the interest of the group or holding company gets priority over that of the subsidiary.

The board of the holding company needs to determine whether all companies will have the same governance structure or each subsidiary can determine its own governance system. The parent board has to also decide how it will monitor governance of the subsidiaries and what will be the extent of oversight. Questions such as 'How many common directors will there be' or 'will they have the same chairman' have to be answered. Subsidiaries may be categories in terms of level of investment, strategic importance and risk to the group and accordingly appropriate governance mechanism established.

Corporate Governance in Multinationals

In multinational groups with companies incorporated in different countries, there is an additional problem of difference in laws and regulations, diversity of culture and disparity of stakeholders. According to a study by Deloitte, governance of oversee subsidiary is viewed different from domestic subsidiary by parent company. While local governance regulations are to be compiled by the foreign subsidiary, its governance system must be aligned with the holding company for smooth functioning. Robust corporate governance is backbone of the success of multinational enterprises. Corporate governance is an important contributor to the global competitiveness of MNCs and affects their strategic choices. Some of the issues that may arise:

Governance Model: As we know, each country has adopted its own form of governance model. Now imagine a Japanese company that adheres to a hybrid model of corporate governance has subsidiaries in the USA, India, China and Germany. Not only will the MNC have to deal with subsidiaries having different governance models—one-tier and two-tier but the intricacies in each will be different.

Board Structure: The size, composition and functions of boards vary in different countries. The degree of independence of boards in each subsidiary and the expected role of independent and executive directors would differ. Then there is the contentious issue of diversity on board. If we take an example of just gender diversity, the percentage of women in 2021 in Japanese-listed companies was less than 10% and about 35% in Norwegian firm. The group will have directors from different countries. Both parent and subsidiary country can be expected to have international directors on the board. Based on resource dependency theory, diversity of foreign directors should enhance board effectiveness, although difficulty in understanding language, cultural differences and variations in regulatory and accounting practices reduces monitoring effectiveness.

Shareholding Patterns and participation rights—Large-listed companies in UK are more likely to have dispersed shareholding compared to Japan or India which are characterized by concentrated holding. The extent of involvement of institutional investors are more dominant in countries such as the USA. The level of state ownership and control also varies across countries. The protection of minority rights, restriction on block holding, voting rights, access to capital market have to be handled in their own way in each region.

Regulation and Accounting Framework: The legal systems are not the same in countries that are regulated by civil law such as Spain and in common law countries such as the USA or UK. Apart from corporate governance and market regulations, business and commercial laws also vary. Each country has their own accounting framework and the financial statements are prepared and audited in accordance to them. This creates problem of interpretation for investors and other users, and complications in consolidating of accounts. Most countries have now adopted a variant of the international financial reporting standards which helps in uniformity of reporting practices.

Corporate Culture and Practices: A country's culture directly impacts how it conducts business. The work ethos of each country is institutionalized by their legal, social and cultural environment. Popularly discussed are organizational hierarchy, business etiquette, communication style and concept of time. In terms of governance, other issues that may need deeper consideration include superior—subordinate relationship, gender sensitivity, acceptable working hours, employee leave practices and compensation. Belgium has introduced a four-day workweek and other countries are experimenting with it. In India many companies still follow a six-day working week. Japan offers one full year of paid parental leave exclusively for fathers. On the other hand, Germany has no paternity leave policy. (It is expected to grant two weeks paid leave to new fathers from 2024.) How is a German employee likely to react if he learns his counterpart in his company in Japan got a full year paid leave on becoming a father and he doesn't get any. Difference in pay packages is quite significant between developed and developing nations even after adjusting for purchasing parity. This can create challenges especially for cross-country transfers. MNCs to succeed have to adopt to multiple sub cultures. From a governance standpoint, it is incredibly difficult to frame policies to resolve dissimilarities in cultural practices.

Political risks: Unlike a single country company, MNCs face political risk from each country they operate in. Cross-country wars, civil conflicts, political instability, regulatory changes and economic setbacks in a country can have dire consequences on the operations and profitability of a company. The impact of the Russia-Ukraine war (2022) has been felt by companies all over the world. Supply of wheat and raw material sourced from Ukraine was severely affected. Fuel prices rose significantly. Supply chain via Russia between Asia and Europe were broken down.

Sanctions imposed by governments meant that companies could not do business with Russia and had to shut down operations there.

Stakeholder Expectations—One of the major challenges of multinational companies is how to distribute earnings between the shareholders of the parent companies and those of the subsidiary. When taking decisions regarding transfer pricing, royalty and dividend payments fairness and equal treatment for all shareholders have to be considered.

The behaviour of the subsidiary has a direct bearing not just on the profits but also on the reputation of the parent company and its relations with stakeholders. The subsidiary has to at least meet the ESG standing of its holding firm. When reservations were made about quality of Nestle's Maggi in India, other countries too began to show concern.

Agency Problems: An MNC may raise or use their own funds to acquire or set up a company in a foreign country. Alternatively, the foreign subsidiaries if incorporated as a company can directly raise both debt and equity from their own home country. The complexities of operations and shareholding structure of MNCs mean that they face more significant agency problems. International diversification increases the complications and costs of monitoring. At the same time, significant foreign ownerships and institutional holdings leads to more active monitoring. The high global competitiveness environment of MNC reduces opportunistic behaviour of managers as they have to take decisions that are strategically beneficial for the firm, mitigating agency cost.

GOVERNANCE STRATEGY

The Governance approach adopted by MNCs depends on the business plan formulated to compete in multinational markets. Governance strategies can be classified into four broad categories (Adopted from Keil et al., 2006 and Filatotchev & Stahl, 2015) (see Fig. 12.4).

Global Governance Strategy: This strategy is used where there is pressure for global integration and limited need to respond to local country. MNCs adopt a highly centralized approached where the parent company issues universal standardized policies and code of conduct that are to be followed by all subsidiaries. Such governance strategy is generally used by organizations that have wholly owned subsidiaries and are into industrial products such as gasoline. As such the need to address local shareholders is absent and that of other stakeholders is extremely limited.

Fig. 12.4 Governance strategy approaches for MNCs (*Source* Bartlett & Ghoshal [1989])

Transnational Governance Strategy: This hybrid strategy is used where the pressure for global integration and local responsiveness are both high. As a result there is a conflict between these two demands. Though global frameworks are adopted, they are customized to meet local legal requirements. For instance private subsidiary in India of a USA-based MNC would be required to spend 2% of its profits (if it qualifies under Companies Act 2013) on corporate social responsibility (CSR) in the manner as required by Indian Laws irrespective of their global CSR policy.

International Governance Strategy: When the pressure for both global integration and local responsiveness is low, this kind of approach is used. Subsidiaries broadly follow the global policies and templates but adapt them according to their specific needs and circumstances.

Local Governance Strategy: Each subsidiary has its independent governance framework so that they can be responsive to the concerns of local stakeholders. This strategy is likely to be found in companies that have raised money in local markets and are in consumer-focused businesses such as the food business as they will have to address the need of the shareholders as well as taste and cultural preferences of the customers of the host country.

GOVERNANCE MODEL

The monitoring problem is intensified by the geographic and cultural distances involved in multinational operations. The governance strategy that the group adopts will determine the kind of model it uses. Building on the works of Keil et al. (2006) and Filatotchev and Stahl (2015), four governance models (Fig. 12.5) are proposed for each of these strategies by which the parent company can govern the subsidiary.

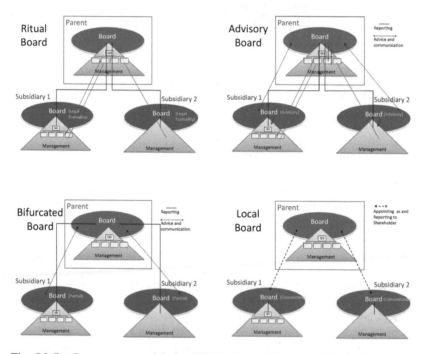

Fig. 12.5 Governance models for MNCs (*Source* Developed by Author)

Ritual Board

In this model, all governance functions are undertaken by the parent company and subsidiary company board exists just for legal formality. This model is used when the group has a highly globalized governance approach. All decisions are taken by the parent board and the subsidiary board rubber stamps them and carries out legal functions such as conducting annual general meeting. CEO and managers may directly report to their counterpart in the parent company (see Fig. 12.5). For instance CFO of subsidiary will report to CFO of parent company.

The benefit of such model is parent company has direct and full control. Consistency in governance practices is followed across all companies and this helps to build trust and goodwill among global stakeholders. The drawback is that it leads to cultural arrogance as parent company may not understand local stakeholder concerns and global policies are applied blindly without taking into account home country's needs.

Advisory Board

This form of governance model is similar to the earlier model in that the parent board retains governance powers but subsidiary board besides being a compliance board plays an advisory role for decisions involving local knowledge and on the ground issues. Associated with international strategy, the advantage is that the parent board is able to develop a better understanding of host country and be more responsive to local stakeholders while ensuring global integration of practices. The correctness of the decisions will depend on the time delay, quality of the advice and effective communication between the two boards. The cost of maintaining an advisory board will be more than that of a ritual board. Directors may be built a sense of dissatisfaction as they have no real decision-making power and their advice may not be heeded.

Bifurcated Board

Bifurcated Board is similar to the two-tier German model wherein governance functions are split between the two boards. The parent board's responsibility involves creating broad common framework, making policies and focusing on strategy. The local board has a larger role in governance functions that benefit from greater local knowledge and contacts such as compliance, networking and stakeholder relationships. The transnational strategy of global integration with localization can be adequately addressed through this model. The local board regularly communicates with the parent board. This enables global consistency, but allows local subsidiaries to adapt according to their local requirements. The benefit is better understanding and quicker response to local needs. The success of the system will depend on the MNC being able to strike an appropriate balance between global consistency and local adaptation. The subsidiary CEO ends up reporting to both the boards. The disadvantage is unclear reporting lines for CEO and overlapping roles of the boards that may result in confusion and duplication of work by the two boards. There is a risk that directors of holding company become shadow directors or regularly overrule directors of subsidiary causing dissatisfaction (Table 12.1).

Local Board

The local board carries out all governance functions as is expected of a board. The parent company as a shareholder appoints the board and monitors the subsidiary through financial and other reports and by decisions taken in general meetings for shareholders. As a major stakeholder, it may appoint its representative on the board. Minimum time and cost is spent in governing of subsidiary. Full freedom to the local board makes it appropriate for multi-domestic strategy so that focus can be on local strategy and meeting stakeholder expectations of home country. The weakness of the model is that parent board has limited control on subsidiary and interests of global stakeholders may be side-lined.

The model used would depend on the extent of control the holding company wishes to exercise and the level of flexibility desirable in a country. This is turn would be affected by how much stake it has in the subsidiary and how much the subsidiary contributes to the consolidated profit. The same parent for a wholly owned subsidiary that contributes say 25% of its profits may use the Ritual or Advisory board but for a 50% joint venture with a local company may need to adopt the Local Board model.

Table 12.1 Governance frameworks for MNCs

Governance Model	Ritual Board	Advisory Board	Split / Bifurcate Board	Local Board
Governance Strategy	Global	International	Transnational	Local
Parent Board	Direct Control on governance functions and makes all decisions	Parent board retains governance function	Split Governance Function – Broad Framework, policies and strategy	Monitoring as Shareholder
Subsidiary Board	Mere Formality—Rubberstamps decisions	Advisory in nature	Local Governance—networking, stakeholder communication	Full Governance functions and decisions
Reporting Pattern	CEO(Subsidiary) to CEO and Board (Parent), Managers (Sub) to CEO (Sub) and Corresponding Manager (Parent)	CEO (subsidiary) receives advice from local board but reports to parent board	CEO (subsidiary) reports to both local board and parent board	Financial and other reports,
Strength	Direct Control by parent Integration helps build global reputation	Global Integration with some effort to address local concerns	Global consistency with greater local responsiveness	Ensures responsiveness to local conditions Minimum time and cost on governance by Parent
Drawback	Disregard for concerns of local stakeholders	High coordination cost and difficult to implement Dissatisfied directors	Unclear reporting lines Overlapping roles of boards Parent board acting as shadow directors	Parent has no control Global stakeholders may be neglected

Source Developed by Author

Tata Sons and the Mystery of Mistry

(S. Jhunjhunwala, 2020, Vikalpa: The Journal for Decision papers, Volume: 45 issue: 3, page(s): 170–182).

The board of Tata Sons shocked corporate India by sacking their chairperson, Cyrus Mistry, on 24 October 2016 (a little less than four years after he was made chairperson), and replacing him with his predecessor, Ratan Tata, as an interim chairperson. The Tatas are the biggest private business group in India, comprising over 100 operating companies spread across six continents. Twenty-nine of these companies are listed with an aggregate market capitalization of ₹ 8,471 billion/US$127 billion (as of 2 March 2017) making their share 7.2 per cent of Bombay Stock Exchange's total market capitalization.

Background of Tata Group

Tata Group was founded by Jamsetji Nusserwanji Tata. It was in 1858 that Jamsetji joined his father's export trading firm soon after graduation. He helped expand the company to countries such as Japan, China, Europe and the USA. In the 1870s, he successfully set up cotton manufacturing mills at Nagpur, Bombay and Kurla. He was the first to introduce hydroelectric power plants in India, which later became part of Tata Power.

In 1901, his vision gave India its first large-scale ironworks—Tata Iron and Steel Company (now Tata Steel)—which became the largest privately owned steelmaker in India and the flagship company of the group. Over the years, the Tatas set up several large manufacturing companies over a range of products including cement, chemicals, watches, trucks and locomotives. The Tata Group converted Jamshedpur (popularly known as Tatanagar) into a large industrial town, with schools, hospitals and other municipal facilities.

The Tatas were equally involved in service industries such as hotels, telecommunication, broadband and financial services. In 1998, Tata Motors launched the first fully indigenous Indian passenger car, the Indica, and in 2008 launched the Tata Nano, the world's cheapest car. Tata Consultancy Services (TCS) was founded by JRD Tata in 1968, long before most people had even touched a computer. It is one of the largest IT service providers in the world, with a market capitalization of ₹ 4,928 billion/US$73.88 billion (As of 2 March 2017), contributing almost 60 per cent of the group's total market value.

Governance Structure of the Tata Group

Tata Sons, as the promoter of the major operating Tata companies, owns significant shareholdings in these companies. Tata companies together are commonly referred to as the Tata Group. The chairperson of Tata Sons is the defacto chairperson of the Tata companies. The companies are further networked through cross holdings (see Exhibit 1), interlocking directors (Exhibit 2), and even trustees.

About 66 per cent of the equity capital of Tata Sons is held by philanthropic trusts endowed by members of the Tata family. The largest of these trusts are the Sir Dorabji Tata Trust and the Sir Ratan Tata Trust, which were created by the sons of Jamsetji Nusserwanji Tata, the founder. Another 18.4 per cent is held by the Shapoorji Pallonji Group, the only other major but non-Tata shareholder in the company. A few of the bigger Tata companies also own shares in the promoter company.

The income of Tata Sons is primarily dividend and brand royalties received from the Tata Group companies. The income of the trusts, in turn, is dividend earned from Tata Sons. Dividend income is tax-free but chargeable as distribution tax (about 20%) to the company distributing the dividend. As a result Tata Sons, whose applicable taxable rate is approximately 33 per cent, does not have to pay any tax on a major part of their income. As charitable organizations, the trusts are exempt from tax. Tata Group is reputed to be an ethical organization with the highest standards of corporate governance.

Exhibit 1 Shareholding Pattern (% Holding)

Company / Shareholder	Tata Sons	Tata Investment	TCS	Tata Motors	Tata Steel	Titan Company	Tata Power	Tata Motors	Tata Communications	Tata Chemicals	Tata Global Beverages	Voltas	Indian Hotels
Tata Trusts	66.00	0.04	0.08	0.05	0.11		0.02	0.06		0.15			7.98
Tata Sons		68.14	73.26	23.00	29.75	20.85	31.05	28.21	14.06	19.35	22.63	26.64	28.01
Tata Industries	0.57		0.02	2.13	0.08		0.17	2.50		0.03	0.12		0.06
Tata Investment Corp			0.03	0.32	0.35	2.01	0.25	0.37		6.11	4.27	3.01	1.35
Shapoorji Pallonji	0.03												
Sterling Investment Corp	9.18												
Cyrus Investments	9.18		0.21							0.01	0.01		0.01
TCS													
Tata Motors					0.45					0.03			
Tata Steel		0.45		2.46			1.45	2.90					
Titan Company													
Tata Power	1.65								4.71			0.07	
Tata Motors	3.06												
Tata Communications													
Tata Chemicals	2.53	0.86		0.06	0.26	1.56		0.07			6.84		0.90
Tata Global Beverages		0.29								4.39			
Voltas										0.08			
Indian Hotels	1.13												

Exhibit 2 Interlocking Directors at Tatas (*Note* This is not an exhaustive list. NE = non-executive, non-independent director; ID = independent director. *Source* Compiled from annual reports and company websites).

Tata Sons	Tata investment	TCS	Tata Motors	Tata steel	Tata power	Tata chemicals	Tata global bev	Indian hotels	voltas	Tata comm	Titan company
Mr. Cyrus P. Misty Chairman		Mr. Cyrus P. Misty Chairman (NE)	Mr. Cyrus P. Misty Chairman (NE)	Mr. Cyrus P. Misty Chairman (NE)	Mr. Cyrus P. Misty Chairman (NE)	Mr. Cyrus P. Misty Chairman (NE)	Mr. Cyrus P. Misty Chairman (NE)	Mr. Cyrus P. Misty Chairman (NE)			C.V. Sankar Chairman (NE)
	Mr. N. N. Tata Chairman (NE)		Mr Ratan N Tata (Chairman Emeritus)					Shapoor Mistry (NE)			N.N. Tata (NE)
Mr. Ishaat Hussain		Mr. Ishaat Hussain (NE)		Mr. Ishaat Hussain (NE)					Mr. Ishaat Hussain Chairman (NE)		
			Mr. Subodh Bhargava (ID)	Mr. Subodh Bhargava (ID)						Mr. Subodh Bhargava Chairman (ID)	
						Mr. Bhaskar Bhat, (NE)					Mr. Bhaskar Bhat, (Managing Director)
Mr. Amit Chandra	Mr. Amit Chandra (ID)										
			Mr. Nusli N. Wadia (ID)	Mr. Nusli N. Wadia (ID)		Mr. Nusli N. Wadia (ID)					
			MR. NASSER MUNJEE (ID)			MR. NASSER MUNJEE (ID)					
		Mr. O P Bhatt (ID)		Mr. O P Bhatt (ID)							
	Mr. Kishor A. Chaukar (NE)									Mr. Kishor A. Chaukar (NE)	
							Mrs. Ireena Vittal (ID)	Mrs. Ireena Vittal (ID)			Mrs. Ireena Vittal (ID)
			Ms. Mallika Srinivasan (ID)			Mrs. Mallika Srinivasan (ID)					
							Mr. Harish Bhat (NE)				Mr. Harish Bhat (NE)

Cyrus Mistry: A Short Stay at Tata House

Cyrus Mistry, a civil engineer and management graduate from London Business School with experience of managing a big conglomerate, was chosen as Ratan Tata's successor in November 2011. He was initially appointed as deputy chairperson of Tata Sons. On Tata's retirement in December 2012, he was appointed as the sixth chairperson of Tata Sons to head the Tata Group. He was selected by a panel comprising of Ratan

Tata, Venu Srinivasan, Amit Chandra, and Ronen Sen (who were later made board members of Tata Sons), and Kumar Bhattacharyya of Warwick, UK (who was a close friend of Ratan Tata). Incidentally, Mistry is the grandson of Shapoorji Pallonji Mistry, whose family holds 18.4 per cent equity in Tata Sons. He joined the board of Tata Sons when his father retired in 2006. According to Mistry, Bhattacharya had courted him to accept the post. Bhattacharyya had described Mistry at the time as 'bright and self-less' and Ratan Tata considered him 'intelligent and qualified to take on the responsibility' as chairperson.

Traditionally, once appointed a chairperson would remain at the helm of affairs until retirement. J. R. D. Tata was chairperson for more than 50 years, and Ratan Tata for 20 odd years until his retirement at the age of 75. Mistry, who was 48, should then have continued for a fairly long time. However, he was unceremoniously removed on 24 October 2016— a few months before his contract was up for renewal. Six board members voted in favour of the resolution to oust Mistry, two abstained and Mistry himself voted to stay. Mistry was neither served any show-cause notice for removal nor given a chance to be heard or defend himself. Surprisingly, no reasons were provided at that time by Tata Sons for this sudden removal. A spokesperson said, '[t]he Tata Sons board in its collective wisdom and on the recommendation of the principal shareholders decided that it may be appropriate to consider a change for the long-term interest of Tata Sons and the Tata Group'. Unexpectedly, some members of the committee who selected Mistry were also among those who voted him out.

It is interesting to note that before Mistry, every chairperson of the Tata Group was a member of the Tata family. As the head of the two Tata trusts, Ratan Tata controls 66 per cent of Tata Sons and hence yields significant control as the promoter shareholder. Before Mistry was made chairperson, the post of the head of the trusts and the chairperson of Tata Sons had always been held by the same person.

Many have questioned the way in which Mistry was removed. It was suggested that he could have been requested to leave when his term was up in April 2017. The Tatas maintain that Mistry had been asked at least on four previous occasions to step down, but he insisted on a board vote. The board was expanded in August 2016 by inducting Amit Chandra, who is also a trustee of several Tata trusts, and two of India's prominent industrialists, Venu Srinivasan and Ajay Piramal, as non-executive directors by Ratan Tata—without even consulting Mistry. It may be recalled that Chandra and Srinivasan were also members of the selection team. These steps suggest the close relation the new members had to Ratan Tata and a possible groundwork for what was to come.

During Mistry's tenure, the revenue grew from about ₹50 billion to over ₹80 billion, and average operating margins by 79 per cent. The market capitalization of the group showed a compound annual growth rate (CAGR) of 18.22 per cent compared to the Sensex's 10.4 per cent. This would have been much higher if it had not been for Tata Steel and Tata Power, which are debt-laden and losing market value. Tata Steel had been accumulating losses since 2009, long before Mistry was made in charge.

Tata Sons, however, claimed that TCS and Jaguar Land Rover were the major profit-making units and that Mistry had not contributed to their success. The revenue and profits of Tata Sons (on a stand-alone basis) during the year 2015–2016 had fallen from the previous year. In the previous year, that is, 2014–2015, Tata Sons had received about ₹11.40 billion as dividend from TCS (the total of others being about ₹6 billon), half of which was because of a special dividend almost tripling their profits from its preceding year. If this special dividend were to be excluded, both revenue and profits of the current year showed an increase. Dividend earned from companies other than TCS had been declining after 2012–2013, when it reached a high of ₹10 billion when Ratan Tata was holding the reins. Under Mistry's chairpersonship, dividend income had grown substantially, but this was purely to the credit of TCS. The overall growth rate of dividend earned was far less than what it was during his predecessors' times (Exhibit 3).

Exhibit 3 Tata vs. Mistry

Financial Parameters	Ratan Tata' Tenure	Cyrus Mistry's Tenure*
Revenue (CAGR)	1.14%	14.43%
EBITDA (CAGR)	21.8%	14.76%
EBITA Margin (Average)	62%	79%
Net Debt / EBITA (Average)	3.86%	12.8%
Return on Capital Employed(Average)	6.8%	1.98%
Market Value (CAGR)	22. 76%	18.22%
Dividend Income of Tata Sons(CAGR)	31.28%**	10.62%
Dividend Received from TCS by Tata Sons (CAGR)	37.89%**	14.86%
Dividend Income of Tata Sons excluding TCS (CAGR)	17. 69%**	-11. 38%

*Upto Financial year ending March 2016
** Calculated From 2006 onwards

The Tata trusts had expressed concern as their philanthropic activities were dependent on dividend income from Tata Sons. The dividend declared by Tata Sons had increased in 2011 and remained constant from 2011 to 2016, except in 2015 when it was much higher as Tata Sons had a bonus income from TCS. Hence, the Tata trusts' income from Tata Sons was not really affected (but maybe marginally reduced, by their direct investment in other Tata companies, such as Indian Hotels, which had not declared a dividend in 2014 and 2015). Meanwhile, the trusts' expenditure on grants and charity had increased more than their income.

Bhattacharyya, in his praise of Mistry in September 2016, just a month before the removal said as follows:

> He is building firm foundations to ensure Tata's expansion lasts not a quarter or two, but a decade and more. Tata Sons is more than just a business—it is an icon, a global symbol for doing business with integrity and long-term vision. As such, it should not be judged by the 'market hawker' standard of quick profits and opportunism.

The Rift: The Mystery Unfolds

Soon after taking charge as chairperson, Mistry replaced Ratan Tata's selected CEOs of Indian Hotels, Tata Motors and Tata Steel with younger persons of his choice. He sold off the loss-making and debt-burdened Corus in the UK. Ratan Tata had acquired the British company. As a result, Tata Steel had become among the top 10 largest steel producers in the world. Tata had acquired the company at an auction for £6.08 pounds per share, a 33 per cent increase from their original quote of £4.55 per share. At the time, the opinion in the business world was that Ratan Tata had overpaid just to win the bid. This suggests it held significant sentimental value for him. However, it was incurring losses almost from the beginning. Uday Chaturvedi, who had worked for more than 40 years with Tata Steel and had a stint as managing director of Corus Strip Products, a unit of Tata Steel Europe, said, 'I had foreseen in 2012 (that would be before Mistry became chairperson) that this would happen. Tata Steel had put in a huge amount of financial resources, but the technical resources were not there'. Tata Steel's former managing director, J. J. Irani, said he was happy that the Tata Steel board had decided to divest the UK business. Tata Sons, in its statement expressed Mistry's inability to turnaround Tata Steel Europe as one of the foremost indicators of his poor performance. When Ratan Tata became interim chair, Tata Steel had to reassure institutional investors that the sale of the UK speciality business would be undertaken as already proposed.

Mistry's biggest mistake was probably wanting to get rid of Nano (operating at just 15% of capacity), the dream project of his predecessor—the *cheapest car in the world* that never really took off. Ratan Tata envisioned providing a *people's car* which the middle-class family in India could afford. The much-hyped car ran into problems from day one. The original factory was meant to be set up in West Bengal. However, due to political agendas and social activists challenging the acquisition of farmers' land, the plans had to be changed. The factory finally relocated, but this led to significant delays and cost escalations. The car had already been priced at ₹ 1 lakh, half the price of the cheapest car anywhere else, making the project unviable from the beginning. Ratan Tata, while unveiling the Nano in 2008, said, '[s]ince a promise is a promise the standard dealer version will cost ₹ 1 lakh'. Later, due to some technical glitches, a few cars caught fire on the road. The Indian customer (who had once lined up to buy the Nano) rejected it.

J. R. D. Tata set up the first airlines in India—Tata Airlines—in 1932. It was later taken away from the Tatas and made the national carrier, Air

India. In the early 1990s, private airlines were again permitted in India. Ratan Tata began trying to set up another airline business. The Tatas re-entry in the airline industry, which hits an emotional chord for the group began with a joint venture with Air Asia in 2013. Overcoming several setbacks, a new airline under the brand of Vistara was finally launched in January 2015 (along with Singapore Airlines, where the Tatas have a majority stake). Mistry, on the contrary, was reluctant to pump more money into the aviation business.

Dissatisfaction with how Mistry handled the Docomo negotiations with the Japanese partners in the telecom business was the final nail in the coffin. The two have very different leadership styles and business strategies. The simmering discontent slowly reached its boiling point. In 2011, when Ratan Tata cherry-picked Mistry, it was seen as the victory of youth. 'Be your own man', was Tata's advice to his then 43-year-old successor. 'But soon, youth was perceived as insolent, precocious and out to destroy the core values that the group stood for, for close to 148 years'. The Tata Sons board claimed that Mistry was removed as they were not happy with his performance. Yet just a few months earlier, on 25 June, the Nomination and Remuneration Committee of the Tata Sons board had put on record an appreciation and recommended a raise for the chairperson, Cyrus Mistry.

Mistry, in a letter to the Tata Sons board the day after his removal, commented as follows:

> Prior to my appointment, I was assured that I would be given a free hand. The previous chairman was to step back and be available for advice and guidance as and when needed. After my appointment, the Articles of Association were modified, changing the rules of engagement between the Trusts, the Board of Tata Sons, the Chairman, and the operating companies.

Mistry has alleged that he was reduced to being a 'lame duck chairman', while Ratan Tata remained a towering figure influencing the decisions even during the board meetings, which forced him to circulate a corporate governance note 'in order to clarify the distinct roles of Tata Trusts, Tata Sons Board and the Boards of the operating companies'. On 25 June, the Nomination and Remuneration Committee of the Tata Sons board had discussed formalizing the governance structure among various entities of the group such as Tata Trusts, the trustees, boards and directors of group operating companies, and the same was up for discussion in the 25 October board meeting.

Ratan Tata, on the other hand, argued that Mistry made it his *personal fiefdom*, took unilateral decisions and did not keep the board apprised of major decisions even though he had been specifically asked to do so, particularly for large capital investments and appointment and pay packages of senior management. Further, they contended that construction dealings with Pallonji Group caused a conflict of interest. Pallonji has historically carried out construction activity for the Tata Group, and most of the projects were ongoing from before Mistry took charge.

His selection of leaders was also questioned. It was argued that he had failed for two years to appoint a CEO for Tata Motors, and the position of group CFO was vacant for three years. Mistry had, in fact, given three options for CEO of Tata Motors; all of them were rejected.

The removal of Mistry from the group is still mystifying. Mahabharata was about the victory of good over evil, but in this case, who is the good one, and who the evil one?

GOVERNANCE CONCERNS OF CORPORATE GROUPS

(S. Jhunjhunwala, 2020).

Companies in a corporate group are part of the same family. They share the same 'family name'. They are interwoven through cross holding and interlocking directors. Inter-company business and trading is prevalent. The entire business and governance structures are built in a way that companies are heavily interdependent. They may use common assets such as brands or software platforms. Companies are dependent on the group for resources such as financial, legal and technical know-how. The Tata group which consists of more than 100 companies has the same chairperson for all its major companies. The purpose of having the chairman of the holding company as the chairman of other companies is that decisions taken all across are in the interest of the group as a whole, even if they are to the detriment of individual companies.

In 2016 in one of the bitterest board room battles witnessed, the then chairman Cyrus Mistry was removed from Tata Sons the parent company (See Box). The decision of Tata Power a subsidiary to acquire Welspun Renewables without informing Tata Sons the parent company was not appreciated and was one of the reasons for firing Mistry. Tata Power's board had unanimously approved the deal. The company's right to make corporate decisions belongs to its board, but the holding company can undermine it. One of the strengths of the Tata Companies is the use of the brand name "Tata" for which they pay royalty, notwithstanding that the brand has been built by the older operating companies of the group. In their attempt to remove Mistry as the chairman from subsidiary companies, Tata Sons threatened to withdraw rights to the use of the brand name and loan guaranties if he was not removed. This would be detrimental to the business of the subsidiaries. In the past it has been seen that when resources, specifically funds and corporate heads, are taken away from healthy profit-making companies to save a sinking ship, the whole group is brought down as a result.

Several proxy advisory firms had recommended the shareholders to vote in favour of the removal of Cyrus Mistry. This, despite agreeing that there was no clear justification for it and that the group had performed well under his guidance. But his continuance would have split the boards into two and this would ultimately affected performance and eroded value. Mehta, an independent director, when questioned by shareholders at the Extra General Meeting of TCS Ltd., said that independent directors supported the move because 'when you have lost the support of the promoter, and when that trust has broken down, it goes beyond performance'.

MONITORING OF SUBSIDIARY COMPANIES

To protect the interest of shareholders of the holding company and at the same time minority shareholders of the subsidiary, appropriate legal provisions are to be established. The most important concern are unlisted companies because they are not subject to same level of regulatory compliance and scrutiny. As seen in several scams, they have been used as a means to transfer assets and funds out of the company. The requirements in India are briefed to throw light on the kind of measures that can be taken.

Board

At least one independent director of the listed company shall be a director on the board of directors of any unlisted material subsidiaries including foreign companies. The minutes of the meetings of the board of directors of the unlisted subsidiary shall be placed at the meeting of the board of directors of the listed company. The management of the unlisted subsidiary shall periodically bring to the notice of the board of directors of the listed company, a statement of all significant transactions and arrangements entered into by the unlisted subsidiary. Significant transaction or arrangement "shall mean any individual transaction or arrangement that exceeds or is likely to exceed ten percent {10%} of the total revenues or total expenses or total assets or total liabilities, as the case may be, of the unlisted material subsidiary for the immediately preceding accounting year" (Reg 24, LODR).

Consolidated Financial Statements

If a company has one or more subsidiaries, associate companies or joint ventures, it shall prepare a consolidated financial statement of the company and all of the subsidiaries, associate companies and joint venture in the same form and manner as that of its own. In addition to the stand-alone financial statements of the holding company, a consolidated financial statement of holding company is to be published to disclose details about subsidiary, associate companies and joint ventures (Sec 129 of Companies Act, 2013). The balance sheet of holding company shall specifically disclose investments in the subsidiaries. The Profit and Loss account of holding company shall disclose (a) dividends from subsidiary companies and (b) provisions for losses of subsidiary companies (Schedule III). The holding company is required to: (a) place separate audited accounts in respect of each of its subsidiary on its website and (b) provide a copy of separate audited financial statements in respect of each of its subsidiary, to any shareholder of the company who ask for it (Sec 136 of Companies Act, 2013). This helps investors to understand to what extent the subsidiary contributes to the financials of the group and highlights loss-making companies that may seriously reduce the profits of the parent company.

At the same time the balance sheet of subsidiary company should disclose shares held by its holding company or its ultimate holding company, or subsidiaries and associates of the holding company or the ultimate holding company (Schedule III).

Audit and Audit Committee

The statutory auditor of a listed company shall undertake a limited review of the audit of all the subsidiaries whose accounts are to be consolidated with the parent company. Besides audited annual consolidated statements, in case of quarterly consolidated financial results, at least eighty per cent of each of the consolidated revenue, assets and profits, respectively, shall have been audited or subjected to limited review (Reg 33, LODR).

The audit committee of the listed company shall also review the financial statements of subsidiaries, in particular, the investments made by the unlisted subsidiary (Reg 24, LODR). The board of a holding company can authorize anyone to inspect the books of account of a subsidiary company (Sec 128, Companies Act 2013).

Material Subsidiary

The listed company shall not dispose of shares in its material subsidiary which would reduce its shareholding (either on its own or together with other subsidiaries) to less than 50% or cease the exercise of control over the subsidiary without passing a special resolution (75% votes), in its General Meeting. Selling, disposing and leasing of assets amounting to more than twenty per cent (20%) of the assets of the material subsidiary on an aggregate basis during a financial year shall require prior approval of shareholders by way of special resolution. Exception has been granted for divestment under a scheme of arrangement duly approved by a court/tribunal (Reg 24, LODR). This is because such actions could significantly reduce the wealth or profit-generating capacity of the holding company.

Every listed entity's material unlisted subsidiaries incorporated in India shall undertake secretarial audit and shall annex the report with its annual report (Reg 24A). This will help to improve compliance of group as a whole.

The policy on material subsidiary shall be disclosed in the company's web site and in the annual report of the company or a web link provided in the annual report. These regulations ensure that shareholders of the holding company closely monitor subsidiaries, especially those whose performance significantly affects the performance of their company.

MNCs: Catalyst for Robust Corporate Governance

Globalization and the liberalization of trade and investment witnessed the growth of global multinational companies with operations across several countries ranging from developed economies of the USA and Europe to emerging economies in Asia to frontier markets of Africa.

From the shareholder primacy proponents of UK to the closed-knit Keiretsu approach of Japan to the state dominance in China, MNCs have businesses everywhere. MNCs in turn have demanded modernization of corporate governance standards. Countries to attract foreign investment to boost their economy have had no choice but to improve their corporate governance systems and bring in better governance regulations.

We have witnessed widespread changes in national corporate governance structures across the world. Japan has undergone a series of reforms reducing its cross holding, introducing a board structure that retains importance of executive directors but is monitored by an independent supervisory and audit board and even brought in an independent director. The bank holding in Japanese companies have gone down from more than 20% in the 80s to about 2%, and foreign investors has shot up from practically none to 30% in the last four decades (JPX, 2021).

When a company decides to raise money in another country, it has to follow corporate governance regulations of that country as well as its own. Subsidiaries too have to meet governance expectations of their holding company. The directors from one country sit on boards of group companies in other countries or interact with their directors. They are exposed to alternative governance practices. This advances the governance system of both companies. These subsidiaries then become role models for other firms in their home country to emulate. A chain reaction leads to overall rise in governance standards.

Internationalization of business and exponential growth of MNCs has let to developments in national corporate governance systems. Though formal convergence of national practices is neither practical nor probably desirable, MNCs have enriched the landscape of corporate governance by raising the bar for accountability of board, fairness and transparency of reporting, rights of shareholders and respect for all stakeholders.

References

Bartlett, C. A., & Ghoshal, S. (1989). *Managing across borders*. Harvard Business School Press.

Companies Act, 2013, India.

Companies Act 2006, UK.

Deloitte (2013). Governance of Subsidiaries A survey of global companies https://www2.deloitte.com/content/dam/Deloitte/in/Documents/risk/Corporate%20Governance/in-gc-governance-of-subsidiaries-a-survey-of-global-companies-noexp.pdf accessed September 14, 2021

Filatotchev, I. & Stahl, G. K. (2015). Towards transnational CSR. Corporate social responsibility approaches and governance solutions for multinational corporations. *Organizational Dynamics, 44*(2), 121–129.

Fischer, D., & Roy, K. (2019). Market entry in India: The curious case of starbucks, Rutgers Business Review Fall. https://rbr.business.rutgers.edu/sites/default/files/documents/rbr-040204.pdf September 14, 2021.

Kiel, G. C., Kevin, H., & Nicholson, G. J. (2006). Corporate governance options for the local subsidiaries of multinational enterprises. *Corporate Governance: An International Review, 14*(6), 568–576. Blackwell Publishing Ltd.

Jhunjhunwala, S. (2020). *Vikalpa: The Journal for Decision Papers, 45*(3), 170–182.

JPX, Japan Exchange Group (2021). Share ownership survey. https://www.jpx.co.jp/english/markets/statistics-equities/examination/01.html.

SEBI. (2015). Listing Obligation and Disclosure Requirements, (LODR).

https://www.mclaneco.com/content/mclaneco/en/about.html#all-business-units accessed September 14, 2021.

https://www.berkshirehathaway.com/subs/sublinks.html accessed September 14, 2021.

Index